Joan Didion and the Ethics of Memory

Also available from Bloomsbury

Philosophy and Vulnerability: Catherine Breillat, Joan Didion, and Audre Lorde, Matthew R. McLennan
Philosophy, Sophistry, Antiphilosophy: Badiou's Dispute with Lyotard, Matthew R. McLennan
The Ethics of Time: A Phenomenology and Hermeneutics of Change, John Panteleimon Manoussakis
Memory and the Built Environment in 20th-Century American Literature: A Reading and Analysis of Spatial Forms, Alice Levick

Joan Didion and the Ethics of Memory

Matthew R. McLennan

BLOOMSBURY ACADEMIC
LONDON • NEW YORK • OXFORD • NEW DELHI • SYDNEY

BLOOMSBURY ACADEMIC
Bloomsbury Publishing Plc
50 Bedford Square, London, WC1B 3DP, UK
1385 Broadway, New York, NY 10018, USA
29 Earlsfort Terrace, Dublin 2, Ireland

BLOOMSBURY, BLOOMSBURY ACADEMIC and the Diana logo are trademarks of
Bloomsbury Publishing Plc

First published in Great Britain 2022
This paperback edition published 2023

Copyright © Matthew R. McLennan, 2022

Matthew R. McLennan has asserted his right under the Copyright, Designs and Patents
Act, 1988, to be identified as Author of this work.

For legal purposes the Acknowledgements on p. viii constitute an extension of this
copyright page.

Cover design by Ben Anslow
Cover image: Joan Didion in Alcatraz Prison
(© Ted Streshinsky / Corbis / Getty Images)

All rights reserved. No part of this publication may be reproduced or transmitted
in any form or by any means, electronic or mechanical, including photocopying,
recording, or any information storage or retrieval system, without prior permission
in writing from the publishers.

Bloomsbury Publishing Plc does not have any control over, or responsibility for, any
third-party websites referred to or in this book. All internet addresses given in this
book were correct at the time of going to press. The author and publisher regret any
inconvenience caused if addresses have changed or sites have ceased to exist, but
can accept no responsibility for any such changes.

A catalogue record for this book is available from the British Library.

Library of Congress Cataloging-in-Publication Data
Names: McLennan, Matthew R., author.
Title: Joan Didion and the ethics of memory / Matthew R. McLennan.
Description: London; New York: Bloomsbury Academic, 2022. |
Includes bibliographical references and index. |
Identifiers: LCCN 2021017372 (print) | LCCN 2021017373 (ebook) |
ISBN 9781350149571 (hardback) | ISBN 9781350149595 (ebook) |
ISBN 9781350149601 (epub)
Subjects: LCSH: Didion, Joan–Criticism and interpretation. |
Memory in literature. | Literature–Philosophy.
Classification: LCC PS3554.I33 Z7735 2022 (print) |
LCC PS3554.I33 (ebook) | DDC 813/.54–dc23
LC record available at https://lccn.loc.gov/2021017372
LC ebook record available at https://lccn.loc.gov/2021017373

ISBN: HB: 978-1-3501-4957-1
PB: 978-1-3502-7186-9
ePDF: 978-1-3501-4959-5
eBook: 978-1-3501-4960-1

Typeset by Deanta Global Publishing Services, Chennai, India

To find out more about our authors and books visit
www.bloomsbury.com and sign up for our newsletters.

*This book is dedicated to Leo's and Moses's grandparents
and great-grandparents.
Anna and I especially want to acknowledge the loving care and support given
to our sons during the pandemic by Louise Legault, Pierre Legault, Christopher
Seifried, Louise Guay and Susan McLennan. The care you've selflessly given
to your grandchildren in turbulent times grounds them firmly in a warm and
loving past, and it helps to safeguard their futures.*

Contents

Acknowledgements	viii
Introduction: Why Didion? Why the 'ethics of memory'?	1
1 'Earthquake weather': Didion's universe	35
2 Memories are what you no longer want to remember: Witnessing, testifying and grieving	63
3 The norm of comprehensiveness: Nostalgia, Forgiveness and Critical Fabulation	105
4 Political memory and memory as politics: Critical political realism and neoliberal life narrative	131
Conclusion: Joan Didion and the future: Philosophical unsettlement and the right to be forgotten	153
Notes	159
Bibliography	186
Index	193

Acknowledgements

Completing a book – in a pandemic, no less – is something I could not have accomplished without the strong support and encouragement I've always been so lucky to receive.

Above all I thank my family, in particular Anna Seifried, Leo McLennan, Moses McLennan, Susan McLennan, Doreen Richmond, Audrey Lundy, Louise Legault, Pierre Legault, Louise Guay and Christopher Seifried.

I am also lucky to be surrounded by supportive friends and colleagues. In the period of researching and writing this book, I received special encouragement as well as moral and critical support from Deniz Guvenc, T. Mars McDougall, Devin Zane Shaw, Julie Paquette, Lauren Levesque, Denis Dumas, Morgan McMillan, Jason Peters, J. Moufawad-Paul, Rajesh Shukla, Tyler Shipley, Lorraine Ste-Marie, Lesley Jamieson, Stephen Stuart, Manal Guirguis-Younger, Monique Lanoix, Sophie Cloutier, Louis Perron, Richard Feist, Natalie Dupuis, Nathalie Poirier, Chris Casimiro, Ephraim Barrera, Sebastian Valderrama-Moores, Darrah Teitel and Susanna Wiens.

I greatly appreciated Lucy Russell, Liza Thompson and the team at Bloomsbury even in the best of times, but they showed exceptional patience, kindness and understanding when the pandemic upended my best laid plans. The book also benefitted greatly from the critical comments of the anonymous manuscript reviewer and anonymous prospectus reviewers.

Finally, Chris Casimiro and Ephraim Barrera provided invaluable formatting and editing assistance. Any errors or omissions in the text are, of course, wholly my own.

Introduction

Why Didion? Why the 'ethics of memory'?

This book has two aims. First, I want to make a good case that the voluminous works of Joan Didion – masterful American essayist, novelist, memoirist, screenplay writer, political journalist and cultural commentator – may be profitably organized and understood through the theme of 'the ethics of memory'. Second, for those of us who are concerned with the drift of modern societies at present and the possibility of better political futures, I want to show how Didion's writings have much to teach us about the overall salience, as well as some specific aspects, of the ethics of memory.

To my mind, the second aim is the more important of the two. As I will explain in this Introduction, Didion demonstrates both the normative importance and limits of memory in a modern historical conjuncture where what public memory there is, is at best contested, and at worst is decaying or coming apart.

I do not want to be misunderstood here: vigorous *contestation* over public memory can be necessary and a very good thing, for example, by allowing a community to commit or re-commit itself to core values through an agonistic if not robustly collective process of revising *how* the past is remembered.[1] Indeed, it may be necessary for moral reasons for communities to overhaul their relation to the past – and this, sometimes, precisely to embody the ideals upon which they tell themselves they were founded, or would like to be founded going forward. Witness on this count, at the time of writing in summer 2020, the widespread questioning, repudiation and vandalism of public monuments to racist historical figures in countries across the world, most spectacularly in the United States but also in my home country of Canada. Note that there is no question here of 'erasing the past', as conservatives complain loudly, and frequently, and in bad faith whenever a Confederate monument is targeted. Since people typically do not learn their history from statues, it is, rather, a struggle over *how* certain elements of the past are either glorified or demonized. Indeed, the very contestation of monuments itself indicates a vigorous engagement with aspects of the country's past, and repudiating a particular historical figure as racist – precisely, by publicly remembering his or her racism and its legacy – is not tantamount to erasing or forgetting.

Contestation, then, is not in and of itself the problem. The *degradation* or, at the limit, the *destruction* or *disintegration* of public memory, on the other hand, would amount to no less than the crumbling of community and hence (I will explain), of ethics itself.

For its part, public contestation of the type just described is inherently risky. Though morally required, it may veer into *disintegration*. A community's ethically fraught revision of its relation to the past may sometimes cross from agonism into antagonism, and this raises the possibility of its splitting into two or more communities, meaning that there are now two or more public memories to be reckoned with.

Public memory may also *degrade* or *decay* through the modernizing process in general, and the imperatives of capitalism and neoliberal governance. After all, if surviving in this world means chasing innovation and recasting myself in my very subjectivity as a kind of walking portfolio (Brown 2015), then it makes little sense to linger on those aspects of the past that are not obviously useful to my forward trajectory. Community history, even family and intimate ties based upon a shared past, may be jettisoned as I move around and always forward searching for new opportunities for self-maximization.

What is more, a community can also have its ties to the past actively targeted for *destruction*, as was the case with First Nations, Métis and Inuit in Canada via the residential school system (Battiste 2013; Truth and Reconciliation Commission of Canada 2015). In this system, children were taken from their communities by the Canadian state, forbidden to speak their mother tongues, and 'educated' in harsh and squalid conditions of frequently deadly abuse and neglect – all with the aim of facilitating settler colonialism by breaking down their cultures, the lifeblood of which was language, tradition and memory.

In all such cases, what is at stake is the crumbling of community through the loss of robust links to a past that individuals could hold in common. Granting her position of privilege and an arguably troubling tendency to partiality, which are issues I will return to throughout the book, Didion offers particularly acute observations and object lessons here. With great clarity, she tracks public memory's contestation in the United States, as well as its degradation and signs of its threatened disintegration or destruction. But she is also remarkable in her refusal to give in to the temptation to reassert and reassume public memory in any crude, reactionary or nostalgic way. On the contrary, she fully assumes the contestation, degradation and threatened disintegration of public memory – to say nothing of putatively 'private' memory, which will also figure prominently in the book – as realities that cannot be magically wished away. She gives us a devastatingly clear if partial prognosis of modern collapse and precarity, but in a pessimistic rather than a nihilistic mode – meaning that she gives full-throated voice to an ambient anxiety and dread, but ultimately abandons neither ethics nor meaning.

Despite certain limitations that I will flag as the book progresses, Didion can therefore be read as a modern moralist, or ethical teacher or exemplar, in the sense that through both her words and her omissions, she indicates what fully facing up to a pessimistic outlook regarding public memory may require of us ethically. This might speak to my own moods and dispositions, but it seems that if we want to transform the world for the better, then we need to read thinkers who at least try to give it to us straight. If 'pessimism of the intellect, optimism of the will' are, indeed, the order of the day as Gramsci and Rolland prescribed (Antonini 2019), then Didion stands out as a crucial and timely resource.

In what follows, I will first unpack exactly what I mean by 'the ethics of memory' and why I think it is so important. Second, I will sketch out a plausible account of Didion's own stance with respect to ethics and/or morality, in addition to briefly mapping out my plan in the book and why Didion is 'good to think with' regarding several key aspects of the ethics of memory. It will become clear why I engaged in this study of Didion in the first place, and why I highly recommend she be read both by disciplinary philosophers and anyone with a philosophical bent. This might be of interest because it suggests how the work of Joan Didion, whose importance in American letters is already widely recognized and celebrated, may be significant in a way that the reader may not have expected.

To show what I have in mind in terms of philosophical issues raised by Didion, I will begin my book on memory with a personal recollection. I recall that one of my favourite professors at the University of Winnipeg, Diane Gall, once quipped that the most important questions to ask in approaching any philosophical text are 'so what?' and 'who cares?'

This claim has stuck with me for over twenty years, and I have often repeated it to my own students. It has even taken on a certain urgency for me as I grapple with the future of philosophy both within and outside of the university. Like Diane, I wager that if you can convincingly get across to your students the 'so what' and the 'who cares' of what they are supposed to be studying, you might get a better buy-in to the task confronting them.

Whether you are an educator, a student enrolled in a philosophy class or an amateur in philosophy, it is always worth repeating to oneself that the philosophy student's task is no easy one. The student of philosophy must invest in patient and earnest readings of difficult texts that in late capitalist societies tend to be dispensed with in one of two ways. On the one hand, philosophical texts are often absorbed and recuperated. This happens when they are trivialized for entertainment or operationalized for teaching mental toughness and the ability to suffer austerity. It also happens when they are tapped for training in lucrative, marketable, flexible forms of thinking. But on the other hand, philosophical texts are also often targeted for disrepute and banishment. This also happens in several ways, for example, through cultural ridicule or by starving the university programmes where they are studied and designating them esoteric, dangerous, 'useless', or remote. It is ever my hope that even faced with such difficulties, and even when the intrinsic value of philosophy *qua* human achievement fails to resonate, I might still be able, through the capture and nourishment of an initial interest, to resist this double pressure, to tie philosophy to vital human activity, and to help keep its practice alive.[2]

On this occasion, I feel keenly how I owe to my readers an answer to the 'so what' and 'who cares' questions up front. What business does a philosopher have writing about Joan Didion, a writer who is usually claimed by literary or journalistic or cultural studies? And why should philosophical readers in general have any interest in her, let alone in my book about her? What, in short, are the answers to the 'so what' and 'who cares' of the text you have started to read? Why read on, precisely, when the pressures of late capitalism make such outrageous claims on your time?

My answer to these questions depends upon two contestable but I think highly plausible claims. First, I claim that *'the ethics of memory' is a salient, even vital topic at present*. Second, I claim that *those of us living in crumbling neoliberal societies are in desperate need of teachers, thinkers and exemplars on this topic*, whether or not they are recognized as 'philosophers' in any disciplinary sense. While it is perfectly conceivable that a reader could find interest in this study purely on account of their passion for Didion's writing, or perhaps even the broader theme of the ethics of memory, I will emphasize throughout the book that there are social and political stakes bound up with its topic. It is from these that I draw my sense of the book's urgency, and they are why I sat down to write it.

'Ethics of memory'

Joan Didion's excellence as a writer, her astuteness as a critical commentator and her overall social relevance are so widely recognized that I believe they require no further defence herein. It is perhaps otherwise with my specific claim that she resonates in our time through the topic of the ethics of memory. I will begin then by defining the titular 'ethics of memory', and I will explain why I claim that it is now so salient. Once I have done this, I can make a provisional link between Didion and the ethics of memory, and then introduce the logic of the chapters that follow. First, let us consider that the notion of an 'ethics of memory' can be taken in a general as well as in a more specific sense.

The general sense

To speak of the 'ethics of memory' in general indicates *that there are normative stakes and standards involved in such actions as remembering and forgetting, as well as memorializing, testifying, grieving, suppressing, recounting, archiving and the like.*

The above list of actions is not exhaustive. It is merely intended to give the reader a good idea of the type of action I have in mind whenever I refer to the 'ethics of memory'. The actions listed certainly differ in some important respects, but they can be plausibly lumped together on account of their shared 'family resemblance' of having to do with memory (Wittgenstein 2001: 32e).

I will not define 'memory' in any comprehensive way, nor do I believe I need to for the book's argument to get off the ground. I will note simply that both in common sense, as well as in a more technical philosophical tradition, memory is 'of the past' (Aristotle 2018: 95). This it is in a dual sense. First, memory is 'of the past' in the sense that it is that which is *oriented* towards what is past, or constitutes *representations* of the past, as opposed to what is future or present. But second, and I believe most importantly, memory *really is* oriented towards, or represents, what *is* past. Psychologists speak of 'false memories' and 'False Memory Syndrome', but these would be best understood along the following lines: if x is a 'false memory', then x is a representation such that it is false that x is a memory. In such a scenario, x is *imagined*. The link to truth, then, is what distinguishes memory from the cognitively similar faculty or activity of *imagination*, wherein representations can be pure fictions. Rejecting the idea of 'false memories' in the strict sense means that memory is bound up with the concept of truth, or that it is a veridical representation of the past – a point that will be important throughout this book (Ricœur 2006: 5–55).

This being said, 'remembering and forgetting' are taken as primary actions in the aforementioned list. The other actions included are derivative; there is no grieving or mourning without memory and the danger – and perhaps, to some extent, the necessity – of forgetting, to take but one example (Ricœur 2006: 69–80; Freud 2011). I will grant in this book that if we keep their salient differences in mind, various memory-related actions can fall together under the rubric of the 'ethics of memory'.

Further commentary is doubtless required, however, on my very use of the word 'actions' in this context, and upon my invocation of 'normative stakes and standards' by which to judge them. I will begin with my use of the word 'actions' in connection with the ethics of memory.

First, a difficulty arises in that some of the 'actions' listed earlier are not always, or do not appear to be, things we actively 'do'. Sometimes they just seem to happen to us, and are therefore better described as 'events' or 'occurrences'. This can be true, first, of the primary terms in the list, 'remembering' and 'forgetting'. A traumatic memory, a particularly strong childhood impression or even a bizarrely trivial bit of remembered information can occupy my consciousness seemingly inexplicably, and when I am totally unprepared for it. Conversely, I may forget something – say, the name of a person with whom I worked daily, years ago in a restaurant, and had warm feelings for at the time – without meaning to, and much to my annoyance, consternation or distress. But derivative 'actions' on the list may also, arguably, occur in a passive rather than active mode. This is true of 'suppressing' memory and of 'grieving' or 'mourning' at any rate – at least if we put stock in classic psychoanalytic theory, which holds that the explanation of both requires appeal to unconscious psychic processes (Ricœur 2006: 69–80; Freud 2011).

Second, some of the 'actions' listed earlier are obviously 'public' and others 'private' in a rough and ready sense. For example, the unveiling of a memorial statue for a famous politician seems different in some respects from taking a moment of quiet reflection to oneself on a train to remember a lost loved one on the anniversary of their death. The former (barring bizarre circumstances) has third-party witnesses, follows definite, publicly recognized rules, and aims at a definite pragmatic and political end or ends. The latter, by contrast, happens without witnesses, to the extent that other passengers on the train may not observe what is going on 'inside' the person reflecting. It also appears not to be bound up with any definite or obviously public rules or expectations. More crucially, it may not be obvious what effects, if any, such reflection has or can have. If 'public' acts of memory such as the statue unveiling are therefore unquestionably *actions*, it is perhaps less certain that 'private' ones are.

With the preceding in mind, I will take for granted herein that remembering, forgetting and their derivatives are not *always* actions, and that this may affect how we judge them relative to normative stakes and standards. But I will also take for granted that it *can*, indeed, make sense to describe an unobservable mental event, such as reflecting on a train, as an 'action', and further, that it can make sense to make a normative claim about it.

Specifically, even if it has no observable, which is to say 'public' effects, a putatively 'mental' event can still in principle be judged according to ethical standards – for example, on account of the goodness it aims at, or commits itself to (or, indeed, that it fails to aim at, or commit itself to).[3] Iris Murdoch's classic example in this connection is of a mother, 'M', who feels hostility to her daughter-in-law, 'D' (Murdoch 2007: 16–22). Supposing that outwardly, M has always behaved impeccably towards D, whom she secretly judges harshly, Murdoch asks us to imagine a scenario in which M nonetheless inwardly improves, in a moral sense, with respect to D. Through self-criticism and 'careful and just *attention*' (Murdoch 2007: 17; emphasis in original), M may revise her assessment of D in such a way as to do justice to the latter's goodness, better qualities and beauty. Here an 'action' has occurred – a work of mental revision of sorts, premised upon rigorous but unbiased attention – that has no observable impact on the world, but which we could nonetheless in principle judge normatively, and find praiseworthy (to the effect that M is now being 'fair' to D, or is showing better character by doing so). Murdoch's example is particularly felicitous for evoking the possibility that M's inner behaviour with respect to D be wholly retrospective; supposing that D has emigrated or even died, M is revising her opinion of D without there being any obvious 'payoff' in the external world. Hers is an ethical action at any rate, on Murdoch's account. But especially if D has died, then it is in one sense an action that would fall clearly under the banner of the ethics of memory. Specifically, in revising her assessment of D, M would be training her attention on the goodness that was really in D while she was alive – thus 'doing justice to the dead', or 'giving the dead their due', if we wish to describe her actions along these lines.

Paul Ricœur (2006) upholds the point I am making here about action in a general way, building his magisterial study *Memory, History, Forgetting* from the ancient Greek distinction between *mnēmē* and *anamnēsis* (2006). *Mnēmē* denotes 'memory as appearing, ultimately passively, to the point of characterizing as an affection – *pathos* – the popping into mind of a memory'; *anamnēsis*, by contrast, denotes 'the memory as an object of a search ordinarily named recall, recollection' (Ricœur 2006: 4). From this distinction, Ricœur cleaves the 'cognitive' side of memory from its 'pragmatic' side:

> the question 'How?' posed by *anamnēsis* tends to separate itself from the question 'What?' more narrowly posed by *mnēmē*. This split into the cognitive or pragmatic approaches has a major influence on the claim of memory to be faithful to the past: this claim defines the truthful status of memory, which will later have to be confronted with the truth claim of history. In the meantime, the interference of the pragmatics of memory, by virtue of which remembering is doing something, has a jamming effect on the entire problematic of veracity: possibilities of abuse are ineluctably grafted onto the resources of usage, of use, of memory apprehended along its pragmatic axis. (Ricœur 2006.)

Note how this very possibility of 'abuse' (perhaps better termed 'negligence' in some cases), is tied up with memory's veracity, which I emphasized earlier. The question cannot be avoided, on account of memory's previously noted cognitive proximity to imagination (2006: 5–55). On this view, it makes perfect sense to ask oneself at any given time if one is actually *remembering* something as it really was, or if one is *imagining* the past, or creatively, wishfully, filling in the blanks. If, to return to Murdoch's example, M had revised her opinion of D according to a positive but fanciful version of how D was in life, then our judgement of her internal action might change for the worse. It seems that remembering 'fairly' implies remembering *correctly* or *veridically* – that, is, *actually remembering*, where one's memory corresponds to reality – so that M's assessment of D either remains morally neutral or becomes worse through its being fanciful. But note how remembering 'fairly' also seems to imply remembering *comprehensively*, to the extent that this is possible. The fuller the picture one has of how the remembered person really was, the better; on this view, truth is not zero-sum but gains the more it is 'filled in' by veridical details. It is, of course, a problem for this view that memory is finite and fragile, a point that we will revisit throughout this book. But fair retrospective judgement implies the ideal of an unvarnished look on the past (a point that will become important when we look at nostalgia in Chapter 3).

It might be accurate, then, to say that an abuse of memory has occurred either by passing off or negligently mistaking imagination for memory, or by refusing to engage in the cognitive rigour required for judicious memory as a pragmatic endeavour. Though it is possible to distinguish cognitive from pragmatic aspects conceptually, we see that in practice they imply each other. Even where it is a question of 'false memory' in the clinical sense, or of forgetting that is apparently *undergone* – pathological 'blocked memory' – we can question and judge the individual's role and efforts in the work of straightening things out, as in the classical relationship between analyst and analysand in psychoanalysis (2006: 69–80).

The possibility of abusing memory – or being negligent with respect to it – therefore speaks to the aforementioned 'normative stakes and standards' that are bound up with memory-related actions. 'Normative stakes and standards' is perhaps just an overwrought way of saying that according to the general sense of 'ethics of memory', it *matters* when and why and how we do all these things. It is to suggest that it matters *what* we remember (or what we forget); that it also matters *how* we do it; and that it matters *when* and *where* (i.e. how and in what venues or jurisdictions we transmit what we remember, and so on). 'Normative stakes and standards' therefore concern the pragmatic dimension of memory through and through, keeping in mind, of course, that the cognitive dimension and the standard of veracity it implies are inextricably bound up with the pragmatic.

Imagine, for example, that I had written this book 'from memory', after a certain initial period of scholarship, instead of patiently rereading Didion's texts and checking my research notes. Certainly, this would raise questions of proper scholarly technique and competency. But it might even be claimed that I had also done something *wrong*, in an ethical sense, as a scholar. At a minimum, by writing the book in this way I would be doing a disservice to my publisher as well as my readers, who are investing their time and effort and perhaps their money to think and to learn about Didion and the ethics of memory. I would also be doing a disservice to Didion herself, whose writings I must strive not to misrepresent if I am to fairly comment upon and criticize them. It *matters*, in other words, how I recall and bind my research together and as the foregoing attests, it is possible to give an account of why and in what ways specifically it matters.[4] Note that at bottom, the cognitive question frames the normative account: Can we trust that the writer's memories of what he researched are *true* – in other words, that they are, indeed, *memories*? And are they as *complete* as possible, giving therefore *as true as possible* a representation of what he researched? We see here the complementary duality invoked earlier – between memory as true because *veridical* and memory as true because relatively *comprehensive* – structuring a normative judgement of how a scholar relied on his memories in the writing of a book.

As philosopher Avishai Margalit rightly points out (2002), the normative aspects of memory and forgetting in general deserve a deeper look. Notably, they often go unthought, or at least unremarked upon, until they are violated in some way – as, perhaps, in the example I have used previously (my publisher *takes for granted* that I will not wing it, memory-wise, and I suppose my readers do, too. The topic has never come up with my publisher, or with my readership.). This should give us pause, since it suggests that the normative aspects of memory and forgetting form part of the broader background web of norms that we usually take for granted. This means, in turn, that we can perhaps learn something general, maybe even something important, about ourselves and about our communities by reflecting upon them. But before we make this move, note how the norms of truth as veracity and truth as comprehensiveness do not paint the full picture of what is normatively important about memories. Ethical judgement of memory actions is not restricted to cases of remembering, and it is not always framed in terms of the questions *Was it veridical?* and *Was it (relatively) comprehensive?* As we have already seen, there are various other memory actions to account for – and though these are derivative of remembering and forgetting, they pose questions and suggest norms of their own, on account of their unique modalities and the different fora in which they occur.

To underscore the usually unspoken aspect of memory norms, Margalit begins his book *The Ethics of Memory* (2002) with a revealing story reported in a local Jerusalem newspaper: an army colonel publicly forgot the name of a soldier killed under his command, and 'There followed a flood of outrage at the officer who did not remember' (2002: 19). There was in this case no explicit public set of rules available regarding when, where and for whom it would be permissible or forbidden to forget a name. The public reaction in this case is nonetheless intuitively understandable, and it can be plausibly reconstructed without too much effort. Given the colonel's life-and-death responsibilities as a military officer, it was thought that the soldier's death should have mattered to him. Retaining the soldier's name in memory was considered to be a necessary condition or sign of this mattering; it was probably quite literally the least the colonel could have done, when a man for whom he was responsible died. In play here are norms not just of veracity and comprehensiveness, but also of responsibility, authority, character and the value of a human life. All of these crystallize around the cognitive question – what *was* the soldier's name that should have been remembered – and they manifest in the community's outrage. The ethics of memory appears therefore to be no trivial matter, not restricted to one's accuracy or comprehensiveness in recalling facts. It is an issue that speaks to, and that can apparently bring to light, a host of other important and deeply held values.

The reader might have noticed, however, that the two examples used thus far – writing a book sloppily 'from memory' of what has been previously researched, and publicly forgetting the name of a soldier killed under one's command – are both obviously 'public' examples. But recall that in my view, we can also in principle judge putatively 'private' examples as well. We might ask whether the colonel in Margalit's example could be judged similarly if he had forgotten the soldier's name privately, 'on his own time' so to speak. My intuition here, following Murdoch's analysis of inner actions, is that the colonel would be equally culpable (though he would not wind up nearly as embarrassed). As to the example of my writing a book badly in the way described, suppose I did so and never tried to publish it – would I have done anything unethical? Perhaps we could speak here of wasting one's time when there were other pressing matters, or failing to strive for excellence or leaving garbage to my inheritors to sort out after I die – but the case is arguably less sure. The important thing is that when we speak of normative stakes and standards relating to memory actions, we can include both obviously 'public' and more putatively 'private' cases. This was, after all, Murdoch's point: just because an action is interior and unobservable, this does not mean that it has no ethical bearing.

Uncovering the kinds of normative expectations or standards attendant to memory actions allows us to do more, however, than simply learn something interesting and important about ourselves, or about our communities. Such an exercise also allows us to submit our background assumptions and those of our communities to further reflection and critical scrutiny – to open them to 'contestation', in the sense used in the opening pages. Could, for example, the public outcry over the colonel's lapse, though perfectly understandable, have focused blame for a preventable human tragedy onto a relatively low rung of responsibility? Would the colonel's *correct* recitation of the fallen soldier's name have served in any way as a fig leaf to the greater truth that the state, as such, generally values 'manpower' more than the person's uniqueness and the full measure of their sacrifice? Such questions can be debated, but the important thing is that they emerge clearly, when the underlying norms of remembrance have themselves been uncovered and clarified.

There is more at stake here, however, than just unpacking the norms we take for granted, important though this exercise might be for our self-knowledge and social knowledge, and our capacity for self-criticism and social criticism. If Margalit's assessment is correct, there is even further interest in digging into such intuitions and the deeper normative stories they tell. Namely, there might be a relatively underexplored story about how the ethics of memory, be it individual or collective, 'private' or 'public', *shapes and in some sense constitutes* the broader norms of the community that its discussion uncovers. Differently put, there might be a significant link between the ethics of memory, and ethics in general.

The specific sense

This brings me to the more specific sense of 'ethics of memory' that I also will keep in mind and refer to herein, as defined by Margalit in the same book

(2002). To my mind, Margalit's picture is useful and philosophically fleshed out, within certain limits (McLennan 2018b). Note, however, that in following him in sketching a framework for my own book, I am not precluding that there could be other or better senses of 'the ethics of memory'. Nor, by highlighting Margalit, am I suggesting that Didion would understand herself through his picture, or have much to say about it – though interestingly there is evidence that she has read him, having noted his 'considerable intellectual subtlety' in commenting on Israel in *The New York Review* (Didion 2003: 23).

By 'ethics of memory', Margalit is referring to *norms of remembrance and forgetting that flow from, and underpin, human beings' 'thick' relations.* By 'thick relations' he refers to our belonging to various, concentric communities of responsibility and care and concern, participating in what might be called 'shared forms of life'.[5] For Margalit, thick relations are, indeed, 'based on belonging rather than on achievement' (Margalit 2017: 55). Under the heading of such 'thick' relations, we would therefore obviously want to include our immediate families and/or our close friends first, where belonging (as opposed to achievement) is usually paramount. At a further remove we would likely also include our extended kinship groups, our more casual friendships and our local communities. We may include our workplace or occupational ties, our ethnic or religious communities, and perhaps our political affinity groups and the like. We might even extend the concept of 'thick' relations as far as our national belongings, though the further out we get from the immediate family and/or close friends, the more 'virtual' a given relation seems to become, and the harder we might need to work to justify our defining it as 'thick'.[6]

Wherever we draw the line, what 'thick' relations all have in common is their constitution through various memory actions. As Margalit put it, 'Thick relations are oriented toward a shared memory of the past' (Margalit 2017: 73). But for Margalit,

> Shared memory does not mean that the individuals who are in thick relations with one another remember the same thing. There is a mnemonic division of labor in thick relations. Those who stand in such relations are plugged into one another and can fill in the memory gaps. What gives thickness to human relations is to a large extent their historical depth. (Margalit 2017)

This leaves the door open for communities of memory at the national level, and quite nicely describes communities of memory even at the smaller scale, where remembering is always a work done in common. Individual people certainly remember, testify, grieve and the like, but memory actions are never simply something that the individual does on their own. On the contrary, such actions also presuppose and, in turn, play a major role in staking out, through the communal construction and maintenance of an ongoing narrative and associated customs, rites and rituals, who belongs and who does not belong on the basis of shared memory.[7] As such, memory and mnemonic practices constitute who is and who is not the subject of (and subject to) specific community norms. As Margalit puts it, 'Memory is the cement that holds thick relations together, and communities of memory are the obvious habitat for thick relations and thus for ethics' (2002: 8).

The ethics of memory therefore deserves a deeper look for the very reason that *memory is vital to ethics as such*. This might help to explain why norms of memory often go unremarked until violated: perhaps they are so much in the background of our ethical experience that they help to *constitute* that experience in important ways. This they do, precisely, by delimiting who belongs and in what way to the group and its ongoing story, and therefore who is a proper subject of care, concern, responsibility and community standards of normative judgement.

This being so, it is worth noting how Margalit (2002) distinguishes the aforementioned thick sphere of 'ethics' from a thinner, more abstract, but also more comprehensive and universalist 'moral' sphere which would comprise care, concern and responsibility for humanity at large.[8] Our duties to humans as such would include, for example, basic duties of respect and personal as well as institutional non-humiliation to all human beings, including strangers. These would flow from a recognition of their inherent dignity, as well as the defence and promotion of their rights (Margalit 2007).

This distinction between ethics and morality is not universally acknowledged, but it belongs to a major tradition of Western philosophy and has much to recommend it.[9] It is helpful, first, because it sheds light on many so-called 'moral dilemmas'. Here Margalit invokes Jean-Paul Sartre's example of a pupil who faced the decision to stay home to care for his mother, or leave for England to join the Free French Forces and contribute to the war effort against Germany (2010: 141–42). What for Sartre boils down to a choice between the claims of 'two kinds of morality', Margalit construes, rather, as a tragic choice between one's ethical duties and one's moral duties (Margalit

2010). It could be that what is decisive in constituting the pupil's dilemma is the starkly different degree of abstraction, or, rather, the question of who is properly included in the ambit of the two choices.

It is also worth drawing the distinction between ethics and morality as Margalit does because it gives us one way to envision healthy forms of community, and to think through and oppose its toxic forms. In short, Margalit's picture allows us to conceive of the value of community in a non-reactionary and even a progressive way, precisely through its theorizing of a universalist moral sphere.

In terms of healthy forms, a given community of human beings will ideally be both ethical *and* moral in its outlook, its self-understanding and its behaviour. This means, first, that it will take care of its own (as constituted and designated through the cement of shared memory). But the community will *also* have a proper basic regard for members of the human race (and hopefully also for members of sentient non-human species) in general.[10] This community regard for humanity at large could take the form, in particular cases, of transforming a thin or virtual relation into a thick or actual one – or differently put, through developing an *ethical* relation to someone who beforehand only stood in a *moral* relation to us. I have in mind here the welcoming of migrants and refugees – not in the abstract, as policy or as a presumptive normative duty, but the act of giving hospitality to real people, welcoming them in their contingency and difference as new or future anterior members of the ethical (which is to say 'thick') community (Brugère and Le Blanc 2017).

In practice, however, there are numerous examples of communities who fall well short of this ideal – and not just with respect to how they treat migrants and refugees. At the limit there are communities that practice 'ethics without moral constraints', a condition that Margalit calls 'tribalism' and which can take aggressive and inhuman forms (2010: 122). Nazism is the obvious historical example, and Margalit makes much of it, but the point about 'ethics without moral constraints' sheds a good deal of light on forms of community constituted through contemporary racisms, xenophobias and other forms of hateful exclusion.[11]

Within this framework, wherein ethics and morality are distinguished, it is therefore meaningful to speak of distinctly *ethical* as opposed to *moral* norms of memory. To be sure, most norms of memory are ethical in the sense of having to do with our thick relations; as Margalit puts it, 'In thin relations there is very little memory' (2010: 121), and 'while there is an ethics of memory, there is very little morality of memory' (2002: 7). Nonetheless, what moral duties of memory there are, appear to be extremely important.

As a community member I may have an *ethical* duty to remember my ancestors in appropriate ways and to transmit the family or the larger community story at certain times and according to certain rules – perhaps simply because this kind of caring and reparative action is what family or community *means* at bottom. It may even be the case that for similar reasons – under certain conditions, and to the extent possible – I have an ethical duty to 'forget' or more accurately, to refuse to revisit particular memories (more on this in Chapter 3). This could be the case, for example, when I wish to preserve thick ties in the face of the transgressions or even, perhaps, the betrayal of a community member, a friend or a loved one.[12] All of this would depend upon memory's constitutive role in cementing my concentric communities, as Margalit has theorized it. But in addition to these ethical norms, according to Margalit I can also have mnemonic duties to those I have never even met, and whose pain I perhaps can never know, even by approximation.

Specifically, I doubtless have a *moral* duty never to forget and always to duly memorialize 'gross crimes against humanity, especially when those crimes are an attack on the very notion of shared humanity' (Margalit 2002: 9). More than being crimes against particular humans, they are also 'inhuman' in their general meaning and import. As such, they have a moral as well as an ethical resonance. Obvious large-scale and systematic examples are slavery, the Holocaust, the Rwandan genocide, the Armenian genocide and the ongoing genocide and dispossession of Indigenous peoples worldwide. But there is also a crime against humanity – a denial of the wronged party's full inclusion in the moral community – in *any* injury to individuals where their race, their gender, their disability or other differentiating factor is a motivating or structural pretext to dehumanize them. In short, there is a crime against humanity whenever someone is expressively 'cast out' of the human community. In duly memorializing such crimes, at any scale – that is to say, in adding them to the stories that matter to me and to my community – I accord a proper if belated respect for the humanity of those memorialized. I thus perform a reparative expressive gesture that would invite them back into the moral community, even if they have died and this is no longer literally possible.[13] This is a gesture that at minimum saves and cements and transmits *my own* humanity, even if the gesture cannot be directly reparative to those who were wronged.[14]

The normative underpinnings of ethical and moral duties of remembrance would therefore be different on Margalit's model – that is, specific community belonging as opposed to recognition of humanity as such – but all of them point to the importance of stressing the 'ethics of memory' in the more general sense, as laid out earlier. Throughout this book, I will always have the general sense in mind. On specific points relating to Didion, however, I will often refer or allude to Margalit's more specific sense.

Ethics of memory in our times

So much then for the definitional question; the 'what' of the ethics of memory should now hopefully be clear. But I have also claimed previously that the ethics of memory is a highly salient topic in our time, effectively addressing the 'so what' and 'who cares' questions confronting the book on its account. No doubt the ethics of memory has *always* been salient, since as Margalit argues, our mnemonic norms have to do with the bonds and boundaries of our communities and therefore with both our ethical and our broader moral duties. I will argue, however, that insisting upon the ethics of memory could today be especially salutary, even vital.

I hope I will be forgiven for assuming a readership that largely hails from late capitalist or 'Northern' societies, wherein a crumbling neoliberalism gives way to virulent forms of political reaction and exclusionary communitarianism.[15] Under such conditions, the choice appears to be between a rear-guard shoring up of neoliberalism, or a communitarian retreat and retrenchment or finally some form of universalist social and political emancipation. It therefore becomes vital first to articulate, but then also to strive to observe, proper norms of remembering, forgetting and related mnemonic actions. In broad terms, nothing less than both our 'thick' community ties and our 'thinner' relationships to human and perhaps even non-human (McLennan 2018b) strangers are at issue. The following account is not exhaustive, but it should give a good indication of what is at stake.

First, the crumbling of the neoliberal consensus (Mouffe 2018) in an age of new media takes shape as a fracturing, targeting and overloading of information, much of it false and misleading. This is combined with an unprecedentedly rapid news cycle. There are palpable risks here in terms of public memory; quite apart from the question of truth and 'post-truth' (McLennan 2018a), the failure to track our sources, to 'keep our receipts', could have grave social and political costs. One thinks naturally of the news cycle in the United States, which at the time of writing described a seemingly endless political nightmare. In a context of pandemic and acute racialized conflict, to say nothing of the comparatively 'normal' times during his presidency, Trump and those in his orbit simply fabricated claims, many of them about the past or the recent past. This itself became news, and required breakneck fact checking. The obvious risk here – aside from widespread illness and risk of death exacerbated by misinformation – was of a slide into further ignorance, scepticism, hopelessness and endemic conflict. This produced a certain blackmail effect: absent meaningful public alternatives, corporate and partisan media had to be trusted to perpetually and faithfully constitute the archive of the present. In broad strokes, and as the example of the US forcefully suggests, it matters greatly how and through what channels we bear witness to the events of our time, and how we archive and organize them into a narrative not just for our personal coping and social cohesion, but also for our political empowerment.

Second, and lest we feel too comforted by countervailing tendencies to the acceleration and amorcelation of information and the crumbling of mnemonic culture, we must be clear that the political aspect of memory can cut both ways. Specifically, if there are ways to perform remembrance as emancipatory and empowering, then there are also ways to perform it as an ideological prop to embattled neoliberalism, or as a constitutive element of virulent and exclusionary communitarianism.

Regarding neoliberalism in particular, take, for example, the thriving North American culture of literary first-person testimony – the 'memoir boom' in book publishing described and theorized by Leigh Gilmore (2018), to say nothing of blogs, podcasts and the like (I will revisit Gilmore's analysis in Chapter 4). As Gilmore reconstructs it, after a brief period of memoir playing a critical social function in the 1990s, the North American book market is now awash with first-person testimonies that overwhelmingly foreground the bootstrapping ethos of disciplined neoliberal subjects. These narratives shift focus away from structural inequalities and meaningful social change, and they nourish a culture of individual responsibility or 'responsibilization'.[16] In doing so, they implicitly blame the poor, the oppressed and the sick for their predicaments.

Considering its sheer volume and the cultural and political effects published memoir can engender, we are therefore in desperate need of clear standards and a way to distinguish principled egalitarian from perniciously ideological forms of memoir and testimony: not just 'the facts' of a given life or events, which is to say the cognitive side of memory, but also the right facts at the right moment, as per the pragmatic side; not just testimonies to overcoming adversity, but also a range of diverse testimonies giving a clear picture of both triumphs and failures, and of the different structural inequalities impinging upon people's life stories.

In terms of exclusionary communitarianisms, I have already noted how the cement of memory offers sinister possibilities beyond the nurturing forms of affiliation it typically encourages. Specifically, we have seen in many quarters a doubling-down if not a resurgence or spreading of exclusionary and inhumane definitions and attitudes. This might be described, borrowing Margalit's terms, as a global retreat from the moral perspective into the narrower horizon of the ethical.[17] In face of this shift, it will not do simply to tout the superiority of the moral to the ethical. This is because as Margalit reminds us, the ethical is our natural home as communitarian beings, and it is in any case the developmental base from which accession to the moral point of view is even possible.[18]

It is extremely important to get things right, for example, when it comes to national history. In my own country of Canada, at the time of writing, Truth and Reconciliation with First Nations, Métis and Inuit ran aground upon a deeply rooted colonial mindset in settlers, and widespread indigenous mistrust. While a thin 'morality of memory' is no doubt of the essence in combating anti-indigenous racism, it will never flourish without the patient 'ethical' work of remembrance – that is to say, of looking truthfully into the nation's colonial past and present, to the point of questioning and then justly, if not more inclusively, constituting thick relations. As Margalit points out, 'In thick relations there is depth, created by shared memories' (Margalit 2010: 121). 'Shared' cannot, however, simply mean that 'both settler and indigenous communities remember it'. As Ricœur put it, 'What we celebrate under the title of founding events are, essentially, acts of violence legitimated after the fact by a precarious state of right. What was glory for some was humiliation for others. To celebration on one side corresponds execration on the other. In this way, symbolic wounds calling for healing are stored in the archives of the collective memory' (2006: 79). In this light, the vociferous indigenous resistance to

'Canada 150' celebrations in 2017 was unsurprising (Bascaramurty 2017). The very idea of thick relations between settler and indigenous communities, arguably implied by the notion of Truth and Reconciliation, is premised upon revising what is publicly celebrated and then making new memories *together* – for example, through solidarity actions and active settler involvement in decolonizing and indigenizing. Failing this, as Ricœur points out (2006: 79), there will continue to be so significant a historical cleavage between oppressors and oppressed that while both may remember the same events in a rough sense, any shared history would be impossible.

Note how nostalgia, a kind of wistful and wishful recollection, can figure as precisely the opposite of such an honest work of ethical remembrance.[19] The problem with nostalgia is its affective investment in only some aspects of the past; as a kind of *memory*, nostalgic representations do not run afoul of the ethical norm of truth as *veracity*, but they do violate the norm of relative *comprehensiveness*, often quite spectacularly. Fixation on the good times, which were often good for some people but not for others, requires a work of editing, wherein uncomfortable or painful aspects of the past are sacrificed. Such editing can amount to *a second-order falsification of the past*, in the sense that the nostalgic person or community, invested only in good memories, erases or downplays truths that should be remembered and therefore distorts recollection.

This operation can occur at the individual level, for example, when a person pines for the good times with their former lover while downplaying or suppressing the toxicity of their past relationship. But it can also occur at the collective level. Nostalgia can provide a source of affective belonging, in the sense of mobilizing feelings to nourish communities of incomplete and deluded memory. It may also encourage a retreat from the political challenges of the present, or a flight into reaction. In the US, the preposterous slogan 'Make America Great Again' conjures up through a mix of falsification and very partial reminiscence the image of a peaceful and prosperous white community and uses it to ignite the racial resentment of poor whites. But some those critical of Trump made a comparable error when they cast retrospective, nostalgic praise on George W. Bush – a president who was less brazen and guttural, true, but also by any reasonable measure a war criminal who drastically expanded the scope and powers of the police state and destabilized the wider world. In Canada, such uncritical, nationalist nostalgia often takes the form of a pernicious exceptionalism. Commonly heard self-satisfied claims that 'we are the nation that invented peacekeeping' or 'we have never been as bad as the US when it comes to racism', for example, serve to paper over our ongoing colonial, imperial and racist history and promote complacency at a crucial time of historical reckoning.[20]

The costs of nostalgia in terms of communitarian reaction and lost opportunities for social and political progress can already be gleaned from what I have said earlier. But it is also striking that via nostalgia, the imagination – which we saw is very close to, but crucially different from memory – itself appears to be at risk of being blunted, and this means that political possibilities might be foreclosed.[21] It seems perhaps a petty concern to point out that with notable exceptions, movies and television, for example, have devolved into an endless series of remakes and reboots – but this is not unrelated to the bigger question of the scope and powers of the collective social imagination. What are the social and political costs when we stop dreaming of the future and retreat, instead, into past comforts? What would it mean, instead, to use the best of the past to envision the future as a real alternative?

Finally, with all the emphasis on remembering, do we do a disservice to ourselves by omitting the positive ethical salience of *forgetting*? Shoshana Zuboff (2019) describes in chilling terms the risk we now run of losing our very 'right to the future tense' by accepting the Trojan horse technologies of surveillance capitalism into our intimate lives. In a world where everything about us is rendered and sold to corporations banking on their total prediction if not control of our future behaviour, does it not make sense now to insist precisely upon our 'right to be forgotten', and thus our right to the wildernesses and opacities of the human lifeworld? Does the 'ethics of memory' not rightly include a robust reflection on our claim to a certain sanctuary of oblivion?

In such a climate, facing questions such as these, we would do well to encounter thinkers who challenge and provoke us to clarify our norms of memory. More specifically, we need to encounter those who, far from embracing either reactionary communitarianism or some version of 'post-truth', give the fracturing of national and smaller community narratives their due but also teach patient and disciplined handling of facts in the face of rapid information turnover. We need, moreover, exposure to those who challenge us to look clearly and painfully at the legacies of the past. And finally, we need an encounter with those who unsettle our nostalgias and spur us to tarry with a psychologically costly, but also politically productive or even perhaps saving mindset of uprootedness or homelessness, where the possibility if not the very right to a future community and a future tense itself are articulated and upheld.

Transition to Joan Didion

The reader should now have a good idea of what I mean when I speak of the 'ethics of memory', and why I believe it is so important. Assuming that my two initial claims are plausible – that the ethics of memory is a highly salient theme in our times, and that we need teachers and exemplars with respect to it – let us turn, finally, to Joan Didion. Having sounded the alarm on the question of public memory, I submit here my study of Didion, arguing that she responds, in some small if vital way, to our needs. Doubtless, this book represents my attempt to *interpret her works* by means of the theme of the ethics of memory (first aim). But more importantly, I will also attempt to *draw lessons and insights* on that theme from those works (second aim). Didion thus appears in these pages first as an author to be interpreted, or at least as a problem to be approached. But second, and more importantly, she appears as a philosophical and, especially, an ethical thinker. She can be approached as a teacher, perhaps one to be emulated on some points, though like any teacher she is human, and we will have to note her limitations as a resource for thinking the ethics of memory as we go.

For the remainder of this Introduction I will do two things. First, I will add an important missing ingredient: a rough overview of how *Didion herself* arguably understands what she calls 'morality', and how her own basic outlook on ethical and/or moral issues should prepare us for the chapters to follow. Second and finally, I will map out the structure of the remainder of the book according to the modest claim that Didion is 'good to think with' in connection with a variety of issues arising from the ethics of memory.

Ethics and/or morality in Didion

I have spoken of both the general and specific senses of the 'ethics of memory', and have claimed that I will make the connection to Didion in this book. The general sense, simplifying considerably, stipulated that our memory actions matter. The specific sense adopted from Avishai Margalit, again simplifying considerably, stipulated that shared memories constitute our thick relations, and that thick relations are the natural home of ethics – so that memory is particularly salient through its bearing on ethics in general. Margalit's picture also left open the possibility of a comparatively thin 'morality of memory', wherein what matters is to affirm human dignity and bear witness to its violation. This mostly translates into commemoration and mourning of gross crimes against humanity. The moral plane in Margalit gave us, first, a way to untangle many so-called 'moral dilemmas', that is, dilemmas between ethical and moral duties. But second, and more importantly, it gave us a way to evaluate existing communities according to their commitment to humanity, and to envision and work towards better ones.

It might seem that I risk little or no interpretive violence against Didion if the general sense of 'ethics of memory' alone is at issue. To say that it 'matters' in some way when we remember, forget and the like is vague enough that Didion would doubtless agree. She demonstrates, precisely, that memory actions matter in various contexts, and she does this on numerous occasions in her works. But in imputing an 'ethics' to Didion, or 'moral' views or positions, and further by distinguishing between them as Margalit does, this nonetheless raises the question of how *she herself* would likely understand these terms. What, for Didion, are ethics and/or morality in general? And what ethical or moral outlook, if any, does she adopt – both in general, and in connection with remembering and related actions? Even the general sense of 'ethics of memory' raises these questions, but using Margalit's framework to shed light on Didion increases the risk of drowning out her voice. It is therefore important to at least briefly discuss how ethics and/or morality are treated by Didion herself, and to keep this treatment in mind throughout my analysis.

One obvious source for something like an ethical or moral viewpoint in Didion is the short 1965 essay 'On Morality' (Didion 2006: 120–4). Another is the earlier (1961) essay 'On Self-Respect' (Didion 2006: 109–13). As we will see, they help – along with other early essays, from which I will borrow – to form a basic template that Didion refers to and critically negotiates as her career progresses. We have to be careful, because these are comparatively early works, containing views that appear to be nuanced by Didion as time goes on (Nelson 2017; McLennan 2019). Nonetheless, the early works stake out in a particularly clear fashion the major normative themes that will affect or be in play concerning Didion's ethics of memory throughout her career.

In 'On Morality', Didion evinces a characteristic *moral scepticism*. To be clear, this is not moral or ethical nihilism, which would be the lack of belief in any moral or ethical code. Rather, Didion advances a highly circumscribed notion of what she calls 'morality' and cordons off anything more robust – more abstract, more general, more ideal – as dubious, if not highly dangerous. She recounts how when *The American Scholar* asked her to think 'in some abstract way' about morality, her mind veered 'inflexibly toward the particular' (Didion 2006: 120). This is a notable claim, since particularity will be an abiding theme and concern in Didion, affecting her choice of subject matter but also her very style. As she recounts of her time as an undergraduate at Berkeley, she states that

> I tried to think. I failed. My attention veered inexorably back to the specific, to the tangible, to what was generally considered, by everyone I knew then and for that matter have known since, the peripheral. I would try to contemplate the Hegelian dialectic and would find myself concentrating instead on a flowering pear tree outside my window and the particular way the petals fell on my floor. (Didion 2021: 46–7)

The particular is, then, in some sense also the peripheral. This stakes out Didion as a writer who will champion the concrete, the marginal, at the expense of the abstract, the ideal and the widely touted or recognized. As Nelson recounts, Didion also lays down a description of her stylistic strategy in her 1976 essay 'Why I Write' (Didion 2021: 45–57), a strategy which is in line with her own understanding of moral particularity: 'Writing is . . . a process of induction (the thing speaks for itself), obliquity (the periphery rather than the center comes into focus) and impersonality (even the "arrangement of words" has more cognitive agency than the writer)' (Nelson 2017: 154). As Nelson goes on to argue, however, this strategy does not position Didion the writer as in any sense passive: rather, she considers 'confronting "evil" to be a writer's moral obligation' and explicitly aligns herself with George Orwell's notion of the dual aesthetic and partisan nature of writing (Nelson 2017: 154–5; Didion 2021: 45–6). Remarkably, Didion goes so far as to claim that

> In many ways writing is the act of saying I, of imposing oneself upon other people, of saying *listen to me, see it my way, change your mind*. It's an

aggressive, even a hostile act. You can disguise its qualifiers and tentative subjunctives, with ellipses and evasions – with the whole manner of intimating rather than claiming, of alluding rather than stating – but there's no getting around the fact that setting words on paper is the tactic of a secret bully, an invasion, an imposition of the writer's sensibility on the reader's most private space. (Didion 2021: 45–6, emphasis in original)

Overall, Didion therefore interprets herself to be *pushing the reader, through her words and the grammar of her sentences, to look hard at particularity – that is, at the thing itself, which is to say the periphery*. Not incidentally, this stance explains the principal limit or caveat to treating her as a teacher or exemplar in the ethics of memory; at stake in her writing is not simply the particular – the raw material of memory as both veridical and as relatively comprehensive – but also her 'sensibility'. In describing this sensibility in terms of what Nelson calls induction, obliquity and impersonality, Didion therefore appears to want things both ways; by bullying us into a way of looking where 'the thing speaks for itself', she simultaneously defines her point of view while effacing it *as a point of view*. Put differently, in defending the particular, Didion ironically elevates her own viewpoint to the level of the universal. But – perhaps precisely because she has no truck with the dialectic – this can manifest in her writing as an aristocratic and false kind of 'universalism', one that can seem closed to other and unknown points of view on the particular. As the book progresses, we will encounter moments where precisely this stance in Didion seems to prevent her from seeing things differently or more richly, and we will see why this is a limitation where the ethics of memory is concerned.

Circling back to 'On Morality', the example Didion gives of a *moral* particularity is revealing. She tells of a car crash on a desert highway, and of someone who stayed with the body all night so that coyotes did not devour it. This refusal to leave the body, for Didion, derives from no abstract moral theory but, rather, a basic social code, sometimes referred to pejoratively as 'wagon-train morality', that Didion as a child absorbed through 'graphic litanies of the grief awaiting those who failed in their loyalties to each other' such as the Donner-Reed Party and the Jayhawkers (Didion 2006: 120–1). Aware of how none of this rises to the status of a moral theory, she goes on:

You are quite possibly impatient with me by now; I am talking, you want to say, about a 'morality' so primitive that it scarcely deserves the name, a code that has as its point only survival, not the attainment of the ideal good. Exactly. Particularly out here tonight, in this country so ominous and terrible that to live in it is to live with antimatter, it is difficult to believe that 'the good' is a knowable quantity. (Didion 2006: 121)

Because of her moral scepticism, it is with 'ethics' in Margalit's sense, rather than 'morality', that we should expect Didion to mostly engage. This is, indeed, what we find in her writings, first in 'On Morality' itself. Didion insists that 'we have no way of knowing – beyond that fundamental loyalty to the social code' that helps us to survive together '– what is "right" and what is "wrong", what is "good" and what is "evil"' (Didion 2006: 123). She gives no philosophical argument for this position; rather, her essay is above all a warning about the dangers of 'true believers' and their moral certitudes. She asks us: 'Except on what most primitive level – our loyalties to those we love – what could be more arrogant than to claim the primacy of personal conscience?' (Didion 2006: 122). Margalit's 'thick relations', or perhaps more accurately, Ricœur's 'close relations' (2006: 131–2), are above all what is at issue when one reads these lines.

This is not to say that Didion is completely insensitive or closed off to any more abstract notion of human worth and dignity, or to more expansive normative values and duties. To repeat, she is a moral sceptic, not a moral nihilist. As any cursory reading of her works will attest, the scope of her ethical *concern* is not narrow, ranging far beyond her 'close relations'. In her famous 1967 essay 'Slouching Towards Bethlehem' (Didion 2006: 67–97), for example, she demonstrates a serious concern for young people who are doubtless members of her own American society, but who are also in no obvious sense 'close'. As Didion tells it,

> we were seeing something important. We were seeing the desperate attempt of a handful of pathetically unequipped children to create a community in a social vacuum. Once we had seen the children, we could no longer overlook the vacuum, no longer pretend that the society's atomization could be reversed. This was not a traditional generational rebellion. At some point between 1945 and 1967 we had somehow neglected to tell these children the rules of the game we happened to be playing . . . . They are less in rebellion against the society than ignorant of it, able only to feed back certain of its most publicized self-doubts . . . their only proficient vocabulary is in the society's platitudes. As it happens I am still committed

to the idea that the ability to think for one's self depends upon one's mastery of the language, and I am not optimistic about children who will settle for saying, to indicate that their mother and father do not live together, that they come from 'a broken home'. They are sixteen, fifteen, fourteen years old, younger all the time, an army of children waiting to be given the words. (Didion 2006: 93)

What Didion is articulating here is a society's failure with respect to equipping a whole generation of children for life. As I have argued elsewhere (McLennan 2019), anxiety over children *in general* is an index of the other-regarding and hence properly ethical, if not moral, orientation of her works. The theme of the vulnerability of children crops up again in 2003, for example, in her discussions of the Lakewood High School scandal (Didion 2006: 1019–26). In her fiction, moreover, anxiety over children is pervasive, often taking nightmarish forms (Didion 1970: 96–7; Didion 1977: 148–52).

Such concern for others is arguably never absent in Didion, even when she is at her most austere. To take a case in point, in the classic essay 'On Self-Respect', she articulates an ethic of individualism that *at the very same time* recognizes some minimal concept of abstract human worth, having import far beyond the individual whose trajectory she describes. Arguably, even when she is at her most 'individualist' – having been a Goldwater Republican in her youth (Didion 2006: 735–6) – Didion's position is other-regarding well beyond the scope of her thick or close relations, not only on account of recognizing the very existence of such worth, but also through her exhorting certain character traits from the broad public of her readers.[22]

Opening the essay by recounting her disappointment in not making the grade cut-off to join a sorority, Didion describes how being 'driven back on oneself', in the sense of having to look at oneself, being left to one's own devices, seems to her 'one condition necessary to the beginnings of real self-respect' (Didion 2006: 109). This is because 'Most of our platitudes notwithstanding, self-deception remains the most difficult deception' (Didion 2006). Living without such self-deception requires cultivation of self-respect through 'character', (Didion 2006: 111) and having self-respect ultimately amounts to having a sense of one's own 'intrinsic worth' (Didion 2006: 112). Through the contents of her essay, but also through its very address to the public, Didion is staking out values that will play an exhortative but also a *critical* function. The themes of self-respect, character, toughness, self-delusion and intrinsic worth, all of which figure in the essay, allow her in other contexts to chastise as immature those who refuse to 'accept the universe' (Didion 2006: 258) – a notion that we will return to, as it will be important in Chapter 1. As an example of the critical function of such values, on the basis of them Didion elsewhere drubs the women's movement of the 1970s. She does this on account of what she claims is its cult of the 'dolorous phantasm' everywoman who is 'everyone's victim but her own' (Didion 2006: 261). In this respect, the Didion of the 1960s and 1970s is often writing against the grain of seismic cultural shifts and movements – thus laying down potentially expansive values, but using them precisely to attack putatively progressive positions.

The essay on self-respect is also extremely revealing in that it crystallizes Didion's ethos not just as a moral individual recounting her formative past, but also as a writer. In Chapter 2, we will have the chance to explore further how 'self-respect' – in the form of refusing self-pity, refusing to be a victim – generally animates Didion's public-facing persona and her ethos as a writer, only to be severely challenged when she loses both her husband and her daughter in quick succession. Suffice it for now to follow Nelson in her judgement that for the earlier Didion, 'The inability to tolerate one's own pain – that is, to "control" one's own self-pity – begins the slippery slide from moral softness to stylistic sloppiness to self-delusion. To "impose" that self-delusion, rooted in self-pity, on others in the act of writing is, for Didion a violation of the writer's public trust' (Nelson 2017: 154).

Taken together, these essays show how the earlier Didion espouses a kind of 'frontier' ethic of individualism, particularity, self-respect and unsentimental clarity. This is both an *ethos*, in the sense of a personal code of conducting oneself, and an *ethics*, in the sense of appealing to values in exhorting, judging, and in some sense – through writing – serving other people. It is also basically an *ethical* outlook, in Margalit's sense, of being focused on thick or close relations and minimal social codes, as opposed to abstract, universal *moral* values. But as we have seen, Didion was no moral nihilist, and her writings contain clues that she is open to more expansive, perhaps universal, human values – if only through her expressed concern, or the wide public address of her exhortations. This openness eventually leads the way to questioning and self-criticism. In *Where I Was From*, a collection of essays wherein Didion tries to revise her understanding of her home state of California, she centres the dictum of Donner-Reed Party survivor Virginia Reed: 'Remember, never take no cutoffs and hurry along as fast as you can' (Didion 2006: 999). As she puts it, 'When you jettison others as not to be "caught by winter in the Sierra Nevada Mountains", do you not deserve to be caught? When you survive at the cost of [the children who are left behind], do you survive at all?' (Didion 2006: 974) Ethical individualism in Didion, or even a predominant focus on one's very closest relations, is at best unstable. And as we will see in Chapter 4, the later Didion becomes more *political*, in the sense of making the underlying power interests of her society her central concern. The ethical import of this shift should be obvious: Didion develops, at least up until her memoirs on grief (Chapter 2), through the progressive expansion of her ethical scope.

Bearing in mind, then, an ethic of clear-minded toughness – a basic template that becomes nuanced as Didion ages and develops as a writer – we can also anticipate some important aspects of how she intersects with the ethics of memory, both in the general and in the specific sense.

We can anticipate, first, that when it comes to memory – where, as we saw, the cognitive meets the pragmatic – Didion will draw our attention to the *particularity* of what is past, which is to say to the things in all their concreteness, and their apparently peripheral features. Above all, Didion will prize the *veracity* of memory – Ricœur's cognitive sense, explored earlier – interpreted as faithful attention to such particularity. But this also implies the necessity of relative *comprehensiveness*, which Didion champions explicitly under the guise of wanting 'life expanded to a novel, "not a window on the world but the world itself", a view with 'everything in the picture' (Didion 2021: 69). To this end we see her attending to neglected aspects of local or national history to challenge or set the dominant narrative straight. As Ricœur reminds us (2006: 209–16), different details emerge at different 'scales' of history (or of memory, in general). In this spirit, while Didion is known for transmitting the broader history of the present, or at any rate its moods and preoccupations, she often does so in a surprising way by homing in on the particular, the peripheral, the neglected. The bedrock memory-ethical values of veracity and relative comprehensiveness are therefore in play in Didion in obvious ways. To be sure, these are undermined to an extent by what I earlier called an aristocratic universalism that emerges ironically from her partisan 'sensibility' of the particular. Nonetheless, her investment in the two main values is demonstrable and even her limitations with respect to them are instructive.

These values raise a further issue, however, that I will address at some length in Chapter 3. Earlier, I raised the possibility that in some situations there could be a positive ethical duty to 'forget', or more accurately to refuse to revisit a given memory. The interest in doing so would be in repairing our thick relations. Short of these being shattered altogether through betrayal (Margalit 2017), I might want to put poor treatment by a loved one or friend or community member behind me. If the person in question has expressed and demonstrated a sincere commitment to repairing our relations, and if, for example, there are important traditions or caring concerns at stake – for example, raising children in common, or reproducing a society in which being given a chance to redeem oneself is an important value – then it might make sense to look largely, or perhaps even only forward. Forgiveness might have something to do with leaving certain memories locked away, if not actively forgetting. Didion, however, would arguably repudiate this possibility. Her commitment to 'the particular' and to the truth over any supervening values would seem to preclude it. Moreover, as suggested by 'Slouching Towards Bethlehem', one gets the impression that it is through vigilant guarding and transmission of the truth, not wilful or lazy obscurity, that one actually protects those whom one cares about.

We will see throughout the book that Didion's commitment to clear, truthful, relatively comprehensive and unsentimental memory leads her to adopt a number of positions requiring certain virtues of fortitude. It leads her to reconstruct and transmit the meaning of her loss and grieving, even if this devastates her. It leads her to repudiate nostalgia, and to engage in rigorous self-critique about her past sentimentality. Finally, it leads her to fight political amnesia in a time of acceleration and forgetting. In short – as I will presently explain – Didion evinces several value positions with respect to memory, and this makes her 'good to think with' concerning the ethics of memory.

Thinking with Didion

To add a final element to the context of my intervention, it helps to know that in my previous book (2019), I stipulated a definition of philosophy. The definition was that philosophy is the *self-conscious activity of the mastery of one's being mastered*. Though I did not cite it at the time, Didion in 'Why I Write' gives an excellent encapsulation of what I meant by this: 'Had I been blessed with even limited access to my own mind there would have been no reason to write. I write entirely to find out what I'm thinking, what I'm looking at, what I see and what it means. What I want and what I fear' (Didion 2021: 49). Didion was one of three thinkers from whom I drew to illustrate that definition (the others being Audre Lorde and Catherine Breillat). The book was in part meant to provoke, in that neither Didion nor Breillat nor Lorde practise philosophy in an academic or 'disciplinary' sense; for one thing, they typically use methods or media uncommon to the discipline, and for another, they are not typically recognized as part of the canon. Didion's inclusion as a 'philosopher' in that book was thus an invitation to refresh or inspire the discipline through non-canonical sources, as well as a reminder that much deep thinking happens 'out of bounds', and that academic philosophers ignore it at the discipline's peril.

I view the following study as supportive of my previous argument that Didion is in some sense a philosopher, since it provides supplementary demonstration of her philosophical thinking in action – that is, 'philosophical' as I construe it. But it is also detachable from the previous book, and I believe that it can be profitably read on its own. My argument is simply that Didion offers profound, fertile and politically timely insights into the theme of the ethics of memory, and that even her limitations are instructive. At the limit, and simplifying even further, I will use a formulation favoured by Donna Haraway (2016): it will suffice for me to show that when it comes to the ethics of memory, Didion is 'good to think with', and therefore on that account (to say nothing of other reasons), she is worth the reader's patient engagement.

Note that in methodological terms, Haraway's formulation offers a certain trade-off. Saying that it suffices that Didion is 'good to think with' on matters of the ethics of memory frees me up considerably because it takes me off the hook for defending any strong or even particularly expansive interpretation of her works (for example, to the effect that 'the ethics of memory is *the* key to understanding Joan Didion'). Rather, the interpretation given in these pages is relatively 'weak' in hermeneutic terms. I am confident that the book provides a productive point of entry to Didion in general, but it remains a point of entry only. This methodological limitation might seem to be more of an issue than it is, and for two reasons. First, as I pointed out at the beginning of this Introduction, I am simply less interested in the coherence, sense or lack thereof of Didion's corpus than I am in what I identify as the ethical and political salience of what an encounter with her can provide. But second, in the wake of decades of post-structural literary critique, it would be a bold gesture, indeed, to insist upon the claim that Didion is a self-identical author presenting us with a coherent body of work (Foucault 1977, Gilmore 2001). Remarkably, and as I will explain later in the book, Didion herself often gives evidence of what might be called a post-structural or at least hyper-critical approach.[23] That is, she frequently turns radical criticism upon herself, questioning the efficacy of narrative in general and undercutting her own authorial status repeatedly in her writings (I have suggested earlier, though, that this effacement pretends to let the particular as she sees it 'speak for itself', and thus ironically permits the emergence of an 'aristocratic' universalism in the guise of her own 'sensibility'). For my purposes, this approach is highly revealing, since for one thing it gives the contemporary decomposition of the ethical, in Margalit's sense, its due. As I will explain, however, this critical angle is problematic and Didion tempers it later in her career. Whatever we make of it, she often seems reticent regarding the possibility of robust interpretations.[24]

The loss then, such as it is, is that the book will offer a weak interpretation of what is going on in Didion's corpus. There is no master key here, though I think I can defend the weaker claim that the ethics of memory provides a promising approach. But what, then, are the gains of adopting Haraway's formulation? In what ways, in other words, is Didion 'good to think with' when it comes to the ethics of memory? While I do not claim to exhaust all the ways in which an encounter with Didion might be salutary regarding the ethics of memory, I think she is good to think with in at least five ways – and these determine the structure of the remainder of the book.

Didion is, first, good to think with when it comes to diagnosing and conceptualizing the decomposition of the ethical. The connection to memory is key here because if Margalit's conception is granted, such decomposition both causes and is caused by the loss of both individual and community memory. It is notable on this count that throughout her works, Didion seems to present a fundamentally indifferent, entropic and precarious vision of the universe and our place in it as individuals, and therefore also as individuals comprising a human society (Chapter 1). Though she offers no philosophical arguments on this issue in the traditional sense, her 'metaphysics', if I can call it that, seems to be primary to her worldview and seems also to cannily describe something like the 'postmodern' vision that is often blamed by conservatives and old-school Leftists alike for American social decomposition in the late-twentieth century and beyond. Assuming we take a 'disenchanted', moreover indifferent, entropic and precarious view of the universe, as Didion does, what does this entail for ethics in general? Does it entail an embrace of narrative breakdown, as she seems to indicate, and therefore an acquiescence to memory loss and the foundering of ethical communities? Or does it provide a saving opportunity to free ourselves from pernicious forms of memory like reactionary nostalgias, and thus look more soberly upon the social and political tasks confronting us?

Second, Didion is good to think with when it comes to forms of witnessing, trauma and grieving (Chapter 2). The aforementioned bleak world view, often described as 'frontier' or 'Western' in its character, leads Didion early in her career to expound a rigorous individualist ethos. This is tempered, however, by an anxiety and dread belying a fierce and palpable sense of responsibility and duty to care for her loved ones – and one often detects in her writings, for the vulnerable of her society in general. I will show how this sense of responsibility and care, in the face of an indifferent universe, eventually manifests in Didion's moving, clear-sighted and cutting writings on mournful practices of memory – in particular, *The Year of Magical Thinking* and *Blue Nights*. Here Didion serves as a teacher and a courageous exemplar to the grieving individual. But as I will also indicate, building upon the work of Jill Stauffer, Judith Butler and Leigh Gilmore, there is the opportunity to interpret Didion in terms of less particular, and more public forms of grief and testimony as well. In reaching out, through her writing, does Didion not indicate a pathway to forms of solidarity in the face of the universe's indifference?

Third, Didion is good to think with against the perennial temptation of nostalgia (Chapter 3). As mentioned earlier, nostalgia is costly in terms of communitarian retrenchment, but also in terms of its potentially dampening effects on the imagination and social and political invention. To show what Didion has to offer on this theme, this chapter focuses primarily upon the gap between her first novel, *Run River*, and her later collection of essays on California, *Where I Was From*. I will reconstruct how in the latter, Didion performs a far-reaching self-critique, demonstrating an ethos of guarding against nostalgic impulses and their tendency to wrap everything up in a ready-made interpretation. Here we glean some possibilities for using Didion as an exemplar and a prescient resource in nostalgic times. But since nostalgia is perhaps best understood as a failure of the relative comprehensiveness of memory, we are confronted by the question of whether Didion has anything to offer in terms of forgiveness (where it may be precisely a question of sacrificing accuracy or comprehensiveness to preserve a thick relation), or the 'critical fabulation', to use Saidiya Hartman's term, that historically oppressed peoples may have to engage in when relative comprehensiveness is not even an option.

Fourth, Didion is good to think with when it comes to public and expressly political aspects of memory (Chapter 4). Drawing from her later novels and political essays I will agree with other interpreters that she makes a 'political turn' in later writings, effectively enjoining her readers to dig beneath the narrative breakdown she earlier diagnosed and to focus in on the underlying and persistent backroom *political* story that actually ties contemporary life together. A key part of this chapter will be to show how Didion resists the surface effect of 'post-truth' before the letter, all the while managing to accurately diagnose and critique the phenomena that the latter has come to name. A second key part of the chapter will be to show why the memoir aspects of Didion's writings do not on balance place her in the pernicious ideological category of 'neoliberal life narrative', as Gilmore calls it (2018: 85–117).

Finally, in the Conclusion, I will suggest that Didion – through the theme of the ethics of memory – is good for thinking about the future and futurity. This might seem a counter-intuitive claim, but it will emerge that the future is, indeed, beholden to the past, in the sense that we foreclose possibilities precisely by letting the past get the better of us.

1

'Earthquake weather'

Didion's universe

To gauge Didion's contributions in terms of the ethics of memory, I believe it would be helpful first to grasp her view of the *universe*, or *reality* or the *world*. Using these terms synonymously, I intend to refer both to Didion's take on the social universe and to the broader 'natural' universe in which human society is embedded. Perhaps more accurately, and in keeping with the methodological caveats of the Introduction, I should put it as follows: I claim in this chapter that it would be helpful to grasp the overall universe, or reality or world that Didion *appears to present* in her writings, or that can be *gleaned from* them – whether or not she can be said to consistently believe in it – in order to later draw lessons on the ethics of memory from her body of works.

I claim that starting here is pertinent because Didion's thoughts on how ethics intersects with memory, which I will start to unpack in the next chapter, appear to be absolutely coloured by the picture of reality that can be gleaned from her writing – that is to say, by the 'ontology' or 'metaphysics' her writing suggests, though I hesitate to rely on these terms for two reasons.

First, as I argued in *Philosophy and Vulnerability*, Didion is a 'philosopher' but in a 'pre-disciplinary' or 'existential' sense (2019). There I defined such baseline philosophical activity as Didion engages in as 'the self-conscious activity of the mastery of one's being mastered', and I showed how she often grapples with finitude (her own, and that of her loved ones and communities) using finite tools (thinking through the medium of writing, her attention directed at particularity). In sum, Didion through her writing engages in activity that could be considered philosophical on my definition, though she cannot be considered a disciplinary philosopher (in fact, she 'resists belonging to any class narrower than "writer"', and though she studied English as an undergraduate at Berkeley, returning there for a fellowship in the late 1970s, she had a tenuous foothold in the academy (Parker 2018: ix)). For these reasons – the continuity of my interpretation, and Didion's own self-interpretation – I will go easy on terms suggestive of disciplinary philosophy, except where these are especially helpful in illuminating some aspect of her works. Whenever I do use technical philosophical terms, I will try to be clear that it is me and not Didion who is construing things in that manner.

Second, and related, the use of the terms 'ontology' and 'metaphysics' might tempt us into pursuing technical philosophical questions about the very nature or 'depth' of nature itself in Didion. In theory these are interesting questions, but what she provides is more thematic than systematic. It is more useful for my purposes to speak straightforwardly of 'reality' in what could be construed as a naïve way – especially considering Didion's sensibility of 'induction' from particularity, wherein as Nelson puts it, 'the thing speaks for itself' (Nelson 2017: 154).

On such a straightforward view there is simply 'reality' and 'illusion', and the two are mutually exclusive. But immediately a problem arises: if Didion gives evidence of adhering to such a view, she also appears to derive no epistemic comfort from it. What I have called the 'aristocratic universalism' of her sensibility notwithstanding, she punctuates her writing with doubt. She does this even as she insists that it is the 'shimmering' picture in her mind, and not her, that 'dictates the arrangement' of her sentences (Didion 2021: 51). Referring to such pictures and arguably interpellating her reader, she claims that if 'you' look hard enough at them, 'you can't miss the shimmer. *It's there*' (Didion 2021: 49–50, emphasis added). But this, of course, leaves open the question of whether and to what extent pictures 'in the mind', even those that are apparently clear and self-evident to her, *really do* map onto reality. Interestingly, the earlier Didion seems at once to affirm a straightforward view of reality and to suggest that it is practically untenable: 'I have as much trouble as the next person with illusion and reality,' she tells us (Didion 2006: 32), if not more so – as intimated by her claim elsewhere that though the images feeding her writing really do 'shimmer', they also shimmer for people on hallucinogens, and for schizophrenics (Didion 2021: 50). The partisanship of the particular she describes in 'Why I Write' is, after all, about 'the imposition of the writer's sensibility,' (Didion 2021: 46) and a sensibility is not the same thing as a coherent philosophical programme. It is important, though, to stress that Didion's scepticism is still far from radical; she qualifies her adult life as 'a succession of expectations, misperceptions, that . . . dealt only with an idea that I had of the world, not with the world as it was. Reality *does* intervene,' and in doing so it nourishes a particular outlook or affective colouring, as I will describe (Parker 2018: 34, emphasis in original). In this way, Didion delivers not merely a perspective on the particular, but also a perspective on *the world* and on its power to impinge upon our lives.

To be sure, the same Didion who ironically elevates the particular to the universal and in doing so disavows her perspective *as perspective*, also at times gives the unavoidably perspectival nature of her outlook its due. She is self-conscious, despite invoking 'reality', about her limitations as a knower and a thinker and a writer, and of the limitations of writing in general, as a means of encapsulating and expressing it:

> I was trained to distrust other people's versions, but we go with what we have.
> We triangulate the coverage.
> Handicap for bias.
> Figure in leanings, predilections, the special circumstances which change the spectrum in which any given observer will see a situation.
> Consider what filter is on the lens. (Didion 1995: 124)

In this vein, Didion claims for writing *both* a kind of straightforward realism and a self-reflexive function related to deriving 'meaning' from the encounter with the particular: her only '"subject"' or '"area"' (scare-quotes in the original) is actually 'the act of writing' itself (Didion 2021: 46), and she adds that 'I write entirely to find out what I'm thinking, what I'm looking at, what I see and what it means. What I want and what I fear' (Didion 2021: 49). But notably she ends the essay 'The White Album', reflecting on aspects of the end of the 1960s, with the claim that 'writing has *not yet* helped me to see what it means' (Didion 2006: 212, emphasis added). I think that this fault line is emblematic of her approach to writing in general; even if nothing should seem to be exactly given or clearly rendered, the 'not yet' of meaning contains at least a suggestion of a possible match between the world as it really is and the subject who writes. After all, reality *does* intervene in a person's life, even if belatedly – as Didion describes of her own case (Parker 2018: 34). This stance puts her squarely in line with the definition of philosophy as a precarious but by no means pointless activity that I have previously defended.

To return, finally, to the claim that questions of reality are a good place to start in approaching Didion, I will argue in this chapter that she gives something approaching a perspective on the universe, whatever we wish to make of her doubts and the reflexivity of her writing. Her universe – or at any rate, the universe that is there to be gleaned from her writings, the one that apparently 'intervenes' to shape her thinking – is, overall, *indifferent, entropic* and *precarious*. The universe is *indifferent* in Didion to the extent that it neither centres nor 'holds' the human being and what she cherishes. The universe is *entropic* in Didion to the extent that order and life and community are eked out, hard won and likely only ever temporary, being finally at the mercy of natural forces. Finally, the universe is *precarious* in Didion to the extent that imminent disaster is the norm rather than the exception, lurking even in the everyday.

In this chapter I will give my reasons for drawing this picture from Didion. Chapter 2 will then explain how precisely it bears on memory and the ethics of memory; Chapters 3 and 4 and the book's Conclusion will thereafter take this bearing for granted. In brief, the set-up in this chapter allows me to claim in the remainder of the book that 'Didion's picture of reality', which reflects a radical or even abject modernism, makes her good to think with when it comes to the increasingly palpable decomposition of the ethical, in Margalit's sense, and what that has to do with practices of memory today.

The sense in which I describe Didion as a 'modernist' is philosophical rather than literary and will be further unpacked in Chapter 2.[1] For now, note that her 'modernism' is a self-critical version of the post-metaphysical and forward-facing time-consciousness largely shaping and driving our age. Focused on the present and future and largely jettisoning the past, such a consciousness is vulnerable to ethical decomposition, and, indeed, may contribute to hastening it or to inviting reactionary communitarianisms, at least if it fails to articulate something like Margalit's moral viewpoint. It is in this sense that Didion appears to imbibe, reflect and spread the much-discussed disenchantment and anomie of the postwar period, especially evident in the 1960s and thereafter. Reading Didion, we appear to enter a universe that does not hold us *in general*. We fear with good reason, perhaps, that there is no cosmic meaning or personal survival after death. This would make other humans our only means of survival after death, and fragile ones at that (Chapter 2). Such a scenario endows communities of care and concern with grave ethical importance, as we earlier saw Margalit has suggested. But reading Didion, we also note that contemporary American society (and by extension, other late capitalist societies) increasingly lacks any fixed, unifying meaning or narrative beyond the neoliberal one of economic maximization. This is an issue because narrative, as a practice of communal memory, grounds the ethical community. We therefore see that existing societies, like the universe that fails to hold them, are, rather, in a perpetual process of ethical decomposition and, perhaps, increasingly dubious ethical recomposition (Chapter 3) – though as I will discuss in Chapter 4, the later Didion, from about the 1980s on, appears to reconsider the extent to which there is, indeed, an underlying narrative or political logic to the comparatively chaotic social surface.

All of this matters, I have argued, because Didion demonstrates how in a period of ethical decomposition undergirded by a precarious vision of reality, it is still possible to stay clear-headed and resist the urge to move towards a bad-faith, reactionary recomposition of the ethical community. She provides a model wherein coping with anomie, with sociological 'postmodernity', is not simply to beat a fetishistic retreat into fantasies about the community and its past. As we will see, taking this option suggests the character flaw of self-delusion; it betrays *veracity*, which is a cardinal point in Didion's ethical orientation, as well as the memory-ethical value of relative *comprehensiveness*, which pushes her to want 'life expanded to a novel' rather than 'life reduced to a short story' (Didion 2021: 69). And this might add up to more than just an ethical concern: though avowing that the situatedness of her telling and its focus on particularity always problematizes it, Didion's commitment to the truth and to 'giving it to us straight' – her posture of *universalism*, however ironic or 'aristocratic' – points to an enlarged ethical community and perhaps even the *moral* in Margalit's sense, in other words that which she believes she owes us *qua* human beings, irrespective of our particular ties to her. But there is also room here, as we will explore further in Chapter 2, for discussion of *character traits* or *virtues* required to sustain such an ethical and perhaps moral point of view. Ultimately, the universe gleaned from Didion allows her to suggest how an ethics of memory is necessary, while not being cosmically sufficient, to preserve something of people and places past. Her ethics of memory is therefore in some sense 'courageous', 'heroic' perhaps, but at a minimum it is obstinate. And it is self-consciously so, because it posits its own necessity even after taking the full measure of its ultimate, cosmic futility.

This chapter, in sum, forms the backdrop against which Didion's ethics of memory will emerge with clarity. An important further aspect of the chapter however will be to look at how space, place and, eventually, politics inform Didion's view of the universe, and how they link up with her notion of time and memory. Specifically, I will look at her framings of 'South' and 'West' – the former including not just the southern United States, but also real and imagined Latin American locales and political fault lines that she problematically invokes to underscore her entropic vision. Since Didion's universe is embedded and expressed in tropes that can be challenged, it is also worthwhile to take this discussion as a more general commentary upon her limitations; it is not always advisable, for example, to take a literary depiction as an argument and therefore the overall gesture of this book is hypothetical. *If* we adopt an entropic and meaningless cosmic perspective, *then* Didion has much to teach us – though as she herself seems to realize as her thought develops, this perspective is open to challenge and nuancing.

Didion's atmosphere of dread: indifference, entropy, precarity

The three elements of Didion's universe identified here, indifference, entropy and precarity, form something of a thematic knot in her writings. The knot is at once conceptual, affective and symbolic.

Conceptually speaking, the three elements go together in Didion and are somewhat artificially separated in my analysis. *Indifference*, for example, manifests in her texts through the fact that the universe exposes us (to put it awkwardly) to *precarity* and irretrievable loss through *entropy*, and because it does not ultimately redeem our suffering on account of these through progress or posterity.

The same is true of the knot considered in its *affective* dimension. Reading Didion can often be unsettling, particularly her novels but also classic pieces of social reporting like the 1967 essay 'Slouching Towards Bethlehem' (Didion 2006). An atmosphere of *dread* arises from the fact that she pays significant attention to the *precarity* of everyday life and the lives of empires, the *entropic* slide into greater and greater exposure to said precarity, and the *indifference* of a universe that offers no remedy or consolation.

Finally, regarding the claim that indifference, entropy and precarity form a *symbolic* knot in Didion, one searches for a 'tensor sign' in Jean-François Lyotard's sense: an over-determined sign which gathers multiple meanings and thereby multiple intensities into itself (Lyotard 1993). Here the meteorological and geological metaphors that frequently crop up in Didion help. If the universe is at all predictable in Didion, it is predictably unstable, dangerous, even cataclysmic at times and it strikes indiscriminately.[2] There is perhaps no better stand-in for her take on the universe than her invocation of 'earthquake weather' – a remarkable Californian folk concept, in which two orders of natural phenomena that are usually considered to be mutually exclusive overlap.

'Earthquake weather' receives more than one definition or expression in Didion, but all converge around the necessity of living with precarity – California being a land of 'extreme local possibilities' including 'imminent devastation' (Didion 2006: 657). Earthquake weather is 'a sultriness, a stillness, an unnatural light; the jitters' (Didion 2006: 374). It is a yellow cast to the sky, associated with the Santa Ana winds – hot, whining, maddening winds 'drying the hills and the nerves to the flash point', portending wildfires and driving people into anxiety and unhappiness (Didion 2006: 162–3). As Didion describes them, 'the violence and unpredictability of the Santa Ana affect the entire quality of life in Los Angeles, accentuate its impermanence, its unreliability. The wind shows us how close to the edge we are' (Didion 2006: 164). To this effect, she recalls that her grandmother believed 'an amorphous bad mood' to be adjunct to earthquake weather (Didion 2006: 374). And as the name itself suggests, actual earthquakes, again a quintessentially Californian phenomenon, also index the feeling of dread that can be gleaned from Didion. She describes how 'I have lived all my life with the promise of the Big One, but when it starts going now even I get the jitters' (Didion 2006: 616).

Note that 'earthquake weather' names neither the winds nor the earthquakes themselves, but a meteorological phenomenon and a feeling portending them. As such, as the term is usually used, it is less openly violent than suggestive of violence. It is this quality that I think best captures Didion's universe: its sinister cast, the immanent *possibility* of disaster and 'the jitters' foretelling of it.[3] The obvious objection would be that as a meteorological phenomenon and the jittery feeling it causes, 'earthquake weather' is abnormal – precisely, it is unusual, it is *not the norm*. As such, it could not possibly stand on its own for a 'universe', if we take this term to mean anything approaching a coherent view of reality. But in Didion, even when the jitters are muted, the possibility of disaster is very clearly built into the normal, the everyday. This is evidenced, for example, by post-traumatic shock and incredulity:

> Have you noticed?
>
> The way people always describe the ordinary nature of the circumstances in which the disaster occurred?
>
> The clear blue sky from which the plane fell?
>
> The way the children were playing on the swings as usual when the rattlesnake struck from the ivy? (Didion 2007: 33)

It is also worth mentioning the traumatized, dissociating character Maria in *Play it as it Lays* – arguably in certain respects a projection of Didion – dreading 'the peril, unspeakable peril, in the everyday' (1970: 100).

Again, the geological aspect of 'earthquake weather' steps in to clarify things further. If the earthquake is a disruption, a disaster even, its obverse is *the normalcy that is only ever a transitory compromise*. Characteristically inserting herself as the 'not quite omniscient author' (Didion 1996: 5) of her novel *Democracy*, Didion describes how

> as the granddaughter of a geologist I learned early to anticipate the absolute mutability of hills and waterfalls and even islands. When a hill slumps into the ocean I see the order in it. When a 5.2 on the Richter scale wrenches the writing table in my own room in my own house in my own particular Welbeck Street I keep on typing. A hill is a transitional accommodation to stress, and ego may be a similar accommodation. A waterfall is a self-correcting maladjustment of stream to structure, and so, for all I know, is technique. (Didion 1995: 18)

As such, the norm in Didion is the transitory balance of violent forces. If there is any creative aspect to her universe, it is the kind that is premised upon a longer view of entropy and destruction. Even the ego, she recognizes, is a precarious compromise.

'Earthquake weather' could therefore be described as a moment when we become cognizant of the universe's underlying or *normal* entropy, indifference and precarity. It is as though nature's ever-present violence crystallizes, momentarily, as dread. Following Didion in highlighting symbols like earthquakes, wildfires and rattlesnakes, however, here is a certain risk of misunderstanding. One should doubtless avoid artificially separating 'nature' from humans and speaking as though precarity is only a function of the disasters that befall our species from some exterior zone of being. In an era of climate emergency, it is necessary to remember that 'natural' disasters are mediated by human activity. The COVID-19 pandemic, Hurricane Katrina and scores of other disasters demonstrate that 'acts of God' are both socially and politically driven, and unequally impactful. Perhaps the reason why we often fail to recognize our handiwork in putatively 'natural' disasters is that it comes back to haunt us in an alienated, almost unrecognizable form, a phenomenon that Jean-Paul Sartre named the 'practico-inert' (Sartre 2004). Thankfully, Didion's universe seems to make room for recognition of such alienated activity and underscores the human-driven nature of different types of disaster. Franny Nudelman (2016) reminds us, for instance, that a fruitful way to track Didion's development is through the topic of *nuclear* dread – Didion having grown up in the shadow of nuclear war and annihilation. Moreover, Didion drops clues to the effect that between 'natural' and 'human' entropy, she prefers the former; hence her oddly and eerily *favourable* description of Alcatraz Island as 'a ruin devoid of human vanities, clean of human illusions, an empty place reclaimed by the weather' (Didion 2006: 156).

In fact, a certain pessimism of *human* nature emerges in Didion, going a long way to enriching her account of 'earthquake weather' and explaining her expressed political and ethical commitments.[4] Having come of age just prior to the revolutionary ferment of the 1960s, she describes in the 1970 essay 'The Morning After the Sixties' her alienation from the new social movements she would later famously go on to critique. Feeling hers was 'the last generation to identify with adults,' (Didion 2006: 330), Didion describes

> the ambiguity of belonging to a generation distrustful of political highs, the historical irrelevancy of growing up convinced that the heart of darkness lay not in some error of social organization but in man's own blood. If man was bound to err, then any social organization was bound to be in error. It was a premise that still seems to me accurate enough, but one which robbed us of a certain capacity for surprise. (Didion 2006: 329–30)

Given this dark view of human nature, which Didion still more or less identifies with at the time of her essay, 'the personal was all that most of us expected to find' in life (Didion 2006: 330). But more than that, 'the exhilaration of social action seemed to many of us just one more way of escaping the personal, of masking for a while that dread of the meaningless which was man's fate' (Didion 2006). Here we are in proximity with the ethic of truth-telling and living without self-delusion that I have ascribed to Didion: what is wrong, exactly, with masking the dread of the meaningless if that feels better for a while – unless we can only do so at the cost of self-delusion, an ethically salient betrayal of 'the personal'? And since 'the personal' is emphasized, we are also arguably proximate to the minimal, 'wagon train' morality described in the Introduction. Note, however, that just as I argued there, Didion points here too towards more substantive values even as she despairs of them: 'If I could believe that going to a barricade would affect man's fate in the slightest I would go to that barricade, and quite often I wish that I could, but it would be less than honest to say that I expect to happen upon such a happy ending' (Didion 2006: 331). Here we see the value Didion *would place* in a purely hypothetical social and political efficacy. This indexes her apparent belief that despite the built-in darkness of humanity, it is not meaningless at least to pine after the chance to make sacrifices for humanity's good.

The important point is that Didion shows an abiding preoccupation with 'natural' forces and dangers, both human and otherwise. So it is perhaps not surprising that her frequently expressed interest in design and infrastructure, particularly water infrastructure, forms the other side of the coin. Hailing from an arid climate, Didion claims to be particularly attuned to water and the question of its delivery. She relates that perhaps the best definition of the American 'West' she has ever read is one emphasizing its aridity, and she claims to have a 'passion for seeing water under control' (Didion 2006: 225). She goes so far as to say that the way dams are to her, their beauty, 'almost makes me weak' (Parker 2018: 29), and she expresses regret over never having worked at a reservoir, calling it 'the only vocation for which I had any instinctive affinity' (Didion 2006: 223). Note how Didion dissolves the elements of the very notion of 'control of water' into an interpretation of water's importance: 'Water is important to people who do not have it, and the same is true of control' (Didion 2006: 225). This accounts for why, visiting the Operations Control Center for the California State Water Project in Sacramento, she is impressed by the 'prodigious coordination, precision, and the best efforts of several human minds' its operations require (Didion 2006: 222). Her comments on 'the symbolic content of swimming pools', particularly in drought-prone California, are similarly revealing:

> a pool is misapprehended as a trapping of affluence, real or pretended, and of a kind of hedonistic attention to the body. Actually a pool is, for many of us in the West, a symbol not of affluence but of order, of control over the uncontrollable. A pool is water, made available and useful, and is, as such, infinitely soothing to the western eye. (Didion 2006: 224)

Clarifying the notion of 'control over the uncontrollable', Didion concedes that water is 'the only natural force over which we have any control out here' (Didion 2006). California remains relatively inhospitable to permanent settlement, and its apparently easy or laid-back life is illusory (Didion 2006: 225). Water is therefore such an important value in Didion precisely because its infrastructure in California represents a victory over the uncontrollable. Having lived through flood and drought, however, she knows that this control is only ever a precarious one. And it is also important not to miss how Didion, 'granddaughter of a geologist', frequently deploys the image of water to suggest the inevitability of erosion, drowning, 'the end to which even the island will eventually come' (1995: 18, 84).

Other images of design and infrastructure, gaining a modicum of control over 'external' natural forces or human nature, are frequent in Didion. She describes, for example, being kicked out of 'one greenhouse or another' all her life, craving their 'particular light and silence' (Didion 2006: 337). It also pays to recall that when she was younger, in New York working for *Vogue* magazine, she studied 'shopping-center theory' by correspondence (Didion 2006: 312). Her plan was to finance her fiction writing through a career building shopping malls. This was a decision that was certainly economic, but also indexed the peculiarities of her personality.[5] Malls were likely privileged sites for Didion because they stood as 'climate-controlled monuments' to the 'peculiar and visionary time' after the Second Word War, when 'For one perishable moment . . . the American idea seemed about to achieve itself' (Didion 2006: 311). It is not simply the order and behavioural control implied in shopping-center design that stands out here, but also her stressing that such monuments were 'climate-controlled'. Didion, the famous writer, admits to wishing she could 'be' the great theorists of shopping-centers whom she studied (Didion 2006: 314), much in the same way that she wishes she could work at a reservoir.

Note that for all she writes favourably of control over nature, Didion also appears at times wary of control for control's sake, seeing something ultimately pointless, if not inhuman, about it. This emerges in her imaginary picture of the Hoover dam, after humans are all gone, as 'a dynamo, finally free of man, splendid at last in its absolute isolation, transmitting power and releasing water to a world where no one is' (Didion 2006: 326). She also famously skewers the 'spectral circularity' of bureaucratic reason underpinning Los Angeles freeways (Didion 2006: 240), intimating that human control over nature is ultimately undermined by human decision-making – after all, itself only another aspect or region of nature.

The question that intrudes at this point, suggested by the possibility of the Hoover dam 'finally free of man', is that of any possible *valuation of life* in such a universe. I am speaking here both of any value that life *as such* could have, and of the value that the individual person could find or make in *their own life*. Didion gives less of an answer to this question than a series of suggestive anxieties and moods. Though she arguably does not write within the loose family of genres that includes science fiction, speculative fiction, horror or weird fiction, both her fiction and non-fiction resonate loudly at times with the literary type of 'cosmic horror'. The latter evokes the unthinkable vastness and the fundamental indifference of the wider universe to human affairs. Properly grasping this fact confronts the reader with the ultimate futility of human striving and the question of whether there can be any significant values at the human scale. As such, tarrying with the cosmic perspective provokes feelings of dread, loneliness and despair. Cosmic horror can claim to root itself in the scientific realm of modern cosmology, which confronts us with such eventualities as heat death and the eternal blackening of the sky through the accelerating expansion of space. It fails as genre, however, unless it can mobilize these eventualities to provoke us and disturb us at the level of our affects. Arguably, though vastly more 'down to earth', Didion is in this way constantly leveraging her knowledge of earth science, the weather, fire, infrastructure and human psychology to disrupt our patterns of settled feeling, and thereby our 'fixed ideas' (Didion 2003).

To describe Didion as a fellow traveller with the genre of cosmic horror is not, however, to suggest that she is a nihilist – and this is a key claim in the account that I am giving here. 'Nihilism' describes an outlook according to which there is no meaning – or, in a more explicitly ethical register, it describes an outlook according to which there are no values and no right and wrong. Simon Critchley (2013) distinguishes between active and passive nihilism: the passive nihilist takes a quietist approach to life, whereas the active nihilist destroys. The common thread, however, is the belief that the universe is worthless, and that nothing of value can be made of it.

A nihilistic outlook might seem to flow naturally from the perspective that the universe is indifferent, precarious and entropic. Moreover, the earlier Didion arguably adds fuel to a nihilistic interpretation by referring, for example, to 'the meaninglessness of experience' (Parker 2018: 5). But Didion, as I explained in the Introduction, displays throughout her writings a principled if minimal ethical stance, and a fierce protectiveness when it comes to at least some values at the human scale. Even when earlier in her career she alludes to how 'moral disgust' with others led her to work for herself alone (Parker 2018: 8), this is a shift premised upon values and standards to which she still holds others. It does not in and of itself entail the abandonment of an other-regarding, hence ethical, stance.[6]

It is instructive to consider how Didion handles the theme of children. Though it is common to underscore her 'toughness' or 'coolness' (Nelson 2017), a reading that Didion herself encourages in such essays as 'Doris Lessing' and 'Georgia O'Keefe' (Didion 2006), it pays to remember that despite this stylistic posture she gives hints and explicit indications that she is wracked with agony and arguably even undone by the vulnerability, suffering and deaths of children – not just her own child, but those she hears about in historical accounts and in the news, those she imagines and those she encounters in the course of her journalistic work. Didion expresses doubt, for example, over whether her generation has adequately prepared the next one for the exigencies of modern life (Didion 2006: 67–97), and the most horrific elements of her fiction converge upon imagery of abortion and fetal tissue clogging drains (1970: 96–7, 104), as well as infantile disability, illness and the death and dismemberment of children through accident (1970: 99–100, 1977: 147–52). Perhaps emblematic is Didion's protagonist Maria in *Play it as it Lays*:

> She could not read newspapers because certain stories leapt at her from the page: the four-year-olds in the abandoned refrigerator, the tea party with Purex, the infant in the driveway, rattlesnake in the playpen, the peril, unspeakable peril, in the everyday. She grew faint as the processions swept

before her, the children alive when last scolded, dead when next seen, the children in the locked car burning, the little faces, helpless screams. The mothers were always reported to be under sedation. In the whole world there was not as much sedation as there was instantaneous peril. (1970: 99–100)

This thematic of sedation, contrasted with reality's peril, offers insight into Didion's ethics, and it helps to better understand a discordant note that the reader may have noticed. Recall that Didion starts to get the jitters whenever an earthquake starts going, despite waiting for 'the Big One' all her life (Didion 2006: 616). But positioning herself as the 'geologist's granddaughter', she coolly keeps writing as the 5.2 earthquake wrenches her writing desk (Didion 1995: 18). The second source is a novel, *Democracy*, so it is possible to read too much into the discrepancy – though I would draw attention to the fact that *Democracy* is a novel into which Didion intrudes ('Call me the author') referring to herself in the third person, by her own name (Didion 1995: 16). What I find interesting is that she seems to suggest in *Democracy* that it is *possible* to live with peril, to benumb oneself to it, *so long as we take the long view* suggested by geology (more on this in Chapter 2). It is, of course, also possible to drop this viewpoint, and to take the earthquake personally. In fact, the ethical might even demand this of us. Maria in *Play It As It Lays* again offers material for reflection:

> a Pentecostal minister . . . had received prophecy that eight million people would perish by earthquake on a Friday afternoon in March. The notion of general devastation had for Maria a certain sedative effect (the rattlesnake in the playpen, that was different, that was *particular*, that was punitive), suggested an instant in which all anxieties would be abruptly gratified . . . she felt a kind of resigned tranquility. (Didion 1970: 104, emphasis added)

We see that there is more peril in the world than sedation. But there is, nonetheless, a kind of resignation and even a relief in the idea of 'general devastation', counting bodies in the millions, to see that one's anxieties have finally borne fruit. The same is not so with the devastation following the death of the *particular* child. It turns out that 'earthquake weather' is modulated by what we might call the 'ethical' sphere, or the sphere of one's 'thick' or 'close' relations – as one might expect, given the ethical framework explored in the Introduction.

What is remarkable about the horror of Didion's writings, then, is that it indexes not the absolute fatalism of a nihilistic outlook but, rather, an acute anguish over the seemingly 'punitive' particular disaster, exemplified in the one that strikes children – especially one's own. Her oft-remarked toughness and coolness are only one side of the story, and they should not be taken to mirror the universe's indifference. Rather, they approach stoicism, not as doctrine but as an ethical practice (Hadot 2004) – namely, in terms of meeting the harshness of the universe with clarity, without self-delusion, but in such a way that she can strike a kind of 'transitional accommodation' with the knowledge of the impending and inevitable loss of those she values.

Didion is therefore, I believe, not a nihilist but an 'extensive (but not unmitigated)' pessimist, in David Benatar's sense (Benatar 2017: 4). As Benatar puts it about his own outlook:

> I think that that there is no cosmic meaning. If I am right about that, then calling me a nihilist about cosmic meaning is entirely appropriate. However, my view is not nihilistic about all meaning because I believe that there is meaning from some perspectives . . . . Life is meaningless, but it also has meaning – or, more accurately, meanings. There is no such thing as the meaning of life. Many different meanings are possible. One can transcend the self and make a positive mark on the lives of others in myriad ways. These include nurturing and teaching the young, caring for the sick, bringing relief to the suffering, improving society, creating great art or literature, and advancing knowledge. (Benatar 2017: 62–63)

Didion, in short, shares with cosmic horror the theme of the universe's indifference. She parts ways, however, at the point where this is supposed to end in nihilism at the human scale – whether by this we mean a total lack of faith in meaning, or a total lack of faith in value. Her reference to the 'meaninglessness of experience' in an early interview (Parker 2018: 5) nourishes not so much a *nihilistic* interpretation as a persistent exploration of the theme of *the failure of narrative* to make much sense out of life. Such failure is perfectly compatible with *pessimism*, where certain values persist and are staunchly defended.

Part of the mystique of Didion is precisely her ironical and clear-eyed detachment from the social upheavals of her times – a stance that allows her to punch both left, against new social movements, and right, against the American state – as well as her scepticism with regard to edifying, even potentially saving, narratives. In 1969, welding the ethical salience of the *particular* disaster to the social fact of the crumbling of narrative, she describes herself as

> a woman who somewhere along the line misplaced whatever slight faith she ever had in the social contract, in the meliorative principle, in the whole grand pattern of human endeavor . . . alert only the stuff of bad dreams, the children burning in the locked car in the supermarket parking lot, the bike boys stripping down stolen cars on the captive cripple's ranch, the freeway sniper who feels 'real bad' about picking off the family of five. (Didion 2006: 277)

Here Didion characteristically expresses a shift of focus to the particular, the peripheral, in terms of resistance to mainstream, edifying narrative. This narrative unmooring could be interpreted cynically, as a culturally savvy 'postmodern' pose, but Didion stresses on the contrary that it is a process or event that *happens* to her, and she intimates – through the device of a 'flash cut' – that it is in some sense pathological, as something she underwent in spite of herself. Didion, who it must be recalled earned part of her living as a screenwriter, 'cuts away' to her psychiatric report, occasioned by an episode of 'vertigo, nausea, and a feeling that she was going to pass out' (Didion 2006: 187). The report paints a picture of Didion as alienated, isolated and steeped in the pessimism I have described. It details her

> fundamentally pessimistic, fatalistic, and depressive view of the world around her. It is as though she feels deeply that all human effort is foredoomed to failure, a conviction which seems to push her further into a dependent, passive withdrawal. In her view she lives in a world of people moved by strange, conflicted, poorly comprehended, and, above all, devious motivations which commit them inevitably to conflict and failure. (Didion 2006: 187).

Characteristically, however, Didion demurs: she offers that 'an attack of vertigo and nausea does not now seem to me an inappropriate response to the summer of 1968' (Didion 2006: 188).[7] And elsewhere: 'I am not the society in microcosm' (Didion 2006: 278), meaning that she makes no claim to extrapolate from her often-morbid fixations on the particular, at the expense of narrative, to society at large.

Didion will even claim at one point that she is neither an optimist nor a pessimist (Parker 2018: 4), though she will later describe a kind of 'turn' in her outlook that places her squarely in the pessimist camp:

> I am more attracted to the underside of the tapestry. I tend to always look on the wrong side, the bleak side. I have since I was a child. I have no idea why. I'm rather a slow study, and I came late to the apprehension that there was a void at the center of experience. A lot of people realize this when they're fifteen or sixteen, but I didn't realize it until I was writing *Play It As It Lays*. And until around that time . . . that it was possible that the dark night of the soul was . . . it had not occurred to me that it was dryness, that it was aridity. I had thought it was something much riper and sinful. And I think that *Play it As it Lays* was a way of working that out, dealing myself with the idea that experience was largely meaningless. (Parker 2018: 34)

I am inclined to classify Didion as a pessimist both on account of this self-interpretation, and for the reasons given herein. And as we will see in Chapter 4, Didion does not give up all hope in people, retaining a minimal faith that if people knew the truth, the inconsistencies between the official and the underlying narrative, then there could be political change.

So, what then exactly is going on when Didion becomes unmoored from narrative? She famously tells us in the titular essay of *The White Album* that 'We tell ourselves stories in order to live,' how 'We live entirely, especially if we are writers, by the imposition of a narrative line upon disparate images, by the "ideas" with which we have learned to freeze the shifting phantasmagoria which is our actual experience' (Didion 2006: 185). Even faced – or perhaps because we are faced – with the universe described by 'earthquake weather', we continue to do this: as Didion suggests, 'We look for the sermon in the suicide, for the social or moral lesson in the murder of five' (Didion 2006). But having set 'us' up, writers certainly, but apparently people in general, as narrative animals, a species of optimists who survive by means of their storytelling capacities, she goes on to describe how she began to doubt the very premises of all the stories she had ever told herself, in a period running roughly between 1966 and 1971. In this period, Didion loses 'the plot', but retains vivid 'flash pictures', likening the experience not to a movie but to 'a cutting room experience' (Didion 2006: 186). Significantly for my purposes, she signals here that in this period, she becomes aware of the ethical stakes of telling stories, and thus – implicitly – the ethical stakes of memory, as an expression of the doubly cognitive and pragmatic activity theorized by Ricœur: 'I wanted to believe in the narrative and in the narrative's intelligibility, but to know that one could change the sense with every cut was to begin to perceive the experience as rather more electrical than ethical' (Didion 2006).

In this spirit, Didion confronts the cosmic, narrative optimism of career politicians, folk singers, hippies and communist revolutionaries with demonstrable irony. In my view, however, it will not do to overplay this aspect of Didion's writing. Doing so enables her recruitment to reactionary positions – of the type that revolutionaries and youth are perennially foolish, and so on – that fail to see her nuance, and the fact that she emerges in later years with a renewed interest in *political* narrative, as a critic of the American state. In her writings critical of new social movements, Didion in fact admits to 'appreciating', but not adhering to, what the disciplinary philosopher might call metaphysical or ideological systems that could assuage her abiding sense of dread by giving an order and a meaning to being. For her such systems are (merely, the reader surmises) 'opiates'. Writing of the marginalized militant communist Michael Laski in 1967, Didion tells us

> I am comfortable with the Michael Laskis of this world, with those who live outside rather than in, those in whom the sense of dread is so acute that they turn to extreme and doomed commitments; I know something about dread myself, and appreciate the elaborate systems with which some people manage to fill the void, appreciate all the opiates of the people, whether they are as accessible as alcohol and heroin and promiscuity or as hard to come by as faith in God or History. But of course I did not mention dread to Michael Laski, whose particular opiate is History . . . . The world Michael Laski had constructed for himself was one of labyrinthine intricacy and immaculate clarity, a world made meaningful not only by high purpose but by external and internal threats, intrigues and apparatus, an immutably ordered world in which things mattered . . . . You see what the world of Michael Laski is: a minor but perilous triumph of being over nothingness. (Didion 2006: 53–5)

It would be easy to chalk these comments up to ironic, politically centrist detachment – and it might still be possible on the strength of such comments, though not very plausible, to claim Didion today as an exemplar of the pretension to rise above partisan politics and other so-called 'doomed commitments'. But a richer interpretation, I believe, is that Didion is genuinely sympathetic to Laski. The real irony here is that despite her apparent disbelief in Laski-type systems – demonstrated perhaps by her ironical deployment of the word 'opiate',[8] and her analysis of his revolutionary communism as only one such possible system – Didion in some sense *wants* to believe, because she understands perhaps better than others what such systems promise.

It is here that we begin to better understand my claim that Didion takes seriously a disenchanted perspective and then embodies an ethos of refusing to reconstitute the ethical in a reactionary way. Knowing that Laski-type systems are desirable for providing 'an immutably ordered world in which things mattered' (Didion 2006: 54), she cannot commit herself to sheltering in any one of them. One way to view the problem is through the values of truth and relative comprehensiveness, which I explored as primordial to memory ethics in the Introduction. Though Laski's system seems comprehensive, it is so to a fault. It is comprehensive at the cost of violence to particularity; in effect, particularity as such ceases to exist when it is reduced to an element of the system.[9] This reduction, in turn, has a suppressive effect on *truth as surprise or exception*; truth is always already what the system dictates, and this accounts for the danger that Didion detects in moral systems in her essay 'On Morality'.[10] As such, when she sits down to interview Laski, he already believes he has her pegged, and significantly admits that he only let her interview him to provide the public with a record of his existence. Laski, Didion tells us, 'did not feel as close to me as I did to him' (Didion 2006: 53).

Sectarian communism, it should be stressed, is not the main issue. Rather, it is any intellectual system that would gain victory over 'nothingness' at the expense of nihilating particularity. Though, as mentioned, Didion tends to punch left in her early writings of the 1960s and 1970s, this is born out of her *moral* scepticism as much as any lingering *political* conservatism. Her problem is with those who fail to 'accept the universe' (Didion 2006: 258) – the universe of earthquake weather, which tends towards a conservative ethical rather than an expansive moral stance. But in later works, as we will see in Chapter 4, Didion levels much of the same critique on American 'fixed ideas' (Didion 2003), and their proselytizers on the political right.

Thus, in sum, Didion's vision resists while simultaneously yearning for any comprehensive system that would give meaning to human existence. Moreover, hers is a universe where contingency, entropy and the folly of human endeavors perennially wreck the practical steps that people can take to impose order. In addition to the dread I have described throughout, there is therefore, finally, often a weariness in Didion, a failed romanticism or a melancholy predicated on loss (Nowak McNeice 2019) – a 'sense of not being up to the landscape' (Didion 2017: 117), a sense against which she has to constantly fight if she is to continue to bear witness to her times.

South and West

The risk I take in privileging 'earthquake weather' as a tensor sign for Didion's precarious, entropic and indifferent universe is that it might strike the reader as too specific to California. Perhaps Didion's picture of reality is reducible to a kind of regional sensibility that it would be inappropriate to extrapolate from. Perhaps her comments on earthquakes, fire and water, for instance, help us to understand her character and her outlook, or something about regionalism in American literature, but do not constitute anything approaching a picture of reality or a world view.

I believe such an interpretation would be too conservative. While for reasons already expressed, I hesitate to turn her atmosphere of dread into a metaphysics, what 'regionalism' there is about Didion is aspirationally bigger than her and her home state. It is purposely trained beyond California, on her country at large (and, eventually, beyond). In *South and West*, pulled mostly from a travel notebook from 1970 but not published until 2017, Didion, the Westerner, makes the claim that the South represents America's future. This is jarring, because as Didion depicts it, the South 'is a true earlier time' (Didion 2017: 43). She describes her

> dim and unformed sense, a sense which struck me now and then, and which I could not explain coherently, that for some years the South and particularly the Gulf Coast had been for America what people were still saying what California was, and what California seemed to me not to be: the future, the secret source of malevolent and benevolent energy, the psychic center (Didion 2017: 14).

Tellingly, this shift of the future from West to South is marked by a difference in ethos that is undergirded by the community's memories and its relation to nature:

> When I think now about New Orleans I remember mainly its dense obsessiveness, its vertiginous preoccupation with race, class, heritage, style, and the absence of style. As it happens, these particular preoccupations all involve distinctions which the frontier ethic teaches western children to deny and to leave deliberately unmentioned, but in New Orleans such distinctions are the basis of much conversation . . . as if talking about anything at all could keep the wilderness at bay. In New Orleans the wilderness is sensed as very near, not the redemptive wilderness of the western imagination but something rank and old and malevolent, the idea of wilderness not as an escape from civilization and its discontents but as a mortal threat to a community precarious and colonial in its deepest aspect. (Didion 2017: 21–2)[11]

In general, the American South for Didion represents a zone marked by traditional distinctions, deep memory and memorialization.[12] In *South and West* she describes seemingly static systems of gender and racial exclusion,[13] and invocations of mythology and enduring feudalism also crop up suggestively in the text. There is a 'time warp' in this land, where 'the Civil War was yesterday, but 1960 is spoken of as if it were three hundred years ago' (Didion 2017: 104). How could this represent the future? Reading the book in the year it was published, 2017, was a jarring experience for me because in many ways it had turned out to be quite prescient. The United States is now in a period of acute communitarian fracturing and retrenchment, where traditions are weaponized and democratic agonism slides into open antagonism.

The whole point of contrasting 'South' with 'West' was initially to understand something about California; Didion admits, however, that it took her time to realize that what she was really interested in was 'the South as a gateway to the Caribbean' (Parker 2018: 116). The latter theme will become important when Didion shifts registers into a critical political realism trained on Washington's connections in Latin America. For now, note how looking at the South potentially sheds light on California's unusually amnesiac, future-oriented character – and whether the latter is ultimately sustainable, or will give way to a return of the repressed. As Didion describes, 'In the South they are convinced that they have bloodied their place with history. In the West we do not believe that anything we do can bloody the land, or change it, or touch it' (Didion 2017: 117). But despite the putatively Californian optimism where 'the future always looks good . . . because no one can remember the past'

(Didion 2006: 13), Didion drives home throughout her works that we cannot ever truly escape from our histories. And ethically (as well as sometimes morally) speaking, we often must cultivate our memories, rather than letting them wither. To this extent, invoking the South in the way Didion does is a salutary move. It is especially so in the context of the Americas, where nations are built upon ongoing legacies of genocide and slavery.

Things appear to go wrong, however: as I interpret her, there is evidence of a slippage from 'the past' to what I will call 'the immemorial' in Didion's writings on the American and Latin American South, and this opens her to critique on the grounds of replicating a certain colonial irony. By 'colonial irony' I mean the Northern mindset or attitude according to which Southern zones are inherently chaotic and entropic to the point of intractability. As such, colonial irony can either be a pretext for abandoning the South to its fate or for continuing to reap colonial spoils from it. Didion 'goes wrong' in replicating this irony by means of a slippage into the immemorial, to the extent that she suggests an image of the South as stillborn, incapable of historic achievement. To be clear, I make no claim that Didion expresses this image in terms of a coherent viewpoint or argument, or that she actively supports colonialism in the South. She explicitly names, for example, 'the acute tyrannies of class and privilege by which people assert themselves against the tropics' (1995: 22). Rather, I am suggesting that her writing replicates tropes that are concerning enough to flag as dangers and limitations, especially in the context of reading her as a moral or ethical teacher or exemplar.

By 'the immemorial' I have in mind what is suggested by the verminous, putrescent jungle imagery often populating Northern novels with tropical settings, like those of André Malraux.[14] The idea is that human endeavours and the modern ideal of a more or less *linear* progress through history are sapped and ruined by a primordial, *cyclical* time of generation and decay. Empires are swallowed back by the encroaching forest, and literary images of human failure are sharpened against a backdrop of sweltering, rotting, uncontrolled growth. Calling such fertile decay 'the immemorial' underscores the idea that when time is construed as rigorously cyclical, nothing truly happens that is worthy of being remembered.[15] On this view there is no narrative to speak of if nothing occurs beyond the cycles of nature, and human striving gives way to fatalism. It is a fatalism that rubs off even on the visiting traveller; even the writer's craft, her 'reporting tricks', 'atrophy' in the South (Didion 2017: 90). The connection, of course, extends far beyond Malraux and the tradition of colonial novels. The thematic of the South as fatally entropic or as emblematic of nature's revenge on history has a long lineage not just in literature but also in philosophy, political science, policy studies and beyond. To take but one other literary point of reference, Didion frequently cites Joseph Conrad as a significant influence, and frames *Salvador* with a famous passage from *Heart of Darkness*. Indeed, she claims of El Salvador that 'In many ways race remains the ineffable element at the heart of *this* particular darkness' (Didion 2006: 389, emphasis added).

Didion contributes to this literary vein, particularly in her 1977 novel *A Book of Common Prayer*. Though she tells a lecture audience that it was sparked by no more than a one-hour stopover at the Panama airport at 6.00 am – comprising the entirety of her experience in Central America up to that point (Parker 2018: 18–9) – it is also redolent of more substantive encounters, in other locales, with tropical illness, political froth and colonial decay.[16] It dramatizes and aestheticizes the full-blown pessimism that had bloomed in Didion by the end of the 1960s. The aestheticization and 'working out' of her pessimism in *A Book of Common Prayer* occurs precisely in the idiom of colonial irony I have sketched earlier. Characters come to grief in an imagined equatorial country, Boca Grande, depicted as dark, devouring, ruining: 'The bush and the sea do not reflect the light but absorb it, suck it in, then glow morbidly' (Didion 1977: 14). Memory is swallowed up by the immemorial in a country that 'has no history': 'Every time the sun falls on a day in Boca Grande that day appears to vanish from local memory, to be reinvented if necessary but never recalled' (Didion 1977: 14). Termites eat away presidential palaces, fly larvae suppurate flesh and wriggle across human eyeballs in 'an amniotic stillness in which transformations are constant' (Didion 1977: 155). Thus depicted, the immemorial is a stillness but one of constant, issueless movement. Everything is boiling with a fermentation that undermines fixed categories of identity, and even of life and death: 'A banana palm is no more or less "alive" than its rot' (Didion 1977: 155). Perhaps most problematically of all, but in the same vein, evenings with certain characters are described as 'essentially Caribbean', meaning 'volatile with conflicting pieties and intimations of sexual perfidy' (Didion 1977: 165).

In her non-fiction, too, examples abound of what in *Miami* Didion calls 'tropical entropy . . . defeating grand schemes even as they were realized'

(Didion 2006: 428). Miami is down to its very terrain 'liquid', 'provisional' (Didion 2006: 429–30). Of El Salvador, she describes how 'The campus of the National University is said to be growing over, which is one way contradictions get erased in the tropics' (Didion 2006: 394–5).[17] Along the Gulf of Mexico, where everything 'seems to go to seed' (Didion 2017: 30), hurricane devastation 'has something inevitable about it: the coast was reverting to its natural state' (Didion 2017: 27). The stagnation of the immemorial is also represented through a connection of two of Didion's frequently used symbols, water and snakes: 'I think I never saw water that appeared to be running in any part of the South. A sense of water moccasins' (Didion 2017: 62–3).

Of New Orleans, Didion describes 'the sense of swamp reclaimed to no point' (Didion 2017: 22), suggesting the futility of building where nature will claim its due. The June air there is 'heavy with sex and death, not violent death but death by decay, overripeness, rotting, death by drowning, suffocation, fever of unknown etiology' (Didion 2017: 5). She reaches for the trope of 'darkness' here, describing the city close to terms she will use again later (1977) as 'physically dark, dark like the negative of a photograph, dark like an X-ray: the atmosphere absorbs its own light, never reflects light but sucks it in until random objects glow with a morbid luminescence' (Didion 2017: 5–6). It is an atmosphere that slows everyone down 'as if suspended in a precarious emulsion, and there seems only a technical distinction between the quick and the dead' (Didion 2017: 6). Didion describes the city's time-consciousness or temporality as 'operatic, childlike, the fatalism that of a culture dominated by wilderness' (Didion 2017: 8). That she ties a 'childlike' mindset to untameable wilderness is, of course, a long-standing colonial trope.

Once more, in the context of a trip to Bogotá, Didion puts the trope of Southern decomposition into play in comments about narratives and memory – all the while replicating the association with childishness. She describes how 'when Columbians spoke about the past I often had the sense of being in a place where history tended to sink, even as it happened, into the traceless solitude of autosuggestion. The princess was drinking pink champagne. High in the mountains the men were made of gold. Spain sent its highest aristocracy to South America. They were all stories a child might invent' (Didion 2006: 317). Further, she describes 'the residuum of European custom so movingly and pointlessly preserved' in the ritual of lunch service at the Hostería del Libertator (Didion 2006: 323). Columbians are here depicted as incidental to the putatively decayed traditions and histories they 'pointlessly' preserve, and the question is not posed as to what value or use they themselves might still derive from them.

What if, then, the spatial or geographical understandings – or misunderstandings – characterizing Didion's depiction of the earthquake weather universe are simply part and parcel of the radical modernity that I have ascribed to her, and its historical investment in colonialism? What if, precisely through her filiation to the expansive and expansionist 'western' or 'frontier' point of view, Didion betrays through her work the anxiety of entropy and rot that shadows this expansion in lockstep?

It is not likely that simple. Tropes of 'South and West', though problematic given their long history and often her specific uses of them, will arguably give way to a reinvigorated critical political realism in the later Didion. Following *A Book of Common Prayer* (1977), Didion's next novels – *Democracy* (1995) and *The Last Thing He Wanted* (1996) – similarly feature Southern and island locales, but with a much more muted invocation of tropical entropy. The non-fiction book *Salvador*, published in 1983, may represent an inflection point in this movement. Compiled of Didion's observations on the ground in the wake of the El Mozote Massacre of 1981, *Salvador* arguably renders the 'earthquake weather' universe as both explicitly social and political, and more immediately as opposed to implicitly violent. We shift from *dread* or *anxiety* to *terror*, in full recognition of both the affective and political implications of the term: 'I did not forget the sensation of having been in a single instant demoralized, undone, humiliated by fear which is what I meant when I said that I came to understand in El Salvador the mechanism of terror' (Didion 2006: 356).

However bleak 'nature' ultimately is, even in its putative tropical extremes – that is, however disappointingly it refuses to hold us, or centre us, or care for our works and our projects and our values – it does not terrorize us in the specific sense of using violence to degrade and dehumanize, to *communicate* to us our nothingness. El Salvador in 1982, according to Didion's depiction, is 'a state in which no ground is solid, no depth of field reliable, no perception so definite that it might not dissolve into its reverse' (Didion 2006: 347). 'Terror is the given of the place' (Didion 2006: 362); put differently, 'Any situation can turn to terror. The most ordinary errand can go bad' (Didion 2006: 409). As such the visitor, to stay safe, to stay alive, must sharpen her focus on details – particularities, in other words, in a hypertrophied version of Didion's writerly ethos – at the expense of past and future concerns, as though 'in a prolonged amnesiac fugue' (Didion 2006: 347). In a place that 'brings everything into question' (Didion 2006: 362), such fearful, forced and humiliated focus on the particular strangles any attempt at inductive irony, if not narrative itself (Didion 2006: 363). This is much more sinister than the 'atrophy' of her journalistic craft that Didion elsewhere ascribes to the South (2017: 90). Rather, the problem is that the 'texture of life' in such a situation reveals itself to be 'essentially untranslatable' (Didion 2006: 407). As she suggests, for example, about the Spanish verb *Desaparecer*, there is 'no equivalent situation, and so no equivalent word', for being 'disappeared' in English-speaking cultures (Didion 2006: 377). It occurs to Didion that in El Salvador, for the first time in her life, she had been in the presence of obvious writing 'material' but 'felt no professional exhilaration at all, only personal dread' (Didion 2006).

Remarkably, in *Salvador* Didion reaches for the metaphor of earthquake weather to make sense of her surroundings and her difficulties with witnessing and writing about them. She recalls having been seized by an amorphous bad mood for several hours preceding a major earthquake (Didion 2006: 374). But for Didion, 'there was no particular prescience about my bad mood, since it is always earthquake weather in San Salvador, and the jitters are endemic' (Didion 2006: 374). This may strike the reader as odd, given my interpretation in this chapter. Have I not implied that in some sense it is also 'always earthquake weather' in Didion's universe in general? What then is so special about San Salvador? Here it pays to recall that on my reading, 'earthquake weather' may be viewed as a 'tensor sign', gathering, binding and concentrating several meanings and affects. It is not necessary to hold that she literally always fears for her life or safety, or even that she feels dread or garden-variety anxiety at all times, to suggest that in the final analysis, her universe is *much like* what 'earthquake weather' describes. What is remarkable about San Salvador, in Didion's experience, is that it takes the source of her dread and both concentrates and weaponizes it to an unlivable degree. In a sense, it affirms that it takes human evil, conflict and political organization to unleash the very worst of the indifference, entropy and precarity the universe has in store.

The risk here is that Didion could fall back on her aforementioned suspicion of *human* nature, and simply naturalize Salvadoran terror in a racist mode – a possibility suggested by the Conrad epigraph. But this is thankfully not the route she takes. If we have crossed into a social universe in which 'earthquake weather' is grotesquely amplified and made permanent through human design, then there might be a *political* as opposed to racial story to tell about who foments violence, who becomes truly *fodder* for the indifferent universe and who has the safety and luxury to escape it to meditate upon its indifference. Arguably, the experience of reporting to write *Salvador* was both a traumatizing and invigorating experience for Didion, spurring her to sharpen her critical political realist vision in her next non-fiction book *Miami* and subsequent ones as well. Whereas 'South' was arguably mined for its questionable *symbolic* value in a manner suggestive of colonial irony, it nonetheless becomes drastically important for Didion on account of its centrality to the *underlying political narrative* of her own country and hemisphere. This links the book to the ethics of memory in the sense that it helps to envision politically efficacious witnessing, even where witnessing is drastically hampered if not impossible on account of the atmosphere of terror in which it is supposed to occur.

If I have been successful in this chapter, the reader will now have a picture of the universe in Didion as precarious, entropic and indifferent – as well as a sense of how she frames this universe using problematic but, perhaps, characteristically modern spatial or geographical tropes. Though indicative of the limitations or even dangers of using Didion as a moral or ethical teacher or exemplar, these give way to a critical political realism that will animate her career from at least the late 1970s onwards. My aim in setting up this picture of Didion's universe, however, has primarily been to lay the groundwork for an interpretation of her memory ethics as thoroughly modern, responding to the past as at once *retrievable* through witnessing, testimony and grieving, but also metaphysically or cosmically *irretrievable*. This will frame the analysis in the chapter that follows.

2

Memories are what you no longer want to remember

Witnessing, testifying and grieving

'Earthquake weather', as per the preceding chapter, is a fitting term for the mood of anxiety, precarity and dread that one often encounters reading Didion. I went so far as to tentatively ascribe a 'universe' to her writings based on that mood and her several comments supporting it, specifically one that is *indifferent*, *entropic* and *precarious*. I argued that Didion's universe is indifferent, to the extent that it neither centres nor 'holds' the individual human being and the people and things she cherishes. I argued that Didion's universe is entropic, to the extent that order and community are only temporary achievements from the cosmic perspective. Finally, I argued that her universe is precarious, to the extent that imminent disaster colours or haunts even the everyday. While levelling criticism at the literary tropes of South and West used throughout her works to uphold this vision, my aim in Chapter 1 was primarily to lay out the background assumptions against which Didion's ethics of memory, as I perceive it, makes sense.

For this reason, Chapter 1 was essentially preparatory. At this point, we enter the discussion of the ethics of memory proper in Didion's works. I will begin the remainder of the book by examining the deceptively 'intimate' and 'individual' sphere of memory constituted by first-person witnessing, testifying and grieving. I believe that some commentary on this choice of where to begin is necessary.

In the Introduction, I covered the sense in which remembering, forgetting and related actions can, indeed, be called *actions* (and therefore, be subject to 'ethics' or normative judgement). I also covered the idea that such actions can be more or less private and more or less public. It is possible, for example, to participate in a public memorial monument unveiling, or to quietly remember a lost loved one on a train. We saw that while both are actions, they are different in important respects. But the choice of examples, which served above all to illustrate the point I was making at the time, raises important questions: Are *remembering and forgetting*, which I construed as the primary mnemonic actions in my rough list, first or fundamentally or perhaps even always private – that is to say, done at the inner, and individual, level? Is it only *related and derivative actions* such as testifying, archiving and the like that one would be capable of doing in public?

Because of its 'inner' aspect, remembering a lost loved one on a train is, indeed, in one sense, something I do 'by myself' – even if there are other passengers. But I would resist overemphasizing the distinction between types of action here, for the simple reason that much if not most of my inner, mental life – including active remembering and forgetting – is at least *framed* (Butler 2020) for me (which is not to say strictly 'determined') through public means or resources. These most obviously include language, which is pre-eminently public,[1] but also the whole range of cultural symbols and values in which I am brought up and in the thick of which I persist and act. Put differently, there is, indeed, a phenomenological or 'inner' story to be told about memory actions, accessible only to the person who is performing them. But I believe that this irreducible interiority can only be disentangled from the action *phenomenologically* and *conceptually*. In practice, my *active* mnemonic experiences, at least,[2] are framed and guided if not strictly determined by available public norms, to say nothing of contingent public goods like material artefacts, idioms and fashions.[3] In trying to remember someone's name, for example, I am in all likelihood following, or at least in a kind of dialogue with, mutable public norms about what is and is not important to remember.[4]

By starting the remainder of the book at the seemingly individual or intimate level, via Didion's memoirs on grief, I am therefore not claiming or implying that remembering, forgetting and related actions are *first of all* things people do privately, only later adding up to some kind of public memory. But nor, since I cleave to the idea that memory actions have an irreducibly inner aspect, do I take the opposite view, expressed for example by Huebner (2006) that 'It is not autonomous individuals who remember', but, rather, the community as a whole. To me this seems like a false alternative; in ethical common sense, 'autonomous individuals' do exist and they do remember, but we need to understand autonomy and memory, however we define them, as things that are only made possible and continuously supported through the mediation of the community and the supporting environment in general.[5] As Judith Butler put it,

> every individual emerges in the course of the process of individuation. No one is born an individual; if someone becomes an individual over time, he or she does not escape the fundamental conditions of dependency in the course of that process. That condition cannot be escaped by way of time. We were all, regardless of our political viewpoints in the present, born into a condition of radical dependency. As we reflect back on that condition as adults, perhaps we are slightly insulted or alarmed, or perhaps we dismiss the thought . . . . I want to suggest, however, that no one actually stands on one's own; strictly speaking, no one feeds oneself. (Butler 2020: 40–1)

Relatedly, we must bear in mind, but ultimately bracket for reasons of scope, the possibility of the ontological *plurality* of the named 'individual' who remembers. Throughout the book, I refer to 'Didion' as self-identical when describing how 'she' remembers and engages in ethical memory actions. This could be defended on a Lockean view (Locke 2008), where memory is what appears to hold together the person, or rather constitute the person, as such. On this view, I *know* that the person whose childhood memories I have is me, by virtue of the continuity of memory. But this is an epistemological point only, leaving wholly aside or bracketing the question of whether or not I actually *am* a temporally continuous 'substance' of one kind or another (Ricœur 2006: 102–9). Moreover, there are notable philosophical problems raised by this view. Most obviously, memory fails pathologically, as in dementia, or even through normal age-related 'decline', and this has implications for both identity and ethics. For example, is the advanced Alzheimer's patient a different person now? If so, can we therefore set aside her previous preferences and wishes as not hers, and in some sense unimportant (Malabou 2012; McLennan 2020)? As Annie Ernaux points out on several occasions, it is even possible to radically question the continuity of one's identity, and, indeed, the memory of oneself, in *non-pathological* contexts:[6]

> What's important to me is to retrieve the words with which I thought about myself, and about the world around me. To say what for me was the normal

and the inadmissible, the unthinkable even. But the woman I am in 95 is incapable of placing herself back into [*se replacer dans*] the girl of 52 who knew nothing but her small town, her family and her private school, having at her disposal a reduced lexicon. And before her, the immensity of the time left to live. There is no true memory of oneself. (Ernaux 1997: 39, my translation)[7]

With these kinds of consideration in mind, any view of the self-same individual herein must be taken as philosophically provisional, and the ethical implications of its uncertainty or suspension as unexplored.[8] This caveat lines up with my hermeneutical hedging in the Introduction, concerning my realism about Didion as 'author'. If the reader prefers, I have no philosophical objection to 'Didion' being read herein as a proper name, grouping together a number of texts, rather than as an 'author' in any metaphysically robust, internally coherent sense. Indeed, Didion herself, in the early essay 'On Keeping a Notebook,' supports this more sceptical reading, referring to the people she used to be, their alienation from her, and their power to interrupt and impact her life. For Didion, keeping a notebook allows us

> to keep on nodding terms with the people we used to be, whether we find them attractive company or not. Otherwise they turn up unannounced and surprise us, come hammering on the mind's door at 4 a.m. of a bad night and demand to know who deserted them, who betrayed them, who is going to make amends. We forget all too soon the things we thought we could never forget. (Didion 2006: 106)

To summarize, this chapter makes no claim about the methodological priority of the seemingly 'inner' level of memory in general. And it only takes for granted, for the sake of argument, that one can speak of a self-identical 'Didion' who is engaged in ethically salient memory actions at different times. My reasons for starting out, then, on what *appears* to be the 'individual' or 'intimate' level – essentially, with Didion herself, commenting upon her own life and working through her trauma – are, rather, as follows.

The first is pragmatic. Didion is strongly connected in popular culture or the public imagination with themes of grieving and memoir. This has been the case since the publication of *The Year of Magical Thinking* in 2005, and its subsequent staging as a one-woman play starring Vanessa Redgrave in 2007.[9]

As Leigh Gilmore recounts, 'Didion's ubiquity has led several commentators to observe that Didion is having a "moment" in which she occupies the space of public grief as a style icon' (2016b: 611). Her moment, characterized by the resonance of her works on grief, therefore arguably speaks primarily not to any 'individual' or 'intimate' space of grief, but, rather, to the notion of an 'intimate public', as per Lauren Berlant:

> An intimate public operates when a market opens up to a bloc of consumers, claiming to circulate texts and things that express those people's particular core interests and desires. When this kind of 'culture of circulation' takes hold, participants in the intimate public *feel* as though it expresses what is common among them, a subjective likeness that seems to emanate from their history and their ongoing attachments and actions. Their participation seems to confirm the sense that even before there was a market addressed to them, there existed a world of strangers who would be emotionally literate in each other's experience of power, intimacy, desire, and discontent, with all that entails. (2008: 5, emphasis in original)

To the extent that the concept of 'intimate public' applies to Didion, beginning with the memoirs on grief thus allows me to tap into an affective investment that many people may already have in her. It also helps me to connect it to my theme of the ethics of memory at the outset – thus speaking to the 'so what' and 'who cares' questions discussed earlier in the Introduction.

A second reason for starting here is more philosophical, and it speaks to a challenge thrown down by Didion in her texts on grieving. Whatever we make of the contestable boundary or false alternative between the individual and the community, Didion makes a strong case, in *Blue Nights* (2011) in particular, that there is a moment, or a level, of the ethics of memory where we must face up to the possibility of what I would call our radical, *metaphysical* loneliness. This is the loneliness that is never really assuaged by our proximity to others, since aspects of our inner life remain irreducibly inner, and we cannot, in the final or cosmic analysis, rely on others to centre or hold us. Such loneliness is suggested most forcefully perhaps by our confrontations with death: regardless of the supportive accompaniment we might receive in dying or grieving, to an irreducible extent we must face up to death alone. Doing the work of memory *despite everything* from within this state of abjection seems to me to be the very core or zero degree of Didion's ethics of memory, and for this reason, I believe it is important to begin there.

Unsurprisingly, the point of absolute loneliness that one finds in Didion with respect to the ethics of memory matches up with the 'earthquake weather' universe described in Chapter 1. In what follows, I will therefore first make the connection between 'earthquake weather' and death – specifically, the deaths of loved ones – as an issue for remembering, forgetting and related actions. To do this, I will rely upon both versions of *The Year of Magical Thinking* as well as *Blue Nights*, and I will also draw from Jean-Didier Urbain's *L'archipel des morts* (2005). Urbain will help me to situate Didion in a modern cultural moment where death has become meaningful only *qua* 'accidental' and disavowed, thus underscoring the radicality of her ethical labours.

Second, I will continue to tap *The Year of Magical Thinking* but especially *Blue Nights* in order to highlight the aspect of *work* or 'working through' that is involved in activities like remembering in general but also witnessing, testifying and grieving. This will underscore how Ricœur's 'pragmatic' dimension of memory binds to the 'cognitive,' and how memory as activity is implicitly normative (2006). Through the notion of trauma and the subsequent memory and time lag this entails, and the 'working through' it requires in particular, I will highlight *how* Didion faces up to the ethical challenges of remembering and forgetting from within the very point of abjection she acutely describes. Here I will draw upon resonant philosophical sources such as Freud, Ricœur and Lyotard to make my case. The ethical content of Didion's works will come to the fore especially in this section, but still at a seemingly 'intimate' or 'individual' level. This, to repeat, reflects the possibility of *metaphysical* loneliness sketched by Didion, and not the claim that the individual who grieves is always socially speaking alone, or that the private or intimate level of memory is methodologically prior in general.

Finally, I will therefore have to explicitly introduce the 'public' side of the equation as a separate discussion in connection with grieving. I have already noted earlier that the boundary between individual and community is contestable, and their strict opposition seemingly a false alternative. I have also drawn attention to the idea that Didion's writings belong to, constitute or help to constitute an 'intimate public' as per Berlant. The question naturally arises, then, as to how and why Didion's memoirs on grief resonate publicly *given what else* is going on in her society at the time of their highly favourable reception, with respect to witnessing, testimony, grieving – in short, with respect to key activities evoking the ethics of memory. My main resources in approaching this question will be Jill Stauffer's concept of 'ethical loneliness' (2015); Judith Butler's writings on the 'grievability' of lives (2016, 2020); and, finally, Leigh Gilmore's writing on 'jurisdictions' and 'frames' of testimony (2018, 2019) and her text linking Didion to #BlackLivesMatter (2016b). In brief, the argument will be that it is too easy and, in fact, dangerous to conflate Didion's metaphysical loneliness with an ethical or social idea of loneliness. It is true that in *Blue Nights* especially she writes from a position of modern abjection, a view 'lacking recovery or God' (Kristeva 1989: 228). But this is not to say that Didion lacked social being or social support; on the contrary, her memoirs found an enthusiastic public in a society where not every case of testimony does. As Gilmore points out, Didion's 'moment' is also the moment of highly contested, politicized public grief over the widespread police murders of unarmed African American women, men and children – something that is still rampant at the time of writing, in 2020, where the police murder of George Floyd has served as a catalyst for massive protests across the United States. This connection cries out to be examined, and doing so might shed light on some of the limitations of holding up Didion as a teacher or exemplar when it comes to the ethics of memory.

My hope is that in turning to Stauffer, Butler and Gilmore at the end of this chapter, the stage will be set for further engagements with more obviously 'public' questions in the remainder of the book. The reader should always keep in mind, however, that the ethics of memory – both in the general sense, and in the specific sense theorized by Margalit – is never either wholly public or wholly private in the strict sense. It is always in some sense both.

Memory and the accident of death

It is worth emphasizing that Didion's engagements with death and its relation to memory in *The Year of Magical Thinking* and *Blue Nights* are quite radical by contemporary standards. In the context of a culture vacillating between prevention, hygiene, denial and consolation when it comes to the topics of death and dying (Urbain 2005; Doughty 2015), Didion is here to deliver the bad news. As we saw in the Introduction, she is here to 'bully' us, even, into seeing things truthfully – which is to say, in light of their particularities, their suppressed or disavowed peripheries (Didion 2021: 46–7). Though the success of her memoirs suggests that a wide public has managed to find a measure of solace or strength in reading her and by connecting their own grief to hers, Didion is above all *not* trying to console in these texts. Quite the opposite. She is here to warn us that

> it will happen to you. The details will be different, but it will happen to you.
>
> That's what I'm here to tell you.
>
> Memory stops. The frame freezes. You'll find that's something that happens.
>
> I warned you. I'm telling you what you need to know.
>
> You see me on this stage, you sit next to me on a plane, you run into me at dinner, you know what happened to me.
>
> You don't want to think it could happen to you.
>
> That's why I'm here. (Didion 2007: 1–2)

What exactly is it that will happen? Moreover what – and *why* – does Didion feel that she needs to tell us?

First, there are the facts surrounding the memoir's precipitating event. In the two versions of *Magical Thinking*, she describes her husband John Dunne's sudden death at home on the evening of 30 December 2003, while the two were conversing over drinks and she was making a salad. In the play version, she goes on to recount the details surrounding her daughter Quintana Roo Dunne's death on 26 August 2005 following multiple illnesses and hospitalizations. This will form the basis for the subsequent memoir *Blue Nights*, published in 2011. From a purely factual viewpoint, Didion's losses in this period – her husband and close collaborator of decades, and her only child – are catastrophic. We all lose loved ones, but the memoirs are perhaps inherently interesting and worth sharing based on the relative extremity of the human experiences they together describe.

Those losses, however – the bare facts of our inevitably losing loved ones, and the period of mourning that follows – are not the whole picture. In *Magical Thinking*, Didion speaks up to warn us. She warns not only of our impending trauma, but also of the incomprehension and irrationality that can set in as we grieve. These will arguably short-circuit the mourning process, and possibly unmoor us from modern values we would otherwise uphold.

In this connection, Didion describes the titular 'magical thinking' that gripped her in the wake of John's death: '"Magical thinking" is a phrase I learned when I was reading anthropology. Primitive [sic] cultures operate on magical thinking. "*If*" thinking. *If* we sacrifice the virgin – the rain will come back. *If* I keep his shoes – ' (Didion 2007: 23). Effectively, 'magical thinking' names the temporary suspension of Didion's belief in ordinary causality and temporality following John's death. Her thoughts about having an autopsy performed are illustrative: 'I now see the autopsy as an early example of this thinking. I wanted the autopsy . . . . Here was my reasoning, which for some months remained hidden even from me: an autopsy could show that what had gone wrong was no more than a transitory blockage or arrhythmia. If so, the reasoning went, they might be able to fix it' (Didion 2007:23).[10]

Note that Didion's intervention, putatively a 'memoir' of grief located at the 'intimate' or 'individual' level, emerges as robustly ethical, and in two senses. First, it puts a long-standing personal *ethos* to the test, arguably nuancing or somewhat revising it. Second, it construes its mission – recounting how Didion succumbed to magical thinking and overcame it – as other-regarding, or public.

Turning first to *ethos*, consider 'the question of self-pity' that looms large in *Magical Thinking*. Didion relates how the first lines she wrote after John's death were:

Life changes fast.

Life changes in the instant.

You sit down to dinner and life as you know it ends.

The question of self-pity. (Didion 2005: 3, italics in original)

Deborah Nelson argues that self-pity, 'which Didion invariably pairs with self-delusion, has been the deep subject of her work' (Nelson 2017: 146). According to Nelson,

Self-pity and self-delusion are the moral flaws that underwrite bad politics and bad writing, which for Didion are one and the same thing. Since she began to develop an aesthetic philosophy in the late 1950s and early 1960s, Didion has advocated 'moral toughness' as the antidote to the social and political turmoil of the late twentieth century (Nelson 2017).

This ethos of moral toughness manifests in a dialogue with feeling in general, throughout Didion's career, becoming particularly acute at certain inflection points such as the memoirs on grief and *Salvador*. It is arguably only in *Magical Thinking* that Didion begins 'to understand herself as susceptible to self-pity, seduced by it in certain guises' (Nelson 2017: 170).[11] And it is only in *Blue Nights*, argues Nelson, after Didion has lost everything, that we see her 'Allowing herself self-pity – or the less pejorative emotional self-reflection' (Nelson 2017: 172).[12]

The importance of the question of self-pity is in its being bound up with the question of veracity. As Nelson points out, Didion's relationship to feeling in general 'follows from and leads to an aesthetic moralism and a moral aestheticism' (Nelson 2017: 172).[13] Shifting this notion to the register of the ethics of memory, we see how for Didion, remembering must be clear and truthful, refusing to succumb to the 'abuses' (Ricœur 2006) of sentimentality – even if, as Nelson argues, there is finally a place for feeling in the Didion of the grief memoirs. Once again, the knotting of cognitive and pragmatic senses of memory is manifest: to remember more or less faithfully is already an ethical issue, and feeling is suspect precisely on the grounds that it has the potential to lead us astray from our ethical duty (Nelson 2017: 172).

Turning next to the issue of ethics as properly other-regarding, note how Didion in *Magical Thinking* claims that we *need* to know what will one day happen to us. In this sense, she takes on the task of spreading the bad news, through the lucid reconstruction of her trauma and grief, as a kind of duty. For Didion in general, as Nelson claims, 'hurting the readers' feelings is . . . part of the writer's moral obligation' (Nelson 2017: 151). Since it is part of a moral obligation, this is not causing pain for the sake of causing pain. Rather, by hurting us *in the way she does*, Didion functions as a kind of moral teacher, with all the resonance of mastery or authority that the classical notion of teaching entails. We have seen that she transparently 'bullies' the reader in the interest of seeing things her way, which in this context, means she does it in the interest of spreading what she holds to be the truth about grief.[14] In *Magical Thinking*, Didion evinces pedagogical themes when she gives evidence of having to some extent mastered the situation she went through, italicizing '*I now know*' more than once, and claiming 'I was crazy for a while but I'm not now' (Didion 2007: 3, 44). Since Didion knows, and went through it, she is a kind of authority and we should therefore heed her *now*, and not wait to find out on our own: 'You might think you'll see it straight [when it happens] but you won't' (Didion 2007: 6). The reading through of the memoir therefore gives us access to how from within a place of extreme disarray, Didion 'composes' herself, both aesthetically and emotionally (Nelson 2017: 145). This may prove a lifeline to her readership; it is, in sum, *for our own good* that she unsettles and spreads pain.

Notably, Didion warns us of what's coming – the death of loved ones, and the grief that follows – *as if we did not already know*. This is significant, evoking the theme of 'self-delusion' highlighted by Nelson. Didion made a career out of exposing American self-delusion, and her approach to death is no different. As mentioned earlier, 'Western' cultures such as Didion's generally disavow or hide what they actually know surrounding death and dying, prompting some to call for a new culture of 'death acceptance' and reform of the funeral industry in this direction (Doughty 2015). What is telling about Didion's gesture is that she reports from a location within that very denial of death and dying, having succumbed for a time to a period of magical thinking. She is therefore well positioned to communicate to her contemporaries, exposing both our unpreparedness and our vulnerability to magical thinking in general. But the aim is not, as one finds in Doughty for example, to foster any kind of 'death acceptance'. The aim, I believe, is, rather, to do us the service of witnessing the full horror of what is coming, so that we can steel ourselves for grief and for the ethical memory-work that this entails.

This is where 'earthquake weather', and the previously explored difference between 'general devastation' and the *particular* disaster, are most resonant. It is perhaps the eminently modern theme of the *accident* – and relatedly, as we will see, the theme of *failure* – that does the most conceptual work in *Magical Thinking*, on account of how it unravels Didion's sense of time and causality. Due to the generalized and apparently rudderless acceleration of modern societies, the accident is that which, increasingly, can be expected to befall each and every one of us *in general* (Virilio 2005). But this does not mean that the accident is ever expected in the form of *this* accident; indeed, if it were, it would not be an accident, strictly speaking. Didion is well aware of this characteristic of the accident when she initially feels for the connection between her husband's death and his medical history: she tries for some time to find meaning in the causal story, but as long as she is thinking magically, this gets her nowhere. Similarly, on the evening of John's death – when he and Didion were returning from visiting their daughter Quintana in intensive care – reconstructing the sequence that put Quintana in the hospital, the 'how' of it, does not answer for him the much more important question of 'why' (Didion 2007: 13).

Note precisely how the dread that often colours Didion's texts, the 'earthquake weather' universe, does not prepare us for *this* accident. We have seen how Didion herself knows this, and how this feeds back into her dread:

> Have you noticed?
>
> The way people always describe the ordinary nature of the circumstances in which the disaster occurred?
>
> The clear blue sky from which the plane fell?
>
> The way the children were playing on the swings as usual when the rattlesnake struck from the ivy? (Didion 2007: 33)

As discussed in Chapter 1, nothing short of a general devastation would relieve the anxiety, the exhausting affective tension associated with 'earthquake weather'. The problem is that devastation, instead, befalls us as an everyday particularity.

How Didion's texts handle the theme of the accident, I argue, bears upon *modernity* in general. The definition of 'modernity' is highly contested, but it obviously involves a relation to time. As Jürgen Habermas points out, 'the modern world is distinguished from the old by the fact that it opens itself to the future' (1990b: 6). In modernity, we are no longer in the temporal rhythm of natural cycles and the picture of cosmic order that these suggest. Rather, 'time becomes experienced as a scarce resource for the mastery of problems that arise' in a newly linear conception (1990b). As moderns, we are essentially unmoored from the past – except for where the latter proves 'useful', for example politically. Correlatively, we are essentially unmoored from any traditional model of order or sense. Modernity therefore 'has to create its own normativity out of itself' (1990b: 7). This opens it up to colonization by the form of reason – namely, instrumental, narrowly practical reason – that is arguably best suited to modern time-consciousness, that is, the form which is best suited to solving the problems arising as time rushes by.

From such a perspective, death can only be construed as a kind of accident, and possibly also as a kind of personal *failure*. Since the word 'failure' often carries a moral implication that 'accident' lacks, the terms might seem to be mutually exclusive. They are not, however, at least not in the perverse logic of neoliberalism, arguably itself imbued with certain 'magical' or pre-modern aspects; since one can expect and should prepare for the accident *in general* as the future rushes towards us, we necessarily fail in preventing *this* accident when it eventually, unavoidably, befalls us.[15]

Let us further examine 'accident' and 'failure' in turn. First, regarding death's modern status as *accident*, this flows from the crumbling of pre-modern narratives and cosmic pictures that would have given death a meaning or a purpose. The cost of modern individualism, in which – at its limit – we pretend to rely mostly or even exclusively upon ourselves, and orient our lives around our projects, is to forego metaphysical hopes and comforts.[16] Since life alone becomes the location of sense, death becomes nothing but 'an intrusion of non-sense into life' (Urbain 2005: 82). At best, having no longer any cosmic meaning, death can be reduced to a technical problem like others. As Jean-Didier Urbain explains,

> Death has become an accident: it can no longer be anything but that. It belongs to the order of the surprise, of stupefaction, of one's being stunned. It is often suspect and now it calls forth expertise, investigations, or autopsies, perhaps because, as related by a morgue worker from New York, 'a modern society can't let anyone die without knowing exactly why and how they died!' [in Lahary and Vannier 1980]. Nonetheless, in doing so, this society that looks at death only through a medico-legal lens, contributes nothing to the social reintegration of dying, to its re-inscription in the everyday, to the restoration of a real sociability of death. (Urbain 2005: 75, my translation)

And further:

> death *no longer enters into the circuit of our ordinary social exchanges*. It erupts in my universe as nothing but an appalling error, an unpredictable dysfunction or a murderous incoherence of the environment . . . as an imprudence or an unpardonable negligence . . . as a blind, productivist cruelty . . . or as an intolerable resurgence of murderous barbarism at the heart of modernity . . . . Unpredictable, barbarous or pathological, from this perspective death belongs to chance, to the living past of the world, or to a morbid fringe of the culture: in sum, to a troubled constellation of social and natural anomies (Urbain 2005: 90–1, my translation, emphasis in original).

Regarding death's status as a kind of *failure*, Urbain connects this to the individualization of modern time-consciousness as a personal consciousness of one's projects, and of the necessary investment, preparation and problem solving that these entail:

> one's dying, by interrupting the process of [personal] redemption here-below, becomes the anguishing site of an intolerable personal failure . . . the individual no longer accepts sinking into the anonymous community of the dead, . . . [and] by this fact, dying becomes highly traumatic. (ibid. 2005: 84–5, my translation)[17]

Didion comes to essentially the same conclusions as Urbain. She recalls how during her period of magical thinking, when John was already gone, she fretted over medical studies that had some bearing on the cause of his death: 'As I recall this I realize how open we are to the persistent message that we can avert death. And to its punitive correlative, the message that if death catches us we have only ourselves to blame' (Didion 2005: 206). If Urbain's argument is sound, then Didion uncovers, through the process of disentangling and repudiating her magical thinking, the modern coordinates of death as both accident and failure. Interestingly, in doing so, she also hints at an irrationality provoked by, or perhaps lying at the heart of, the supposedly secular modern outlook – thus suggesting, in some sense, that modernity casts its own pre-modern shadow.[18]

Magical thinking, which you will recall Didion connects to anthropology and to what she calls 'primitive cultures', is, indeed, *unmodern* in the sense that it denies the accident as such. It attempts to wrest disaster back into the ambit of human control, and therefore takes it personally; even if we lack a theological viewpoint, we feel punished when disaster strikes. This speaks to the normative distinction, explored in Chapter 1, between general and particular devastation: as opposed to the prophesied earthquake killing millions, oddly relieving and gratifying in delivering us from our anxieties, the rattlesnake in the playpen could have fallen under our control and was therefore different, particular, punitive (Didion 1970: 104). But if the distinction holds, and if we do take at least some disasters personally, then there is an unmodern current running through our own societies, directly through modern experience. Fascinatingly, this is on Didion's mind years before John's death, evidenced in the narration of the novel *The Last Thing He Wanted* (1996):

> You will notice that participants of disasters typically locate the 'beginning' of the disaster at a point suggesting their own control over events. A plane

crash retold will begin not with the pressure system over the Central Pacific that caused the instability over the Gulf that caused the wind shear at DFW but at some manageable human intersect, with for example the 'funny feeling' ignored at breakfast. An account of the 6.8 earthquake will begin not at the overlap of the tectonic plates but more comfortably, at the place in London where we ordered the Spode that shattered the morning the tectonic plates shifted.

Had we just gone with the funny feeling. Had we just never ordered the Spode.

We all prefer the magical explanation. (1996: 15, emphasis in original)

If this is true, then paradoxically Didion is typically modern when in late 2003 she stands in the emergency room, thinking that 'The only words at hand will have to do with how this can be corrected. Reversible error' (Didion 2007: 6–7).

Interestingly, one of the signs that Didion breaks free of magical thinking comes through her reading of the autopsy report – precisely, the one that she had ordered when she was in magical thinking's thrall – and her recognition of the causal story it had to tell. As she recounts,

Only after I read the autopsy report did I begin to believe what I had been repeatedly told: nothing he or I had done or not done had either caused or could have prevented his death. He had inherited a bad heart. It would eventually kill him. The date on which it would kill him had already been, by many medical interventions, postponed. When that date did come, no action I could have taken in our living room . . . could have given him even one more day.

Only after I read the autopsy report did I stop trying to reconstruct the collision, the collapse of the dead star. The collapse had been there all along, invisible, unsuspected. (Didion 2005: 206–7)

The causal story is a lifeline to a non-magical modernity. Even supposing we abandon magical thinking's pretension to control and reorder events, we are still not out of the woods. This is because any *pure* accident, devoid of the minimal sense gained through causation, might as well be magical, in the sense of being miraculous. In fact, it might be that the only way to make any sense of an accident *at all* from a modern perspective is to link it up to a deterministic story, as Didion does here, and as she suggests in *The Last Thing He Wanted*, about plane crashes and earthquakes. But note that this story – the underlying conditions, the precipitating causes – does not from a certain perspective change the accident's status *as accident*. To repeat, John's own questioning of the 'how' of Quintana's acute illness did not really provide for him what he really wanted, the 'why' of it all (Didion 2007: 13). Didion's reading of the autopsy report, similarly, furnishes a how without a why. All that she gains, from that point on, is the ability to live in a universe imbued with a non-magical *regularity*: 'When a hill slumps into the ocean I see the order in it' (Didion 1995: 18). There is an interesting connection here to her self-framing as 'granddaughter of a geologist', the qualified solace or 'sedation' she finds in geology, erosion and the like, as explored in Chapter 1. What Didion calls 'the solace I found in geology' inheres in

> its promise that the world will change but also continue.
>
> Do I still find that solace?
>
> How about those river views from the ICUs?
>
> Those eddies, those tidal bores, those currents, those floes?
>
> If those aren't about geology, what are they about?
>
> *As it was in the beginning, is now and ever shall be, world without end?*
>
> Do we get more 'comfort' than that? (Didion 2007: 59–60, emphasis in original)

The 'geological' viewpoint provides a bare minimum of comfort – if anything does in a modern perspective.[19] Again, a truly nihilistic perspective vies with what I have called Didion's pessimism in spinning out the implications of a wholly modern outlook: if everything *particular* will end eventually, and arguably only a geological 'immemorial' remains (in the sense of the term used in Chapter 1), then what is the point of the modern orientation to the future as a set of problems? Can it self-justify?

Whatever the answer, Didion comes to accept the *fact* of John's death. This means that he persists from now on only in the circuit of her *memory* proper. Though she dated the beginning of the mourning period to at least the summer of 2004 (2007: 52), it was only when a full year had elapsed that she could finally say to herself the words her magical thinking had made impossible:

> I realized today for the first time that my memory of this day a year ago is a memory that does not involve John. This day a year ago was December 31, 2003. John did not see this day a year ago. *John was dead.*

> I know why we try to keep the dead alive: we try to keep them alive in order to keep them with us.
>
> I also know that if we are to live ourselves there comes a point at which we must relinquish the dead, let them go, keep them dead.
>
> Let them become the photograph on the table.
>
> Let them become the name on the trust accounts.
>
> Let them go in the water.
>
> Knowing this does not make it any easier to let go of him in the water. (Didion 2005: 225–6, emphasis added)

The Year of Magical Thinking, in the end, therefore testifies to Didion's struggle *to remain modern*, that is, to retain the minimal, austere and essentially comfortless world-picture that for better or for worse constitutes her in the face of her terrible grief. But inasmuch as she uncovers some of the magical presuppositions of that very picture, the Didion at the end of *Magical Thinking* has made no simple return; she has learned, and she has arguably gone further. To the extent that she succeeds, the text therefore witnesses a kind of *ethical* success – at least in the terms of 'preservation of an ethos', though as previously noted, this is a preservation-while-surpassing; she is now aware, or more fully, more intimately aware, of the magical lure in modernity, and the door is open to revising the question of self-pity (Nelson 2017: 170). But the text is also, as I have pointed out, properly other-regarding – and through its spectacular success as a publishing and theatrical event, in the end it found its own 'intimate public'. By finally returning to her deeply entrenched modern perspective, in which death is both an accident and a kind of failure – but now, interestingly, with a newly critical eye on that very perspective – Didion sets out to warn us of what is coming for us all, as the future and its problems, *pace* modern time-consciousness, rush towards us.

The work of mourning and the work of testimony: ethics of memory at the zero degree

We have seen how death figures in Didion as an accident, only partly recoverable if at all through a deterministic or 'geological' point of view. We have seen how Didion works through and repudiates, in the course of candidly witnessing, the period of magical thinking that followed John's death. To repeat, this is done for ethical reasons, both in terms of regaining and nuancing her modern clarity, and in terms of warning others of what is coming. But can the accident of death also be recuperated, if not through magical thinking or, ultimately, any 'geological' causal storytelling, then by some other means? This is the point at which the ethics of memory proper reveals itself in all its urgency, from within an abject plane of modern consciousness where a qualified recuperation through memory, but no *ultimate* recuperation, is possible.

Here my focus will primarily shift to *Blue Nights*. As noted earlier, the memoir details and freely meditates upon the death of Didion's daughter, Quintana Roo Dunne, on 26 August 2005 – not long after John's death, in a devastating turn of events for Didion. The book is largely impressionistic. If there is an overarching theme beyond grief, I believe it is the discovery of radical loss, and therefore the full assumption of what I have called the radical or metaphysical loneliness inherent in Didion's modern consciousness. Magical thinking is no longer the primary issue. Didion now turns to the possibility of discovering and facing up to irretrievable loss, with no guardrails. Even the 'geological' perspective is challenged.

The ethics of memory enters the picture here as an urgent issue because memories might be the only means by which any recuperation of loss is finally possible. At a key point in the book, Didion recounts how people would suggest she find consolation in memory – her memories of Quintana and John – as a saving power in face of her double loss. Didion rejects this outright. As she puts it,

> 'You have your wonderful memories,' people said later, as if memories were solace. Memories are not. Memories are by definition of times past, things gone. Memories are the Westlake [school] uniforms in the closet, the faded and cracked photographs, the invitations to the weddings of the people who are no longer married, the mass cards from the funerals of the people whose faces you no longer remember. Memories are what you no longer want to remember. (Didion 2011: 64)

Didion's memories, and the mementos she keeps, are no consolation to her. Quite the opposite: 'In theory these mementos serve to bring back the moment. In fact they serve only to make clear how inadequately I appreciated the moment when it was here. How inadequately I appreciated the moment when it was here is something else I could never afford to see' (Didion 2011: 46). Didion's grief over her mother's death, which preceded the deaths of John and Quintana, is also revealing in this connection. Faced with mementos gathered after her mother died, Didion tells us how 'I closed the box and put it in a closet. There is no real way to deal with everything we lose' (Didion 2006: 1103). Similarly, and in a striking formulation, in *Blue Nights* Didion describes mementos as 'Objects for which there is no satisfactory resolution' (Didion 2011: 45). To the extent that mementos continue to connect us to the past, they also cause the pain of loss and regret. The only meaningful sense in which such objects can be 'resolved' is therefore to be filed away for good, to be lost or forgotten.

At this point it is helpful to once again connect Didion to the modern consciousness explored in the previous section, via Jean-Didier Urbain's ethnography of Western cemeteries and memorial practices. Recall that in Urbain's reconstruction, modernity construes death as an inassimilable accident. From within this perspective, Didion is absolutely right that 'There is no real way to deal with everything we lose' (2011: 45). Death being senseless, and accidental by definition, there is simply nothing to be done with it – and, indeed, any given death, like the objects reminding us of times past, has itself 'no satisfactory resolution' (Didion 2011).[20]

Her situatedness in a bleak modernity therefore frames Didion's ethics of memory. But this situatedness also inhabits its own temporality, taking time to unfold.[21] As I pointed out in *Philosophy and Vulnerability*, a key aspect of *Blue Nights* is how Didion only *belatedly* arrives at the full meaning of her trauma, and faces up to her irretrievable loss. This loss and the process of facing up to it, as we will see, has implications for the ethics of memory. It doubles, in an obvious way, the process of recognizing that one has been thinking magically, and finally facing up to the truth. But here it is more obviously a question of working through *trauma*, and how our reaction to the latter has shielded us, in its own way, from the truth.

Didion's process in *Blue Nights* is arguably occasioned by an affective discovery of her own frailty. Following Quintana's death, she feels herself 'The target of any wheeled vehicle on the scene' (Didion, 2011: 139). She relates eerie experiences of suddenly, unaccountably, feeling old and vulnerable. For example, watching the rehearsal of a Broadway musical:

> I sit on a folding metal chair. Behind me I hear voices I recognize . . . but I feel too uncertain to turn around . . . . As I sit on the folding metal chair I begin to fear getting up. As the finale approaches, I experience outright panic . . . . What

> if I stand up from this folding chair in this rehearsal room on West Forty-second Street and collapse, fall to the floor, the folding metal chair collapsing with me? Or what if – (Another series of dire possibilities occurs to me, this series even more alarming than the last –) (Didion 2011: 109–10)

Didion goes on to link her anxiety to the possibility of a general cognitive collapse (Didion 2011).

It is not as though Didion previously lacked a sense of her own frailty, or the precariousness of things in general. We saw in Chapter 1, on the contrary, that she paints a precarious universe and construes both herself and others as living precariously within that universe. Didion's very slight frame and her nervous ailments, for example, have often enough been noted, both by her and by others; in fact, we saw even that Didion used the same framing device in *The White Album* to uncover why following 'an attack of vertigo, nausea, and a feeling that she was going to pass out', 'A thorough medical evaluation elicited no findings' (Didion 2006: 187). Rather, the claim here is that her frailty takes on a life of its own in the wake of Quintana's death, insistently befalling her as a haunting feeling. One way to read *Blue Nights* is in terms of Didion's process of working out the knowledge, the 'cognitive' aspect, that is ultimately hidden behind or beneath the feeling. That aspect, I will argue, is what bears upon the ethics of memory.

Both the *belatedness* and the *manner* of Didion's discovery are what interest me here. There is a time lag at the heart of her experience of grief. This occurs between the affect of frailty or her 'being-vulnerable' on one hand, and a certain conceptual knowledge on the other. The Freudian mechanism of *Nachträglichkeit* – translated variously as 'après-coup', 'double-blow', 'deferred action' or 'afterwardsness' – helps to shed light on what Didion is describing, though the fit is perhaps not perfect. Jean-François Lyotard gives a particularly illuminating breakdown of the concept, underscoring the 'physical metaphor' of the mind in Freudian metapsychology (Lyotard 1990: 62). Imagine an introduction of inert, harmless particles into a particular mind: 'the first blow . . . strikes the apparatus without observable internal effect, without affecting it. It is a shock without affect' (Lyotard 1990: 15–16). Only later, 'the energy dispersed in the affective cloud condenses, gets organized, brings on an action, commands a flight [fleeing from a store, in Freud's example] without a "real" motive' (Lyotard 1990: 16). With the second blow, 'there takes place an affect without shock: I buy something in a store, anxiety crushes me, I flee, but nothing really happened' (Lyotard 1990). Because buying something in a store – or sitting on a folding chair at a play rehearsal – is apparently insufficient to explain either the affect that arises or its intensity, the latter 'informs consciousness *that* there is something, without being able to tell *what it is*' (Lyotard 1990, emphasis in original). There is, to put it differently, a gap between the '*il y a*' ('the there is') and the '*ce qu'il y a*' ('the what there is'). Didion, for her part, knows that she is not *simply* afraid of falling from a chair, but also of something else: 'When I tell you that I am afraid to get up from a folding chair in a rehearsal room on West Forty-second Street, of what am I really afraid?' (Lyotard 1990: 117).

In the clinical picture of trauma described by *Nachträglichkeit*, the symptomatic affect is therefore accompanied by something like a loss of memory. Or more accurately, the affect indexes a 'time' – though not really a time – in which nothing was 'recorded' to memory in the first place, *qua* cognitive experience (*mnēmē*). Psychoanalysis proposes here a process of 'working through' (*Durcharbeitung*) (Lyotard 1988: 26; Ricœur 2006: 71), wherein the analyst and the analysand collaborate to paradoxically 'chronologize' the first blow – precisely, the one which occurred outside of any diachrony, as far as memory *qua mnēmē* is concerned (Lyotard 1990: 16). Such collaboration, in analysis, requires a plumbing of the psycho-sexual history of the analysand; it requires memory *qua anamnēsis*. Even if the affect or symptom cannot, by definition, be transformed into *memories* in the properly cognitive sense of the term, the retrospective construction of its meaning thus requires a collective *effort* of the pragmatic, and hence ethical, dimension of remembering. Interestingly, Didion herself seems aware that she may be contributing to the blockage of meaning in some way, perhaps through repression and in spite of herself:

> My cognitive confidence seems to have vanished altogether. Even the correct stance for telling you this, the ways to describe what is happening to me, the attitude, the tone, the very words, now elude my grasp.
>
> The tone needs to be direct.
>
> I need to talk to you directly, I need to *address the subject as it were*, but something stops me.
>
> Is this another kind of neuropathy, a new frailty, am I no longer able to talk directly?
>
> Was I ever?

Did I lose it?

Or is the subject in this case a matter I wish not to address? (Didion 2011: 116–17, emphasis in original)

Didion also relates how she later experienced an actual blackout and fall, medically diagnosed as syncope. Again, her account mirrors the mechanism of *Nachträglichkeit* in several respects. The subjective effects of the event were highly significant, seemingly out of all proportion with the medical diagnosis. Didion recounts how the event 'altered my view of my own possibilities, shortened, as it were, the horizon' (Didion 2011: 142). Further, after two nights of 'relatively undemanding hospitalization,' she claims that 'Demoralization happens in the instant' (Didion 2011: 146). When extensive medical testing eventually turns up nothing, Didion is therefore surprised: 'Surprisingly, there were no abnormalities to explain why I felt as frail as I did. Surprisingly, there were no abnormalities to tell me why I was afraid to get up from a folding chair in a rehearsal room on West Forty-second street' (Didion 2011: 148). Evoking the uncanniness of the whole experience, she draws from a different area of medicine: '"It doesn't present as pain," I once heard an oncological surgeon say of cancer' (Didion 2011: 149).

Up to this point, then, Didion's feelings of frailty are insistent and troubling but they remain mysterious to her. I argue that this changes at the book's end. Perhaps the labour of writing *Blue Nights* itself stands in for the psychoanalytical 'working through' that would be required to give her feelings a tentative meaning. There are, of course, limits and caveats to using psychoanalytical concepts in connection with the book; as I will explain there is no obvious 'cure' here in any clinical sense or even in the sense of partial relief, and in this respect what working through there is appears 'interminable'.[22] On the assumption that Didion belatedly understands her feelings of frailty, there is, rather, the grim possibility that finally 'To look for "reasons" is beside the point' (Didion 1970: 3). To quote Maria in *Play it as it Lays*, 'I have trouble with as it was. I mean it leads nowhere' (Didion 1970: 7). Or as Cathleen Schine put it, 'Memories – even these memories, the ones [Didion] has collected in this book – are as fragile and complicated and beautiful as one of the scraps of her grandmother's lace, she tells us. They are as singular and, finally, as meaningless. There is no dress to trim with the old lace. There is no daughter. There is no future' (Schine 2011). Yet, even if Didion ends up in some sense where she started, or worse, at least in terms of the immensity of her grief and her loss, she may have nonetheless made a minimal, cognitive progress – and this will prove essential to describing *Blue Nights* in terms of the ethics of memory.

An important clue to what Didion eventually uncovers is given relatively early in the memoir. She claims that 'When we talk about mortality we are talking about our children' and that 'once [Quintana] was born I was never not afraid . . . . The source of the fear was obvious: it was the harm that could come to her' (Didion 2011: 54). This should be familiar by now in terms of 'earthquake weather', and Didion's tendency to mention children in connection with the particular disaster. But note that when we 'talk about mortality' and thus about our children, we are not solely talking about our *children's* mortality. Didion relates that she used to sometimes swim in a cave near her house with John. The cave figures in her description of bringing the newborn Quintana home, following her adoption:

> I think about bringing her home from St. John's Hospital in Santa Monica and placing her in the bassinette that overlooked the point where the sea ran into the cave.
>
> The cave into which we never again swam after the day we brought her home.
>
> One more improvised way of keeping her from drowning.
>
> You're safe, I'm here. (Didion 2007: 61)

Arguably it is not just a question of Joan and John's forbidding Quintana, as she grows older, from swimming into the cave. 'Keeping her from drowning' in a more than literal sense[23] requires that her parents be there for her to protect and guide her – 'You're safe, I'm here,' or as Didion says elsewhere, 'this had been, since the day she was born, my basic promise to her. I would not leave' (Didion 2007: 35). This is why she says *we* never swam into the cave again after Quintana was brought home. When she 'talks about mortality', and thus about Quintana, she is also describing *her own* mortality, and John's.

The closing words of *Blue Nights* therefore take on a terrible meaning in this light. Didion finally comes to understand her feelings of frailty:

> I myself placed her ashes in the wall.
>
> I myself saw the cathedral doors locked at six.
>
> I know what it is I am now experiencing.

> I know what the frailty is, I know what the fear is.
>
> The fear is not for what is lost.
>
> What is lost is already in the wall.
>
> What is lost is already behind the locked doors.
>
> The fear is for what is still to be lost.
>
> You may see nothing still to be lost.
>
> Yet there is no day in her life on which I do not see her. (Didion 2011: 188)

This passage, perhaps one of the most desolate in modern literature, reveals how Didion, belatedly, discovers that *there is still something to lose of Quintana*. Specifically, in a universe that does not hold us and in which there is no personal survival after death, *Didion's own death will amount to the obliteration of an immense amount of what Quintana once was*. This is so on account of her intimate history with Quintana, having been her mother. Every memory that Didion holds – precisely, those *memories* that she does not want to remember, painful as they are in the light of her loss – will themselves be lost when she dies. This amounts to a destruction of a vast storehouse of traces of Quintana's life, a kind of second death. Didion, as the mother who remembers, therefore becomes *precious* in a way that she was perhaps unaware of before. Precisely this preciousness accounts for her newly urgent and acute feelings of *fragility* in the wake of Quintana's death.[24]

Didion can, of course, write a memoir about Quintana's life to resist this further oblivion. Already in *Play it as it Lays*, she recognizes that the events of the past enter the ambit of metaphysical loneliness and teeter on the edge of nothingness if there is only one person left to remember them: 'In a sense the day they ate spare ribs and drove to McCarran had ceased to exist, had never happened at all: she was the only one left who remembered it' (Didion 1970: 151). In this respect, there is a kind of redemption in the fact that not only *Blue Nights* but also much of Didion's catalogue paints an image of Quintana for posterity, recounting who she was and what happened so that others may 'remember' her in a second-hand way. But even this will never quite do: words in a memoir will never capture the fullness, the irreducibly unique life, the absolute singularity and inexhaustible richness of the lost person. At best, even first-hand memories can only ever approximate this uniqueness, and, of course, they constitutively risk confusion with the imaginary – thus raising the question of their veracity for the author herself, but also for each of her readers (Ricœur 2006: 5–55). In short, though Didion once pined for 'life expanded to a novel', and wanted 'everything in the picture' (Didion 2021: 69), she is forced to face up to the radical inadequacy of remembering and writing to this task.

Why therefore, given her bleak conclusion, did Didion bother to write the memoir at all? In *Blue Nights* she writes under no illusions: there is really no preserving Quintana through her gesture. She even writes of her very failure to write – at least in the sense of writing to communicate with her readers:

> What if the damage extends beyond the physical?
>
> What if the problem is now cognitive?
>
> What if the absence of style that I welcomed at one point – the directness that I encouraged, even cultivated – what if this absence of style has now taken on a pernicious life of its own?
>
> What if my new inability to summon the right word, the apt thought, the connection that enables the words to make sense, the rhythm, the music itself –
>
> What if this new inability is systemic?
>
> What if I can never again locate the words that work? (Didion 2011: 110–1)

In spite of everything, however, Didion later pleads with the reader: 'Let me again try to talk to you directly' (Didion 2011: 134). There is, I argue therefore, significance in the very *saying* of Didion's memoir, even if we admit that the *said* cannot help but fail to bear adequate witness to Quintana.[25]

In particular, I believe it is *the saying* represented by *Blue Nights* that forms the zero degree of Didion's ethics of memory. 'Saying' is in this case, of course, to be taken in the sense of *not being silent* about her memories when Didion could have been. To be sure, silence too can be a kind of saying; to see how, just imagine (or think back to) the experience of telling a person you love them, followed by their silence. It is not always clear *what* exactly a given silence means. But as Lyotard argues,[26] the meaning of a silence has something to do with its addressee, its referent, its sense or its addressor – or some combination of these. As he explains, 'The negative phrase that the silence implies could be formulated respectively: *This case does not fall within your competence* [addressee], *This case does not exist* [referent], *It cannot be signified* [sense], *It does not fall within my competence* [addressor]. A single silence could be formulated by several of these phrases' (Lyotard 1988: 13, emphasis in original).

To follow Quintana's death with silence could, indeed, have been meaningful, on this view. The veracity of Didion's *referent*, Quintana's very life and the events of her death, are not radically in question.[27] But Didion's or anyone's ability to capture Quintana's life and the events of her death more or less *faithfully*, let alone in their entirety, certainly is. And what of the *sense* that could be made of Didion's losing Quintana? How, indeed, could any grieving parent – one who is steeped in modernity, at any rate – make sense of such a catastrophic loss? Perhaps, moreover, Didion – the *addressor* – lacks the capacity to put her loss into words. Or finally, perhaps, her would-be readers – her *addressees* – would lack the capacity to understand it, even if she could say it. Even if we have suffered a similar loss in our lives, what could we know of *this* young woman – when she was a girl, and as she grew up – and of how much she meant to her mother, *this* mother who is now grieving?

Such a silence could therefore have been perfectly understandable in principle, and in some sense also 'forgivable'. *Nonetheless*, Didion *says* in an active sense, through her writing, rather than through silence. It is here that we can speak of an ethics of memory at the zero degree – and here, too, Lyotard is of some help. He allows for saying when one would have had very good reasons for remaining silent, on the grounds that one does not thereby pretend to adequacy – or in Ricœur's terms, does not pass off simple *mnēmē* where an interminable *anamnēsis* is required. As Lyotard put it, commenting on Eli Wiesel,[28]

> It must be sufficient that one remembers that one must remember, that one should; and it must be sufficient that one remembers that one does not remind oneself of it anymore; it must be sufficient to save the interminable and the waiting. *Ordinary memory accomplishes forgetting, covers up the promise.* But the promise is not gone, it is always there. It is this always there that must be reserved in the forgetting that conceals it. A narrative of the forgetting of the prayer would serve the purpose because it preserves the waiting. And the waiting alone can reserve for the promise its time of promise (Lyotard 1990: 37–8, emphasis added).

Didion, to repeat, opts to actively *say*, through her writing, what could have arguably been 'said', through her silence.[29] But in her writing, she shows ample awareness of the limitations of her saying – thus, *refusing to pass off her memoir as ordinary memory*, the kind that unselfconsciously obliterates precisely through representation, falsifies the life through telling about it (Didion 1996:

74), forecloses the infinity or the miracle of the lost person, as in Lyotard's aforementioned sense. Any witnessing of Quintana, any testimony of her life, is by definition a failure – and Didion knows this. It is *only* a representation, literally a *re-presentation* that entails doubt over the initial presentation as well as a labour of editing, and it loses much in translation.[30] As such, it involves and risks editorial choices. These may be, and have been, fairly questioned. Once again, Didion proves to have been preoccupied with these issues much earlier in her corpus than the memoirs on grief. Citing 'the equivocal nature of even the most empirical evidence' (1977: 271), and the fact that 'We all remember what we need to remember' (1977: 259), Didion's narrator bookends *A Book of Common Prayer* with the statements 'I will be her witness,' and 'I have not been the witness I wanted to be' (1977: 11, 272).

But even if such an endeavor is compromised from the outset, it is the only endeavor that will preserve *something* of Quintana; silence as we saw is meaningful, but silence preserves nothing of the referent.[31] Specific memories, in fixing the referent for all time, betray it – which gives further meaning to the claim that 'memories are what you no longer want to remember'. But as Giorgio Agamben comments, 'The survivor's vocation is to remember; he cannot *not* remember' (Agamben 2002: 26, emphasis in original). The question is whether this memory will take shape as silence, or as testimony through speech, writing or some other medium. This is an ethical issue because as Lyotard put it, 'The witness is always a poor witness, a traitor. But [she] does, after all, still bear witness' (Lyotard 1993: 146).[32] Between oblivion and betrayal, the witness chooses betrayal – cognizant, of course, in her unhappy consciousness, of the ethical injunction to minimize that betrayal.

Moreover, an undertaking such as *Blue Nights* gives the only possibility on a desolate plane of modern, metaphysical loneliness, that a community of memory, however fleeting and minimal, might be constituted. As I put it in *Philosophy and Vulnerability*, there can be 'a community of suffering for whom such witnessing is significant' (McLennan 2019: 88). This could be updated to say that even if we grant metaphysical loneliness, such witnessing can nonetheless form an 'intimate public'. After all, the writer's irreducible interiority does not amount to her total *imprisonment* in her interiority. I will have more to say about the scope of such a public, and whom it leaves out. For now, note that the very saying of *Blue Nights* appeals to, if not constitutes, an addressee – Didion herself, as the first reader of whatever she writes, but also a community of memory in which Quintana's life and death, and Didion's suffering over them, matters – or will come to matter, if Didion's writings can be considered to found a tradition.

It may sound paradoxical to claim, first, that one could form a community of memory with *oneself*. For one thing, this cannot really be meant in a sense that would *completely* exclude others existing outside of the self/past-self dyad. On the topic of staying in touch with past selves through keeping a notebook, Didion makes the compelling point that 'we are all on our own when it comes to keeping those lines open to ourselves: your notebook will never help me, nor mine you' (Didion 2006: 107). But I have already expressed well-supported doubt over the idea that there is ever any *strict* boundary between the self and the community, such that even when I am contemplating my past selves, I am doing so as a person and in a world that are shaped through and through by others. To repeat, metaphysical loneliness indexes an irreducibly interior aspect of the person, but this does not amount to saying that all personal aspects are entirely interior. As Jill Stauffer put it, 'what feels like intellectual solitude to a free person is already a form of community; research takes the form of a question, and a question addresses itself to others' (2015: 17). In this light, at least prior to John's death there is a good case that his long-time role as 'second reader' for Didion was so intimate and involved as to implicate him into her 'first reader' perspective (Daugherty 2015; Parker 2018).

In discussing the notion of community with oneself, I therefore have in mind no more than the possible ontological plurality of the named 'individual' who remembers, discussed earlier in this chapter. This is what the earlier Didion expresses through the idea that one can have past selves and 'keep in touch' with them through keeping a notebook (Didion 2006: 107). Regarding Didion as her own first reader drafting *Blue Nights*, at a minimum we have seen how she comments on the writing process as she struggles with it, failing to fully identify with some of her own affective states and inserting the very time that it takes to bear witness into the witnessing itself.[33] She also, as we saw, recognizes her past selves' failing to adequately appreciate the past moment when it was present. What is more, elsewhere Didion often takes such an 'excentric positionality' (Plessner 2019) with respect to her past selves and past writings, most notably perhaps in *Where I Was From* (to be discussed in the next chapter). Not just Didion, but anyone who has written something and looked back on it after a passage of years, months, weeks – perhaps even days – may have had just such an inkling of 'oneself as another' (Ricœur 1990).

To the extent that the past self and the present self who is engaged in reading have anything to say to each other via the medium of preserved, represented memory, there is therefore the possibility – arguably the necessity – of ethics.[34] In fact, even where the memorial act, the saying, is done without any witnesses or hope of preservation, this can still be significant from an ethical point of view. One thinks of those in death camps who, committing something of their fallen comrades' lives and fates to memory, hope that they will one day be able to testify beyond the borders of the camp. For some, even the conviction that they themselves are unlikely to survive does not dissuade them; they commit to remembering on the understanding that if they would get out alive, they would want their later selves to live up to themselves somehow. It is possible to behave as a *future past self*, and to apply normative standards to oneself accordingly.[35] Note again though, that all such discussions of forming an ethical community with oneself are premised upon the idea that the sayer is already validated and held, in some way, by her wider community or a subset of that community. For that reason alone, it is not a creation of community *ex nihilo* – as is also doubtless the case for Didion, whose life has been characterized by wide networks of support, admiration and acquaintanceship (Daugherty 2015). Even when one has good grounds for claiming that they *are* ethically alone, as per Stauffer (2015) – an idea to be discussed in the next section – there remains the possibility that one stands irrevocably in a thin, *moral* community with human (and perhaps non-human) others, as per Margalit's definition, and that saying would remain meaningful even when the community ties it enjoins are so thin as to be virtual.

Whatever we make of the idea of Didion's forming community with herself, we have also seen from the simple fact of her broad readership that she successfully interpellates others ethically through her saying. But here we have to be careful. She cannot be expecting that others will carry forth the memory of Quintana *as would one's thickest or closest relations*. Speaking, I believe, as a member of the comparatively thin but still 'ethical' community of memory she constituted through her text (and other texts, and the commentary that these have produced), I now know something of Quintana's life. And in an oblique way, I am continuing the discussion of that life, giving it over once more to memory, by talking about Didion's books – thus keeping the community alive through memory, at the same time as I keep something of Quintana alive. But my witnessing is a paltry one compared to Didion's, and many readers will leave behind them no testimony at all of what they have read of hers. Perhaps Berlant's concept of 'intimate public', which stresses affect, describes best what usually happens when readers encounter Didion's memoirs of grief: we are moved, and in a broad sense we form part of a community with her, but, above all, what we remember is the *feeling* of reading her, of encountering her saying – not necessarily the details of the lives she recounts.

Even if we downplay the idea that Didion constitutes community, in any thick sense, through her saying, it remains true that reading both versions of *The Year of Magical Thinking* alongside *Blue Nights* is revelatory in connection with the ethics of memory. If the very gesture of writing and publishing *Blue Nights* in some sense demonstrates the ethos or courage required for an ethics of memory on the most desolate plane of modernity, we must *also* notice that 'magical thinking' is doubly bad, both for Didion and for the intimate public whom she warns, because in some sense it violates such an ethics. Magical thinking is self-delusion, which as we saw is a cardinal sin for Didion throughout her career. But more than that, it negates or frustrates the vital work of using one's remaining time on Earth to bear witness to those whom one wants to preserve. Before the publication of *Blue Nights*, but after Quintana's death – in the play version of *Magical Thinking* – Didion describes perhaps a limit-case of magical thinking, *resisting even the memories themselves*, during the period in which Quintana was still hospitalized:

> I cannot think of what is gone.
>
> If I think of what is gone the difference between then and now will take me.
>
> I won't be there when she needs me . . .
>
> If I can keep her alive John will come back . . .
>
> To keep her alive I need to focus.
>
> I need to avoid noticing anything that might lead me back into the past.
>
> Going back has trick currents, unrevealed eddies, you can be skimming along on what looks like clear water and suddenly go under.
>
> Get sucked down.
>
> Get caught in the vortex and let go of her hand.

Lose control.

Lose her.

Feel the water take her. (Didion 2007: 35–6).

Didion thus describes Quintana's illness and the need to care for her as a pretext for persisting in her magical thinking. Earlier, I noted how modernity has its own subterranean magical elements, some of which Didion identifies (if not as such). Her refusal to remember while she is caring for Quintana might be a case in point. If modernity is, as I have assumed here, a form of instrumental or strategic time-consciousness which largely jettisons the past in favour of both the vanishing present, and the future construed as an onrushing set of problems, then Didion's refusal to mourn or even *remember* while Quintana is in danger is eminently modern. Extrapolating freely from Didion's example, the persistent magical element here would lie in the faulty assumption that leaving the past behind will in any way save us, or what we hold dear. On the contrary, I have already argued that *an ethics that is also moral*, in Margalit's sense, would require honest engagement with what is painful and shameful in our societies' pasts. Contemporary disputes over racist monuments and the like clearly demonstrate how it is memory, history and a deep engagement with what is painful that might be the saving grace of a failing modernity, instead of uncritical optimism and forgetting.

Note that it is precisely when Quintana's health appears to be improving that Didion's mourning process actually begins. This happens nearly eight months after John's death, when Quintana is discharged for outpatient neurorehabilitation. In an eerie precursor to the mysterious frailty of *Blue Nights*, Didion describes an episode of anxiety and arguably frailty overcoming her at the 2004 Democratic Convention, in terms strikingly similar to the folding chair episode: 'When it was time to stand for the national anthem I could see myself pitching forward, in free fall' (Didion 2007: 52; 2005: 176–8). Here again, Didion is not at first aware that the process has begun, but she is aware at least that something has happened. The pain of memory and its related actions can befall us, or can be assumed as part of a conscious, ethical project – but it cannot be avoided in any case.

Taken all together, it is possible to draw a set of lessons from the memoirs on the theme of the ethics of memory:

- If we wish to remain modern in the face of grief, which is to say committed to *the truth* of death in a context where it is construed as an inassimilable accident and/or a failure, we must be aware that traps of self-delusion lie in wait for us as we grieve. We must, in other words, be on guard against magical thinking.
- What is more, modernity nourishes its own, subterranean magical currents or prejudices – thus the resolution to 'be modern' may be insufficient for guarding against self-delusion, and we must be doubly vigilant. We must guard in particular against the 'magical' modern prejudice that protecting ourselves from our own memories, staying focused on the present and future only, will save us.
- Staying modern, avoiding the traps of magical thinking, entails, however, that more is ultimately lost than the ongoing presence and futurity of the person whom we mourn. Since we alone are finally the guarantors of her life on Earth, through our memories of her and what we might say about her, then *even more is lost* when we ourselves pass on. Through the impossibility of faithful representation, as well as through the decay of community memory and, indeed, the very limits of life on Earth, everything dear to us will one day be lost, forever.
- The choice thus presents itself between pessimism, perhaps profound pessimism, and nihilism – which, we have seen, is crucially different. *Blue Nights* is a profoundly pessimistic text, but it does after all constitute a gesture, an active saying, and one minimally constitutive of a community of memory – first with Didion herself, but also with the intimate public it appeals to or engenders. We see that the ethics of memory *at the zero degree*, from a thoroughly disenchanted modern perspective, amounts to *gathering the courage to witness, to testify, despite everything*. It demands a hardness, a resoluteness, that is nonetheless trained upon earthly values. Looked at from the deceptively 'private' or 'intimate' sphere of memory actions, Didion is an ethical teacher or exemplar, in the sense of exemplifying virtues required for abiding with the bleakest implications of modernity.

Recall finally, however, that to draw 'lessons' in this way from Didion is hypothetical. I am assuming here that the universe does not 'hold' us. This way of putting it is only metaphorical, of course, but there are numerous philosophical views or systems that would deny that anything of what we cherish is ultimately lost. I am staunchly agnostic about such questions, but note that agnosticism itself is only a refusal to be 'held' by anything that one doubts – and thereby, the agnostic (speaking from personal experience) inhabits a zone between dread and wonder, absolute pessimism and radical hope. This is the very zone of philosophy as I understand it, and it requires – if not courage – a certain obstinacy. Having lost much and testified to it, Didion is both obstinate and courageous in her thinking, and to that extent at least she has much to teach us as we tarry with the possibility that the universe really is as bad as all that.

Didion, public testimony and 'grievability'

We have seen how, situated in a desolate plane of modern, metaphysical loneliness, Didion throws a rope bridge of memory out over the void. In doing so she appeals to, or perhaps even constitutes, a community of memory – first with herself, as her own first reader, and then with the wider reading public. She fails to preserve anything near to the richly particular life of her lost daughter, and she is, in fact, doomed to fail because of witnessing and testimony's status as representation. But if the *said* of her memoir falls sadly short, the *saying* itself is courageous or at least obstinate, and opens onto the ethical – precisely when its author could have succumbed to nihilism.

It might seem natural at this point to leave off with the lessons derived previously, and to conclude the chapter simply, as follows: *Didion is an ethical teacher or exemplar*. All along I have been setting up the idea that she exemplifies the courage it takes to constitute ethics, and hence community, from within a thoroughly disenchanted modernism. This conclusion is certainly not false, but it is far from the full picture.

The problem with breaking off here would be that *the very reception of testimony* is always modulated according to structures of interpretation, or 'frames' (Butler 2016; Gilmore 2018 and 2019). In fact, the very reception of testimony *as testimony* is similarly modulated; that is, not every case of testimony is even construed as testimony at all.[36] If Didion's loneliness by the end of *Blue Nights* can be rightly called 'metaphysical', as I have been doing

– meaning that there is an irreducible interiority to her, and that she is in the final or cosmic analysis alone, an impermanent subject or consciousness in a universe that does not hold her – it still cannot properly be called an 'ethical' loneliness. Not only is her gesture through and through an ethical one, in the terms I used earlier, but perhaps more importantly, her reading public *qua* ethical community largely *precedes* the publication of the book. I have said more than once that she 'appeals to or perhaps constitutes' a community of memory through her gesture. If she *constitutes* one, it is in the sense of creating a tradition in which Quintana's and John's lives resonate as important ones, full of events and particularities to be retold, discussed, retrodden (as I am doing now in my own oblique way). But in the broadest sense, the community of memory she *appeals* to is the one (or ones) in which she, Joan Didion, already belongs and whose testimony is already legible *qua* testimony. It is, in fact, this very community of appeal that allows her, the witness who testifies, to constitute a new direction or tradition – to add a circle to the concentric communities of memory, and therefore ethics, in which she is embedded.

If we are to draw ethical lessons from Didion, or to hold her up as a moral or ethical teacher or exemplar, it is therefore imperative that we guard against a pernicious illusion: *We cannot mistake Didion's metaphysical loneliness for a truly ethical loneliness.* Doing so is committing a grave error, masking the properly social and political dimensions of the ethics of memory. If we fail to give these dimensions their due, then we are construing 'ethics of memory' in an idealistic, in fact ideological manner. Put differently, treating *The Year of Magical Thinking* and *Blue Nights* as canonical representations of grief, full stop, masks the realities of grief and, indeed, grievability experienced by persons in different social locations than Didion's. Precisely where we see universal themes in Didion – and the temptation is very, very strong to see them, especially since she 'bullies' us into seeing things her way – we also have to reckon with really existing inequalities.

My first point of reference in making this argument is Jill Stauffer's concept of 'ethical loneliness' (2015). Starting here helps us to pose the problem I am presenting in the starkest terms possible. Stauffer defines ethical loneliness as 'the experience of having been abandoned by humanity compounded by the experience of not being heard' (2015: 1–2). Significantly, ethical loneliness can be imposed through direct violation or victimization, or structurally, as, for example, in ambient and administrative racism or transphobia. As Stauffer describes, ethical loneliness

> is the isolation one feels when one, as a violated person or as one member of a persecuted group, has been abandoned by humanity, or by those who have power over one's life's possibilities. It is a condition undergone by persons who have been unjustly treated and dehumanized by human beings and political structures, who emerge from that injustice only to find that the surrounding world will not listen to or cannot properly hear their testimony – their claims about what they suffered and about what is now owed them – on their own terms (2015: 1).[37]

Focused as she is on testimony, and themes like repair and revision, Stauffer's text is an extremely rich resource with which to think about the ethics of memory. I will have to restrict my commentary to the titular 'ethical loneliness' for reasons of scope, and in order to drive home what Didion is *not* experiencing, even in *Blue Nights*, even when she is apparently at her very loneliest. Having been neither abandoned by humanity, nor systematically violated by the dominant social set, and having full recourse to explore her grief and to voice it in the public sphere – indeed, where she already finds a receptive intimate public – Didion's loneliness is *merely* metaphysical, in the sense I have used the term. In this regard, what I have characterized as Didion's search for the meaning of her newly urgent frailty takes on a public, hence already ethical, cast. Here again Stauffer's formula rings true: 'what feels like intellectual solitude to a free person is already a form of community; research takes the form of a question, and a question addresses itself to others' (Stauffer 2015: 17).

It is of further significance that John and Quintana, about whom Didion gives her most sustained expressions of mourning, were already widely and publicly legible as lives worthy of mourning at the time of publication (and, in fact, they still are). Here Judith Butler is of assistance through her writings on 'grievability', which is a concept that characterizes lives lost, but is also 'already operative in life' (2020: 59). In Butler's terms, to be grievable

> is to be interpellated in such a way that you know your life matters; that the loss of your life would matter; that your body is treated as one that should be able to live and thrive, whose precarity should be minimized, for which provisions for flourishing should be available. The presumption of equal grievability would be not only a conviction or attitude with which another

person greets you, but a principle that organizes the social organization of health, food, shelter, employment, sexual life, and civic life (2020: 59).

Butler's claim across several publications is that we do *not* live in a society where all lives are equally grievable. If we did, it would not be necessary, for example, to claim forcefully and relentlessly in public that 'Black lives matter'.[38] Rather, it can often happen that

> a life is at the same time actively mourned within one community and fully unmarked – and unmarkable – within a dominant national or international frame. It is one reason why the community that mourns also protests the fact that the life is considered ungrievable . . . . This is one reason why mourning can be protest, and the two must go together when losses are not yet publicly acknowledged and mourned. (Butler 2020: 73–4)

Such mournful protest, or mourning as protest, 'seeks to expose the limits of the grievable and establish new terms of acknowledgement and resistance' (Butler 2020: 106). As such, it is 'an intervention in the sphere of appearance' (Butler 2020: 202) calculated to disrupt entrenched norms of unequal grievability – the very frames by which we judge some lives incalculably precious, others as subject to calculation and others as not even lives at all.

Looking at Didion through the lens of grievability, we thus see that there is an entire dimension of suffering that she does not have to contend with – precisely, the effort that would be required to establish her lost family members' lives as grievable in the first place, were they other than white, affluent and cisgender. Quintana's grievability, for instance, is taken for granted by the reading public. There is, to be fair, an arguable element of *ressentiment* around her, *qua* white cisgender daughter of famous parents. Didion herself in *Blue Nights* raised and then summarily dismissed the idea that Quintana was in any way 'privileged', denying this could have been the case on account of her personal struggles.[39] I have previously discussed this at some length (McLennan 2019), arguing that whatever difficulties Quintana may have had in life, they were demonstrably not compounded by her race or class, and *in this sense* at least she was, indeed, privileged. Even allowing that Quintana had a hard life, in Butler's terms we can say that her grievability was never an issue for her in the way it is for racialized persons navigating their daily lives, at sharply increased risk of discrimination, harassment, violence and death, often at the hands of police.

Finally, Leigh Gilmore's work is helpful here. First, she gives a compelling account of the 'jurisdictions', 'genres', and 'frames' through which testimony passes in the public sphere and as a function of which it is not therefore always held to be credible. As she explores through the figure of the 'tainted witness', 'Testimonial truth is indexed not to facts but to power' (2018: 15), and her primary examples in the book *Tainted Witness* are taken from women's testimony in our time. As she argues, 'Judgment falls unequally on women who bear witness' (2018: 1),[40] and this accounts for the injustice of a range of contemporary cases.[41]

Note how Gilmore's insight is broadly compatible with Butler's analysis of frames of grievability, as Gilmore herself points out (2018: 24; 2019). Just as lives are more or less grievable, testimonies are more or less credible: 'judgment disproportionately affects the vulnerable' (ibid. 2018: 13), and such judgements depend upon framings, which in the end rest upon the power interests that are served by existing inequalities. Just as Butler signals the importance of #BlackLivesMatter in recent iterations of her concept of grievability, Gilmore also draws attention to its power and pertinence in connection with testimony. According to Gilmore, #BlackLivesMatter's use of social media 'may offer a density of testimonial reference and supply historical context missing from the headlines and, through links and hashtags, propel these references forward' (2018: 160). Put differently, it 'establishes both a documentary and a commemorative politics around bearing witness and grieving in public through their integration into everyday practices of social networks' (2018: 160–1).

Interestingly, Gilmore also compellingly links Didion, in 2016, to #BlackLivesMatter. The connection may seem 'startling', as Gilmore suggests, but they nonetheless 'share the space of public grief at the beginning of the twenty-first century and, read together, demonstrate how histories of race, public accommodation, and mourning run parallel to the formation of literary reputation and celebrity' (Gilmore 2016b: 610). Didion's 'moment' – her revival as a style icon, connected in the public imagination to grief and mourning – was declared in 2015, and it overlapped fully with the 'moment' of #BlackLivesMatter (2016b: 611). But as Gilmore points out, 'white women's grief historically occupies a space of privilege in the public sphere, while people of color experience risk and harm there' (2016b). This accounts for why during her 'moment', 'Didion exemplifies the lyric survivor who suffers loss and pain but is not required to assert the value of her loved ones' lives and deaths or her right to grieve for them in the face of the denial of their worth' (2016b: 612).

Interestingly, Gilmore draws attention to how 'in addition to organizing public protests to demand racial justice, #BlackLivesMatter insistently counters the "magical thinking " of white police officers who imagine threat and surge with murderous fear and rage in encounters with unarmed people of color' (Gilmore 2016b: 612). This tracks with my previous comments, to the effect that modernity, though viewed as an ideology of disenchantment, nonetheless bears along with it certain hidden or disavowed magical elements. But here it is not the 'primitive', racialized other who is the exemplar of what it means to fail to be modern (recall Didion's own regrettable use of the word 'primitive' in describing the peoples exemplary of magical thinking). Rather, it is the racist white police officer who is rightly cast as a force of unreason, and in this sense as un- or anti-modern, perhaps 'primitive' even, in Gilmore's handling.

Finally – since I began this chapter by noting that Didion's grief memoirs inhabit the deceptively 'private' or 'intimate' sphere of memory – it is of further interest to note that for Gilmore, it is not simply grievability that is unequal for persons of colour, but also their *privacy*. White privileged families, of which Didion's is perhaps to some extent emblematic, 'may invoke a zone of privacy in which to grieve and carry that privacy with them in public' (2016b: 613), while families of colour, through unequal exposure to the law and racist media frames, enjoy no such right. As the historical example of Emmet Till suggests, African American families have at times even had to vociferously forego any semblance of such a right precisely to challenge the unequal frames of grievability permitting their harassment and murder. Till was tortured and murdered by two white men in 1955 at the age of fourteen, after being accused of whistling at a white woman in a convenience store. He was displayed in an open casket at his funeral at the urging of his mother. Tens of thousands attended, and images of his badly mangled body circulated widely, even internationally, sparking unrest and giving great impetus to the civil rights movement. Such publicity, such utter absence of 'privacy' in mourning, indexes the necessity to shock, to outrage and to disrupt racist frames of grievability. Till's mother, Mamie Till-Mobley, ultimately performed this gesture for the good of her community – and went on to write a memoir of the murder and her grief (Till-Mobley and Benson 2003). The point here is that

Didion's memoirs of grief, protected as her family is by white grievability and the 'zone of privacy' Gilmore identifies, were engendered by no such injustice or existential precarity.[42]

Gathering together the preceding – my gloss on Stauffer's 'ethical loneliness', Butler's 'grievability', and Gilmore's 'jurisdictions', 'genres' and 'frames' – we have a powerful way of describing the agony of the present conjuncture, in the academic language of white authors at any rate.[43] At the time of writing, in the United States and beyond, there is a mass cultural reckoning and political uprising sparked by the police murder of George Floyd in May 2020. Floyd was killed after allegedly passing a counterfeit $20 bill at a grocery store; during arrest, police officer Derek Chauvin knelt on his neck for seven minutes forty-six seconds (Associated Press 2020), and other officers on the scene failed either to intervene, or to treat Floyd once it was clear that medical assistance was needed. Until he lost consciousness, Floyd begged for his life and repeatedly told Chauvin 'I can't breathe'. That the murder was even possible, forming a link in a long pattern of police murders of unarmed Black and Brown persons in the US and beyond, indexes ethical loneliness and the social frame of the unequal grievability of Black and Brown lives. But significantly – though events are, of course, continuing to develop as I write – there is hope that Floyd's murder may be a watershed. The scale and the acuteness of the outrage following it, and following subsequent police brutality against protestors and bystanders, indexes a possible shift in frames, jurisdictions, or genres of testifying to the grievability of a life.

To be sure, there is room for further critical discussion about how the *gendered* frame of unequal grievability (Butler 2020: 118–20) arguably contributed to Floyd's murder being the detonator. Breonna Taylor's earlier death at the hands of Louisville, Kentucky, police in March 2020, relatively underpublicized but just as shocking and demonstrative of the need to defund and dismantle existing forms of policing, is a case in point. But recognition of the intersectional nature of frames of grievability is already built into the theory and practice of #BlackLivesMatter. This critical nuance, as well as the courage to build towards and make good upon the possible watershed moment of 2020, must be credited to the vision of Alicia Garza, Patrisse Khan-Cullors and Opal Tometi, the queer feminists of colour who founded #BlackLivesMatter (Khan-Cullors and bandele 2020). But credit is also due to all activists and organizers of colour who have put themselves on the line to assert genuine equality of grievability and transform the very nature of the modern public sphere.

All told, my claim that Didion is a moral or ethical teacher or exemplar, while I believe highly plausible, must take account of its moment and therefore it must be heavily qualified; perhaps we also learn a good deal from what Didion does not or cannot give us. Assuming that metaphysically speaking, from a bleak modern perspective, everyone faces death and the loss of loved ones alone, then, Didion's courage and obstinacy in witnessing Quintana's life despite her own failure to save or recover it are highly instructive, perhaps worthy of emulation. But this picture is pure fantasy at best and reactionary ideology at worst if we fail to factor in the safety and privilege from within which such a labour of witnessing was even possible. Even if the picture suggested by 'earthquake weather' is true, it would be an obscenity to exhort people of colour to be similarly focused in the context of a world that systematically devalues and targets them. Therefore, without minimizing it, it must never be forgotten that Didion's process of grieving happens at a privileged intersection; she has to argue neither for her right to mourn publicly, nor for her husband's or her daughter's grievability. The project of social justice will in any case never assuage metaphysical loneliness, but it can at least aim to abolish *ethical* loneliness, and with it unequal grievability. We must *build* the world in which Didion's memoirs would have a truly universal import, rather than a qualified and limited 'aristocratic' universality. This means building a world in which the *ethics* of memory lives up to the *moral* point of view.

The reader should now have a good grounding in Didion's ethics of memory, as these manifest at the deceptively 'private' or 'intimate' level. Faced with the loss of her dearest loved ones, Didion's memoirs plumb the metaphysical loneliness of a thoroughly modern outlook. But in doing so, Didion does not succumb to nihilism. In the case of *The Year of Magical Thinking*, she retains a double ethical imperative – first, in terms of preserving while nuancing her ethos, and second, in terms of a pedagogical warning to her public – in witnessing and testifying to her grief following John's death. In the case of *Blue Nights*, where her loss is compounded, Didion's struggle to ward off nihilism intensifies, but she succeeds – at least one last time – through the very gesture or work, admittedly inadequate, of testifying to Quintana's life. This constitutes a community of memory, hence an ethical community, with herself as her own first reader, and with the 'intimate public' she appeals to or perhaps constitutes through her gesture. In both cases, what remains is the very possibility of memory as constituting community, in whatever small or impermanent way, which speaks precisely to Margalit's specific sense of 'the ethics of memory'. This casts Didion's memoirs of grief, and perhaps especially *Blue Nights*, in the light of a heroic engagement with bleak modernism. But as we also saw, the conversation cannot stop there. Didion's status as exemplar is awarded in a community wherein her ethical status, in Margalit's sense, goes unquestioned. It is privileged by frames or structures of interpretation that routinely silence or undermine other types of testimony, and other expressions of grieving. If we are to learn from Didion, we must not mistake her metaphysical loneliness for a truly social or 'ethical loneliness'.

Having thus demonstrated, I believe, the most basic and perhaps most obvious and familiar sense in which Didion's works are, indeed, works of the ethics of memory, it remains for me to explore more specific issues. For the remainder of the book I will therefore take my cue from Stauffer's, Butler's, and Gilmore's analyses, keeping my focus on how Didion's works bear on more obviously 'public' topics concerning the ethics of memory. In the next chapter, the focus will be nostalgia – seemingly also a 'private' issue, but as I will demonstrate, quite public in Didion's handling. From hereon we can take for granted the memory-ethical character of Didion's works at the 'thickest' level of her relations. It will be interesting to see how her memory ethics bears on the wider communities of her belonging, and how precisely at this level the border between ethics and politics starts to become questionable.

3

The norm of comprehensiveness

Nostalgia, Forgiveness and Critical Fabulation

In Chapter 2, the emphasis was on the deceptively 'private' or 'intimate' sphere of memory that is perhaps best encapsulated by the memoirs on grieving. I claimed to derive lessons from Didion on the ethics of memory by engaging both with her writing and with what it elides. The argument built from an encounter with Didion was hypothetical: if we assume a thoroughly modern, disenchanted perspective such as hers, then a *morally attuned ethics of memory* requires a fidelity to veracity and comprehensiveness, certain virtues or moral character traits and a structural analysis of injustice (which, to be sure, she largely fails to provide). Such an ethics, I claimed, resists nihilism without becoming 'magical' and reactionary. Through Didion, we therefore glimpse degree zero of a morally attuned community in a universe that does not hold us.

In this chapter, I will take the zero degree for granted. Though what we do 'in private' will still figure in the conversation, metaphysical loneliness is no longer the issue. Rather, I will stress the more obviously 'public' aspects of the ethics of memory, signalled by my turn last chapter to Stauffer, Butler and Gilmore. I have found it helpful to organize these aspects under the norm of comprehensiveness, which as I claimed in the Introduction, doubles the norm of veracity.

My first task is to define *nostalgia* and discuss how Didion, by her own lights, succumbed to it in her early work and then tried to go beyond it. I will attempt to show that here again, her lessons are of the moment. But the thing to stress is that my definition of the ethical wrongness of nostalgia hinges upon the *partiality* of its representations, rather than their lack of veracity.

Viewed as such, nostalgia goes wrong by committing an indirect rather than a direct falsification of the past, and it does this through selective memory. Didion's self-critique therefore presents an occasion to look at two related topics, where the norm of the relative comprehensiveness of memory is also at issue.

The second topic I will look at is *forgiveness*. I have already intimated that there could be times when the ethics of memory would dictate a duty not to revisit and nourish particular memories. This may seem counter-intuitive, especially considering the analysis in Chapter 2, which foregrounded the zero degree of memory ethics as a precarious, cosmically hopeless but courageous and obstinate preservation through representation. But the notion makes perfect sense in light of Margalit's idea of memory as the glue of thick relations. It may be that, precisely to save a given thick relation, I must attempt to edit out or at least dampen or refuse to revisit a given event in the relation's history. Whether or not this is desirable, or even possible, may depend on the nature of the episode: Was it a transgression in the *moral* sense of being a crime against humanity? And if it was an *ethical* transgression, was it one that the relation could in principle withstand? Or rather, was it a betrayal, precisely an act striking the relation at its very roots?

Finally, I will put Didion and the norm of relative comprehensiveness her critique of nostalgia suggests into conversation with the concept of *critical fabulation*, advanced by Saidiya Hartman. Here the insight is that for some people, historical and structural factors make it difficult or perhaps even *impossible* to achieve the kind of relative comprehensiveness with which I have assumed nostalgia conflicts. Writing of slavery and Reconstruction terror, where systematic destruction of the past was perpetrated as an act of control, Hartman suggests how affective investment and imaginative reconstruction – guided by critical scholarly tools, and between the guardrails of the existing archive – may step in where the archive is partial or silent. Indeed, extrapolating from Hartman, affect and imagination may *have* to step in, if anything like community in Margalit's restricted sense of the ethics of memory is to be envisioned or made possible. To this extent, Hartman provides a corrective to the ethics of memory as sketched thus far, reminding us that we cannot take 'the community' and its assumed, relative intersubjective comprehensiveness for granted.

Nostalgia

I have foregrounded nostalgia in this chapter for two reasons. First, it is a powerful motif in Didion that spans her writings, from her earliest novel to the memoirs on grief. I believe that treating it separately will further solidify the interpretation of her works via the key of the ethics of memory, and it will allow us to flesh out the picture I wish to draw of her as an ethical teacher or exemplar with respect to it. But second, and more importantly, nostalgia is and always has been a significant political problem. The slogan 'Make America Great Again' alone demonstrates that wistful and idealized remembrance can be weaponized as reactionary, racial resentment. Nostalgia is never neutral, since it invests affectively in certain aspects of the past at the expense of others, raising normative questions about the veracity and propriety of this investment. Therefore, if Didion sheds any light on the topic of nostalgia as a topic of ethics, she can also contribute to navigating the current conjuncture.

Nostalgia is a sentimental yearning for the past. It is a mode of wistful remembrance, where we call forth our memories of better times, or gloss certain times *as* better times. In this sense, it is conceptually distinct from regret, where our look on the past is above all sorrowful, coloured by guilt or by lost opportunities to have made a different present. This is not to say that nostalgia is ever free of sadness, or, indeed, of regret. As Barbara Cassin explains, the very word seems to imply them. According to one explanation of its origin, 'nostalgia' is a Swiss–German coinage of the seventeenth century, combining the ancient Greek *nostos*, 'return', with *algos*, 'pain' or 'suffering' (Cassin 2016: 5). The word was originally used to medicalize the homesickness of Swiss mercenaries, who were said to desert whenever they heard the 'ranz of the cows', a celebrated alpine air whose nostalgic powers were discussed by Rousseau in his *Dictionary of Music* (Cassin 2016: 5–6).[1] In this way, it is built into the very concept of nostalgia that it is both powerful and painful. Spending time in the memories or apparently even the musical or other associations of one's putatively better days can call forth arresting negative emotions about one's present, or about the fact that one has lost what was of value, or failed to appreciate it when one had it. Where there is nostalgia, there is therefore an interpretation of the past as in some sense good, or better or desirable – but after all, past. This is precisely why the return is so painful.

In speaking of 'return', I am assuming here for the sake of argument that nostalgia is a kind of *memory*; it is recollection or recall. For this reason, I will not speak of it as *imagining* a better past, even though as we will see Didion criticizes her own nostalgia in terms of having 'imagined' a California that never existed. As explained in the Introduction, I take 'memory' to be 'of the past' in the sense that it *really is* a representation of the past. 'Imagined memories' or 'false memories', though the latter have a clinical meaning, are therefore better described as imaginary representations; they are not 'imagined or false memories' so much as representations such that it is false that they even *are* memories.

Following Ricœur's splitting of memory into its cognitive and pragmatic aspects, we can therefore ask: In what consists the cognitive as opposed to the pragmatic dimension of nostalgia? As suggested earlier, the cognitive aspect amounts to recalling events or times when one was happy, or when things were better, but this recall already has a normative framing; it expresses a judgement we either made at the time or have retrospectively brought to bear on the brute facticity of the past, the bare fact that 'x was the case'. In this way, the pragmatic aspect of nostalgia involves active investment of attention and emotions (or passive succumbing to exploitation of these) in representations from the past that have already been framed for us or by us in a certain way. But what then is the meaning of the normative *framing* itself? Does it have its own type of cognitive content, implicit or explicit, to the effect that 'x is what was good about this moment in the past'?

There is an interesting discussion in Kant on 'homesickness', yearning for the places we were from, where we once enjoyed 'the very simple pleasures of life' (Kant 2006: 71). Revealingly, homesickness can be cured by a literal return, but not because we thereby get what we longed for. Rather, simply by visiting the yearned-for place, we disappoint and disillusion ourselves. This disappointment reveals a possible cognitive content of nostalgic framing: 'it was good because I was young.' Speaking of the well-known homesickness of the Swiss in particular, and therefore in connection with the aforementioned coinage of the very word 'nostalgia', Kant explains that 'they think that [they are greatly disappointed when they visit] because everything there has changed a great deal, but in fact it is because they cannot bring back their youth there' (2006: 71).[2] He goes on to reveal a second possible cognitive content, to the effect that 'it was good because my loved ones were there'. This is implied when Kant suggests that homesickness especially strikes 'the peasants from a province that is poor but bound together by strong family ties', as opposed to those who 'are busy earning money', swept up in the socially fragmenting circuits of bourgeois accumulation (Kant 2006: 71–2). Evidently and quite intuitively, the yearning for the past *as past* – not as lost opportunity, for instance – especially strikes those who held close, healthy relations with the people who were most important to them when they were young.[3] As Margalit and Ricœur suggest, this is as it should be, and our closest relations are precisely what afford us the most obvious and ready-to-hand opportunity to engage in an ethics of memory. Briefly discussing nostalgia, Margalit admits that it 'is an important element of communal memory', giving sentimental colouration its due (Margalit 2002: 61–2). But herein also lies a risk; as he goes on to suggest, nostalgia 'is not as innocent a trait as one might think' (Margalit 2002: 62). Taking a page from Kant, altogether the suggestion here is that our youth – our capacity for enjoyment of 'the very simple pleasures of life' – combines with our strongest affective ties, giving a powerfully seductive colouration to the past.

But how exactly would nostalgia present an *ethical* problem? Here Margalit zeroes in on nostalgia's constitutive sentimentality. Sentiment per se is not the issue, and, in fact, 'collective memory has a great deal to do with retaining the sensibility of the past and not just its sense' (Margalit 2002: 62).[4] As he argues, 'The amazement and horror in watching the collapse of the twin towers in New York, let alone being there, is the kernel of the memory of the collapse and not the ketchup added on top of it' (Margalit 2002: 62–3). As distinct from sentiment, however, sentimentality can distort reality 'in a particular way that has moral consequences' (Margalit 2002: 62). For Margalit, nostalgia is precisely such a sentimental mode of remembering, distorting the past by *idealizing* it: 'People, events, and objects from the past are presented as endowed with pure innocence', when they should not be (Margalit 2002: 62).

Margalit's comments can be developed a bit further. As I see it, two reasons why nostalgia can be ethically problematic are as follows. First, it can be *dangerous*, which is to say consequentially bad. Second, it can constitute a kind of *cognitive or epistemic injustice*, which is to say it can be bad in principle.

The *danger* of nostalgia is first that it encourages us to fall into or back into unhealthy patterns, habits, commitments and beliefs, especially during times of stress. This can entail harm to others as well as harm to ourselves, including harms to our character.[5] Consider the person who falls back in with their ex-partner from an unhealthy relationship. Viewed uncritically, the enchantment of their relative youth and the thickness of their past relationship can blot out the bad times which led to the break-up. Though people and relationships are in principle redeemable, the health and happiness of at least two individuals are at stake, and so it would be unwise, or prudentially bad, to let the affective colouration of nostalgia decide the issue. But lest this example make nostalgia seem like a relatively 'private' issue, consider also examples like the collective pining after problematic and unsustainable pre-COVID-19 social institutions, or contemporary, nostalgic political reaction in the United States and elsewhere.

A second but related danger of nostalgia, which I briefly raised in the Introduction, is that it could blunt our imaginations, and therefore our sense of a possible political (to say nothing of aesthetic) futurity.[6] Memory and imagination, we have seen, both trade in representations. Supposing the representations invested nostalgically offer a ready-made vision of what is desirable and best, then why would we ever strive to experiment in making the world better in untried ways? Why not subjugate our futurity to our nostalgia, and simply remain satisfied with whatever programme promises to make us 'great again'?

The *epistemic injustice* of nostalgia, on the other hand, strikes closer to the terms of an ethics of memory that I have borrowed throughout from Margalit and Ricœur. Inasmuch as it is wistful or wishful, nostalgia affectively invests only *some* aspects of the past and not others. This alone can have a distorting affect. The distortion is not a direct falsification, as would be the case if it were a matter of replacing memories with imaginary representations. In fact, every nostalgic memory, if it is, indeed, a *memory*, would be veridical. The point is that even if we grant this, nostalgia is still problematic from the point of view of the ethics of memory.

As a kind of normative framing or colouration, *the nostalgia of the nostalgic memory* is the problem. It is in relation to the norm of relative *comprehensiveness* that it goes wrong. There were no unalloyed good times, there was never any 'pure innocence'; even if a person was overwhelmingly content or happy during a given period, many other people were not. In the world as we find it, it would even be fair to question whether one's happiness at the time was *premised* upon the misfortune of others, as is the case when one lives off the spoils or simply benefits in whatever way from colonialism, slavery, wage slavery and social inequalities. Editing out the negative aspects of the past can therefore amount to an *indirect falsification of the past*, in the sense that the nostalgic person, invested only in good memories, erases truths that should be remembered for justice's sake and therefore distorts recollection, from a moral point of view. The past that results from nostalgia is in this way more narrowly individual or communitarian than it has to be, and insofar as it is an idealization, and insensate to the demands of justice, then it *might as well have been imagined*.

None of this is to suggest, incidentally, that one's relation to the past must be joyless or unremittingly negative. Far from it; shared good memories and the memory of shared positive sentiment can be a legitimate source of solace, as well as a powerful bonding agent in the interest of building and sustaining more just thick relations into the future. The point, rather, is to remain vigilant and critical about how we evaluate the past, and to maintain a broadly historical outlook to the extent that this is possible. There is even a sense in which to affirm my *present* I have to be aware of and in some sense 'accept', if not similarly affirm, both the good *and* the bad of the past, 'recognizing and taking seriously the horrors on which our own lives are based' (May 2017: 155). Such a view requires us to see ourselves as 'compromised but not necessarily fallen' (ibid.). This helps us to define ourselves in a way that discourages self-delusion, while holding out hope of a better future, perhaps feeling that we owe it to the world to build one on account of our own questionable backstories. Such an attitude requires the uncomfortable 'obstinacy' of a philosophical outlook as I have characterized it, perhaps, but in the laudable interests of refusing to be duped by the past, and of building better times ahead.

Didion and nostalgia

At this stage in the argument, my definition of nostalgia and the forms of ethical badness it risks should now be clear. As I have stated, the theme of nostalgia runs through Didion's writings and comes up for critical scrutiny, making her a good teacher or exemplar respecting it. To take but one highly politically salient example, regarding the terror attacks of 9/11, she incredulously describes how 'People are talking about "America losing its innocence"', asking: 'How many times can America lose its innocence? In my lifetime we've heard that we've lost our innocence half a dozen times at least' (Didion 2003: 71). The reason that the loss of innocence constitutes a refrain in Didion's ears is fairly straightforward: it is easy and comforting to retreat to a narrowly invested version of the past when trauma strikes, whenever it strikes. The idea of America losing its innocence *at all* shows a laughably partial historical self-awareness, if for no other reason than that the country is built upon the twin crimes of slavery and genocide. The person pronouncing the loss of innocence is better interpreted as meaning that the traumatic event has punctuated *their* life, of the life of their community, dividing it into a happy before and an unhappy after.

Turning a critical eye on such notions is one way that Didion exemplifies a laudable resistance to edifying narratives, and to dangerously and unfairly partial visions of the past. This does not mean, however, that she is immune to them, and her own nostalgia occasions a remarkable if not always successful or thorough sequence of self-criticism. It is, in fact, on the topic of California, her own land of nostalgic investment, that Didion is richest, most problematic and most widely known with respect to the topic, and I will focus my energies there.

An indispensable voice in introducing this discussion is Katarzyna Nowak McNeice (2019), who interprets Didion's novels and connects them to her non-fiction according to the themes of loss, mourning and melancholy. Nowak McNeice uncovers why precisely the sense of loss in Didion is problematic, based on what I would characterize as a partial, often nostalgic vision:

> Didion locates the roots of Californian identity in the frontier and suggests that Californian identity emerged as the frontier closed. This signifies a peculiar shortening of historical perspective that characterizes Didion's prose: it is as if history commenced with the first pioneers who crossed the Great Plains; there are no Californios, no Native Americans, there is no Mexican period, no Spanish colonization. This curious and deeply troubling omission results in an exclusionist vision: those who crossed the plains with Didion's family are more entitled than others to the Eden of California. That is the blind spot in her vision. As she mourns the past, she does not acknowledge those excluded in her version of history. (Nowak McNeice 2019: 2)

Further, Nowak McNeice explains how Didion's

> investment is in the endeavor of portraying Californian character in the most comprehensive way, to which the whole of her career testifies. This portrayal, however, is highly exclusivist: it is a vision that silences some agents of history and sentences others to oblivion, while attaching undue importance to the pioneering endeavor; what results is a story of a past that never was, with the loss of illusion at its core, a loss that comes back hauntingly in every piece Didion writes. (Nowak McNeice 2019: 3)

It is important to note that whereas my emphasis is on *nostalgia* as a cognitive and ethical theme, a dangerously and unjustly impartial investment on some aspects of the past at the expense of others, Nowak McNeice finds the theme of *melancholy* more promising. As she describes, 'The concept of melancholia promises more space to discuss the issue of identity, which in nostalgia is firmly anchored to a place. Much of Didion's writing, however, carries melancholic longing for the land while locating pain elsewhere: hence my decision to focus on melancholia' (Nowak McNeice 2019: 4). I agree with Nowak McNeice when she claims that the central aim of Didion's writing 'is to cope with loss, a loss that is often unacknowledged, and because of that, it generates melancholia. Even when the source of melancholia and the loss that occasioned it seem to be clearly stated, there is always a deeper layer of sadness that remains unnamable' (Nowak McNeice 2019: 174). After all, Didion the childhood notebook keeper was *already* engaged in coping with loss, even if only as a 'presentiment' (Didion 2006: 102). I have also explained why her very universe has the possibility, even the immanent certainty, of loss built into it. But as I argued earlier, nostalgia may be inherently mixed with negative affects, and it does not preclude the more encompassing state of melancholia, where unconscious forces are also in play. Taking my cue from Nowak McNeice, I would argue that where Didion invests the past in what I have called a 'nostalgic' mode, she does so from a position of thinking she will lose what is left of it or has already lost it, or at any rate she has a feeling that this is so.

Didion sets the template for the sense of loss of a past that never actually was in *Run River*, her first novel and the book that she would criticize decades later in the non-fiction collection about California, *Where I Was From*. *Run River* recounts the fall of the McClellan family; the marriage and family estate of spouses Lily and Everett, great-grandchildren of white pioneers, are washed away in personal and broadly historical currents. Thinking about her husband and her love interest, and how tiresome she could find the latter, Lily reflects

> admiringly upon people in movies – and it was not only people in movies – who when they could not talk to each other said goodbye, had renunciations, made decisions: started fresh, apparently lobotomized. If there was one thing that she and Everett and Ryder all had in common it was that none of their decisions ever came to much; they seemed afflicted with memory. (Didion 1994: 245–6)

Didion herself later names the novel's 'tenacious (and, as I see it now, pernicious) mood of nostalgia' (Didion 2006: 1060). Its key fault was to have given a vision of California 'as it was', its inchoate intent having been 'to return me to a California I wished had been there to keep me' (Didion 2006: 1067). Significantly, Didion wrote the novel in New York, during a long period of homesickness:

> what I actually had on my mind that year in New York – had *on my mind* as opposed to *in mind* – was a longing for California, a homesickness, a nostalgia so obsessive that nothing else figured. In order to discover what was on my mind I needed room for the rivers and for the rain and for the way the almonds came into blossom around Sacramento, room for irrigation ditches and room for the fear of kiln fires, room in which to play with everything I remembered and did not understand (Didion 2021: 66–7, emphasis in original).

The vision of the novel that resulted is not comforting; it is already one of loss. This suggests that if Didion indulges in nostalgia, as I have suggested, it is a patently melancholic one, as Nowak McNeice's reading underscores. Lily, Everett and Ryder as described previously belong in a *Southern* world more than a Western, if we rely upon the tropes of South and West explored in Chapter 1; oddly then, *Run River* reads like a Southern gothic novel set in California. Lily *admires* the future-oriented, hypermodern, cut-and-run attitudes of the movie characters, the kind of attitude Didion frequently associates with her home state. But neither she nor Everett nor Ryder are fully at home in it; theirs is a world of values and attachments in full decomposition, and they cannot swim with the current. In a striking expression of the lonely, sad modernity I have already ascribed to Didion, the family story 'had been above all a history of accidents: of moving on and of accidents' (Didion 1994: 263) when the protagonists had hoped for something more.

Affect predominates in *Run River*, giving a window onto Didion's homesickness. In *Where I Was From*, by contrast, she seeks a belated and dispassionate *understanding* of California. To this end, she will go on to lay out many of the state's central contradictions, with a view to suggesting broader commentary on the United States. Part of this work involves deconstructing the pioneer fantasy, the one that gave us the 'wagon train morality' examined in the Introduction, as well as the 'local core belief' in radical modernity and individualism from which Didion emerged (Didion 2006: 966). For example, she points out the early-set pattern of 'extreme reliance of California on federal money' (Didion 2006: 966), significantly earmarked to control the hazardous natural forces I emphasized in Chapter 1. As such, *Where I Was From* is at least in part an exercise in self-criticism, and a remarkable document from the perspective of both ideology critique and the ethics of memory.

In this spirit, Didion examines *Run River*'s central contentions that 'Everything changes, everything changed (Didion 1994: 46)', that California itself has 'changed' and that change is in some sense 'decline'. Again, we can detect a problematic vision of the South, in the guise of the immemorial, knocking at the door of the West. But echoing Kant on homesickness, Didion in *Where I Was From* claims that 'Discussion of how California has "changed" . . . tends locally to define the more ideal California as that which existed at whatever past point the speaker first saw it' (Didion 2006: 1070). If this is true, then we are in a world of clashing perspectives, a system of partialities that vainly attempt to constitute anything like a true and relatively comprehensive vision of the past. Didion describes how 'Gilroy as it was in the 1960s and Gilroy as it was fifteen years ago and Gilroy as it was when my father and I ate short ribs at the Milas hotel are three pictures with virtually no overlap, a hologram that dematerializes as I drive through it' (Didion 2006).

The lesson to draw here is not that we should veer from nostalgic idealism to a radical perspectivalism – as though the Native American, Californio, African American and later immigrant histories Didion largely elides are themselves 'only perspectives', equally and therefore unimportantly aspects of another hologram, rather than perspectives clamouring for attention in the construction of a truthful and relatively comprehensive account of the past. Instead, the point that is useful in Didion is how our own positions in space-time can lead us astray when we think back on the past. If she figures here primarily as a sceptic with respect to California – perhaps a belated one this time, notwithstanding her lifelong scepticism on other matters – then the impression of unreality she produces is not an end in itself, but is useful precisely in the sense of unsettling dominant narratives and received ideas.

The very title of *Where I Was From* heralds Didion's partial, uncomfortable but, after all, lucid and *ethical* attempt at reducing this impression of unreality to something more solid. The title is complex, encapsulating the book's main theme in miniature. To the extent that it repudiates a certain vision of California that Didion had once longed for, she *is* no longer from there; she *was* from there, but having finally come to terms with how nostalgia has shaped her she becomes more 'remote' (Didion 2006: 1100). But there is more. Didion describes flying over '*home, there, where I was from, me,* California' following the death of her mother (Didion 2006: 1090, emphasis in original). She relates that 'It would be a while before I realized that "me" is what we think when our parents die, even at my age, *who will look out for me now, who will remember me as I was, who will know what happens to me now, where will I be from*' (Didion 2006, emphasis in original). Three things leap out here: first, Didion from now on will no longer 'be from' California, since with the passing of her mother, her thickest relations there are now gone. As with Kant's comments on homesickness, it is not the land of California as such that holds her, that claims her or keeps her, but, rather, her youth and her 'strong family ties'. Second, Didion implicitly grants the power of nostalgic representation, the great pull it has on us, when she describes California as connected to 'me'; as Lily already expresses in *Run River*, 'I'm not myself if my father's dead' (Didion 1994: 78). Finally, there is an obvious foreshadowing of the end of *Blue Nights* here. Didion wonders 'who will remember me as I was, who will know what happens to me' now that her parents are gone – and we have seen that she belatedly discovers her preciousness as Quintana's parent, an irreplaceable witness to her life.

In the end, revising her vision of California gives Didion an occasion to write one of her most moving passages. She will suggest finally that her only real connections are to her loved ones, and not to times or to places at all – echoing Kant in a way, where the true source of nostalgia is our youth and our thick relations, and not where we were, let alone where we were from. As

Didion puts it, recounting a time she visited her parents with Quintana in the early 1970s,

> Quintana was adopted. Any ghosts on this wooden sidewalk [in Old Sacramento] were not in fact Quintana's responsibility. This wooden sidewalk did not in fact represent anywhere Quintana was from. Quintana's only attachments on this wooden sidewalk were right now, here, me and my mother.
>
> In fact I had no more attachment to this wooden sidewalk than Quintana did: it was no more than a theme, a decorative effect.
>
> It was only Quintana who was real. (Didion 2006: 1099–100).

This seems to Didion, in retrospect, to have been the precise moment where 'all of it' – 'the entire enchantment under which I had lived my life', filtered through her attachment to California, to her family's pioneer history, celebrated and remembered at the expense of other local histories – began to seem remote (Didion 2006: 1100). These lines were published in 2003, a few years before Quintana's death, adding an additional poignancy when read today. They speak to themes I explored in Chapter 2, and again they echo Kant's comments on homesickness: what we miss about the past includes our youth, certainly, but also typically, and perhaps above all, our thick relations. But I should add: not our thick relations *as such*. These are, after all, only abstractions woven from the times we spend with real, particular people. What we miss, primarily, are those people themselves. On the boardwalk in the early 1970s, Didion has a recognition that her daughter, *this* person, is one of the only 'real' things in her life, the only things of value, and that the rest are all ghosts, 'decorative effects'. The past is held in suspension but the entirety of her ethical labours in the later memoirs on grief are thereby foreshadowed. [7]

Surprisingly, perhaps, this foreshadowing stretches back even further, all the way back to *Run River*; 'remember Everett baby remember' Lily exhorts her husband after he has just killed himself, running through a litany of everyday memories. The narrator intercedes:

> She hoped that although he could not hear her she could somehow imprint her ordinary love upon his memory through all eternity, hoped he would rise thinking of her, *we were each other, we were each other, not that it mattered much in the long run but what else mattered as much.* (Didion 1994: 264, emphasis in original)

Here again – and Didion seems already to know this, even in the early novel she would otherwise criticize for its melancholic, nostalgic idealism about Sacramento, and about her home state – not much else matters very much, in the long run, but the people with whom, in love, we weave our ordinary lives.[8]

Forgiveness: Moral transgression and betrayal

To the extent that it undermines nostalgia – and to the extent that we understand nostalgia in terms of memory rather than imagination – Didion's self-criticism can be interpreted as upholding the ethical norm of relative comprehensiveness. But this raises the question of whether there are other aspects of memory practice where the norm of comprehensiveness is mainly at issue. The following two sections go further along this path, and they are, above all, sensitive to what an encounter with Didion does *not* provide us with.

I have already mentioned the idea that there could be ethical (but apparently not moral)[9] reasons to 'forget', or more accurately *not to remember*. To be clear, we cannot speak *literally* of reasons to 'forget', as though it would be somehow in our power to forget on purpose (Margalit 2002: 201). As we saw discussing Ricœur (2006), memory in the cognitive sense, *mnēmē*, includes both the memories that 'befall' us passively, and those that we actively go looking for or call up through memory in the pragmatic sense, *anamnēsis*. It is not so much in my power to forget on purpose, as it is to suspend the *anamnēsis* of certain memories. To speak of ethical reasons to 'forget' is therefore really just a way of saying that in certain contexts there are good reasons not to actively try to remember certain things, or to dwell upon them.

Assuming then that we can speak of ethical reasons not to remember, it is not hard to see how these would apply. If ethics in Margalit's sense is premised upon the existence of communities of memory, then the health of the community requires a modicum of 'forgetting' of certain past wrongs. Both for my own good and for that of the community it might be ethically required of me to dampen or suppress the hold that certain memories have over me, once I have made the decision to forgive. If I cannot literally forget or 'blot them out' on purpose, then I can at least 'cover them up' to the extent that they cease to feed my resentment and undermine my relationships (Margalit 2002: 206–9).

To see how this is so, we need look no further than how we live with our close relations, which is to say our family and our good friends. Despite the shared past, the common values and the aspirations generally holding us together, we are finite creatures with flaws and limitations. We often anger and disappoint each other. We come to harsh words, and sometimes we grow apart or abruptly break off our relations. Sometimes the choice presents itself between severing the relation altogether or agreeing to 'forgive and forget', again not in the sense of forgetting on purpose, but of letting time take its course in swallowing up the memories of what precipitated the dispute. Margalit, to be clear, holds that '"Natural" forgetting of an injury is not forgiveness and has no moral value' (2002: 205). Nonetheless, the ideal implied by forgiveness on his view is 'the restoration of the original relationship between the offender and the forgiver' (2002: 205), and this is something that can be very hard to achieve because of hurt, resentment and the desire to avenge. Thus arguably, even if we resist the idea that natural forgetting has any moral value, the 'and forget' clause in 'forgive and forget' is still crucial. Though we may always have the source of the dispute somewhere in the backs of our minds, in forgiving we conscientiously decide to overcome our resentment of it and therefore do not nourish it as a source of ongoing resentment or animosity. My point is simply that in forgiving we make as Margalit suggests 'a conscious decision to change [our] attitude and to overcome anger and vengefulness' (2002: 193), and this can be helped along, at least at a certain point in our healing process, by refusing to gratuitously revisit the site of the injury.

There are, however, two hard limits to the possibility of an ethical presumption not to remember: the moral perspective, and betrayal. *Moral transgression* is an injury to the moral community, or humanity as such, according to Margalit's view. As we will see, it also affects our ethical ties in rather complex ways. *Betrayal* is, more directly, a *radical* injury to the ethical bond or community. Both types of injury require us *not* to forget, but rather to 'will backwards', wishing that the past were otherwise (Stauffer 2015: 116–7). If we can *all* do this – individuals and institutions, victims, perpetrators and bystanders alike – then forgiveness and community repair, and hence a shared futurity, are in principle possible.[10] If there is to be forgiveness in cases of moral transgression or betrayal, what is required is not 'a present moment in which everyone lets the past be', but, rather, 'a present moment in which everyone wants a time machine' (Stauffer 2015: 123).

Looking closer at moral transgression, we see how the moral perspective on Margalit's view (and according to the Kantian tradition more broadly) dictates that I cannot use my thick relations as a pretext for overriding my duties to others *qua* members of the human race.[11] This includes my moral duties of remembrance. Recall that moral duties of memory are few and far between, and are typically negative: I have duties of memory when it comes to truthfully and comprehensively commemorating crimes against humanity, which is to say crimes where human persons and communities have been treated as less than fully human. There are also arguably positive moral duties of remembrance with respect to human scientific and cultural achievement; but here again the negative examples perhaps resonate the best. Recall, for example, the world outrage when Daesh militants destroyed ancient cultural sites in Syria; these were not human lives, but their destruction elicited powerful global condemnation nonetheless, because they struck at a common heritage of achievement and therefore at something like a global, moral community of memory.[12]

Upholding the moral point of view, recall, is distinct from and makes a greater normative claim on us than our ethical commitments. If I am a white Canadian settler who is kind to his white neighbours and provides a good life for his family but is racist towards First Nations, Inuit and Métis, ignoring or downplaying the historical wrongs perpetrated against them, then I am still failing from the moral perspective. But the argument goes even further. Supposing that I do not consider myself to be racist, and want to foster a kind of friendly, thick relation with my country's first peoples, then I *still* need to acknowledge the wrong of colonialism and work to repair it. This requires, among other things, my engaging with my duties of memory, and it means that *even if I am nice* to first peoples, I can still fail from a moral perspective.[13] Since anti-indigenous racism in Canada is both historic and systemic, I am in the wrong from a moral perspective if I take a 'colour-blind' stance, forgetting about and therefore doing nothing to make amends for the nation's colonial history, even if I behave impeccably in my face-to-face interactions. Building thick, ethical relations in a colonial setting requires acknowledgement of past transgressions of our thin, moral ones; 'truth', especially painful truth about crimes against humanity, is a prerequisite to 'reconciliation'.

The example of colonialism in Canada is highly revealing, because it touches a nerve for many 'nice' Canadians. Tyler Shipley (2020) has made a comprehensive argument for dismantling Canada's self-perception as a tolerant peace-brokering nation, relatively unsullied by the colonial and imperial history that has unfolded elsewhere in the Americas. Canada emerges under his keen eye as a country with imperial ambitions and a colonial past. We can see why his historical reconstructions and media appearances have tended to provoke animosity: they disturb racist communitarians, obviously, but they also unsettle the comforting narratives of Canadians who uphold a 'nice' self-image. The point here is that our moral duties of remembrance often push us to unsettle our ethical communities, opening a process of contestation, however painful or uncomfortable that might be. Though risky, this is not an inherently destructive gesture – or if it is, what it aims to destroy is a pernicious nostalgia. If, finally, our ethical community cannot withstand moral scrutiny, then it is perhaps not worth defending. If such is the case, then it is time to build community anew, where thick ties are premised upon recognition of the moral dimension and the work we will have done to uphold it.

We see then from this example how moral transgression precludes forgetting. As for betrayal, Margalit gives a definition linking it to his sense of the ethics of memory: 'Only when the harm and the offense serve as good reasons for questioning the meaning of the thick relation can we talk of betrayal' (Margalit 2017: 83). Betrayals strike radically at thick relations, and this means that they undermine a shared past. As such, they hasten ethical decomposition, or cause an ethical break. Though betrayals may happen in the wider circles of our thick relations, as for example, when our neighbours collaborate with an invading army, they are perhaps more familiar in the intimate sphere. If my lover or my spouse betrays me with another person, then this will put into question the whole past that I spent with them (to say nothing of what I had hoped for the future). As Margalit put it, 'thick relations are built upon a shared past. The shared past is constitutive of the relation. It is the shared past that is colored by the betrayal . . . Following the betrayal, what is questioned about the past is the sense of belonging: "I thought we belonged to each other, but now I know we didn't"' (Margalit 2017: 93). It is unclear whether I even *could* cover up or suppress the memory and associated feelings of such an injury. It is also far from clear that I ever *should* try to do so: in giving myself over to someone who fails to hold me, what exactly am I preserving?

We can see then why 'forgive *and forget*' is precluded in cases of moral transgression or betrayal. But, then, is *forgiveness* ever possible either? I think the answer is a qualified yes, in both cases.

Margalit's presumption of individual moral autonomy (2007) is crucial here. An individual is morally autonomous to the extent that she could always start again, morally speaking, by committing herself to finally doing the right thing, according to moral as opposed to narrowly ethical values. On the assumption that she is a mature, cognitively average adult (Habermas 1990a), then she is not truly a *prisoner* in the ethical world of thick relations; though these will always exert a powerful influence on her behaviour, she is in principle capable of attaining a moral viewpoint, and acting on the basis of a universalizable perspective. This splitting of the individual along the lines of moral and ethical worlds is why we can condemn everyday people who went along with a genocide but only 'to protect their family', for instance. But it is *also* why in principle we can forgive them, since it is possible both to sympathize with their desperate urge to protect their family, and to allow that from hereon they will strive to do better from the moral perspective. The focus on moral autonomy is also, incidentally, why Margalit (2007) opposes humiliating, dehumanizing punishments, and implicitly the death penalty: its *finality* negates the moral definition of the human being, her constitutive freedom to finally do the right thing, to live in a 'dramatically different way' than she has in the past (Margalit 2007: 73). The very idea of respecting humans – that is, the very idea of *morality*, on Margalit's definition – implies that we never condemn someone definitively (Margalit 2007). Viewed as moral agents, humans are therefore defined by a kind of openness – which is why in principle, they are redeemable.[14]

Jill Stauffer's concept of ethical loneliness (2015), which we explored in Chapter 2, is of further help here. Though we tend to focus on *victims* being cast out of humanity and their testimonies left unheard, *perpetrators* often suffer the same fate; that is, they find themselves exiled from the ethical community on account of their crimes against humanity. The issue of the effects of moral transgression on ethical ties is complicated. It matters, for example, whether the potentially forgiving parties are members of the perpetrator's own community, or members of the community the perpetrator targeted or whether finally the perpetrators targeted their own community. The issue of possible forgiveness is further complicated, for example, by the existence of institutional 'group perpetrators', and 'complex political perpetrators', such as child soldiers (Stauffer 2015: 47, 153–6), where the presumption of the perpetrator's moral autonomy and the burden of blame are in question.

At any rate if we hold both that an individual *wants* to be forgiven, is prepared to earn that forgiveness through moral reform and repair, and that the community also *wants* to give her a second chance, then it is possible in principle that she could be forgiven. This is to say, that she could be welcomed back into an ethical relation with them, to repair and to build a life in common anew. But such forgiveness would be fragile and would require constant work on account of the acuteness and moral meaning of the injury that precipitated it. Crucially, it could not take the form of 'forgive and forget', since our moral duties of remembrance preclude us from *not remembering* crimes against humanity. Stauffer cites the case of Jean Améry, who suffered arrest, torture and interment in Nazi concentration camps. He holds, in Stauffer's words, that 'if you forgive without the proper conditions for forgiving, you participate in a "natural" process – the idea that time heals all wounds. This natural or biological time sense gets analogized into a social one where human beings elect to "forgive and forget" harms or "move on" simply because of the passing of time. *But that process is not moral*' (Stauffer 2015: 121, emphasis added). When Margalit similarly claims that 'natural' forgetting of an injury 'has no moral value' (Margalit 2002: 205), we should let the word 'moral' ring clearly. While I have suggested that there could be a certain *ethical* presumption to 'forgive and forget', there cannot be a moral one.

Let us turn now again to betrayal. This is an ethical as opposed to a moral issue, but forgiveness might still be especially fraught here. The difficulty is that betrayal strikes *radically* at the relationship in question. Think back to the example of lovers or spouses, where one has cheated on the other: what is hurt in the betrayal are not just the wronged party's feelings, but, rather, her trust in the very authenticity and value of the relationship. If the betrayer has ruined the thick relation they had by calling it wholesale into question, it is nevertheless possible to welcome them in the spirit of renewal through a recognition of their moral autonomy. But this would not be a welcoming *back*. The trick here, as with the case of moral transgression, would be to defer to the errant lover's or spouse's inherent capacity to begin again. If they undermined the thick relation of the partnership or marriage, then they have made it impossible and in any case undesirable to aim for anywhere near a 'restoration of the original relationship', which Margalit suggests is the ideal that forgiveness implies (2002: 205). If after all the betrayer wanted to stay with the betrayed partner, then it would be a question of committing to building *a new thick relation* premised upon a new ethical commitment and promise. The betrayed partner would also have to commit to this if she wanted to stay. But because of its ethical radicality, crucially neither partner would be doing the right thing by letting time erode the memory of what happened. The memory of the betrayal could and should never truly be erased, but it might change over time to represent the catalyst for change that it will have become.

Returning to Didion: we see, finally, that my reconstruction of her ethic of truth and relative comprehensiveness when it comes to memory actions cannot be the full story. Relative comprehensiveness, expressed in her youthful desire for 'life expanded to a novel' with 'everything in the picture' (Didion 2021: 69), offers more guidance as a moral than as an ethical norm. In fact, there are cases when upholding it would be positively detrimental, ethically speaking. Perhaps she herself recognizes this when she makes the inevitable editorial choices that are involved in testifying through writing; if she has suppressed anything to the benefit of her thick relations, we would likely not know it, and that would be entirely the point.

Critical fabulation

So far, we have seen that nostalgia *qua* sentimental longing for the past inherently risks running afoul of the ethics of memory. It does this to the extent that memory combines cognitive and pragmatic aspects; memory, as distinct from imagination, is *an exercise in truth*. As such, the ethics of memory is *an ethics of the exercise of truth*, and the problem from this perspective is that there are almost certainly going to be lies of omission committed through nostalgic recall. Setting aside for now the good arguments for a 'right to be forgotten' invoked by Zuboff (2019), the ideal, ethically speaking, would appear to be a commitment to unvarnished and complete recall; hence, nostalgia should be indulged in sparingly, if at all. The problem with nostalgia is that precisely through its affective investment in certain aspects of the past, it incentivizes a biased recall – and a biased recall can be both 'unfair', as we saw when we discussed Iris Murdoch (2007), and also dangerous. This is what I have argued, and yet there are at least two significant problems raised by this view and they seem to push us further than Didion can take us.

The first, as we have already seen, is that if we grant Margalit's view of memory constituting thick relations and hence community, then a commitment to unvarnished recall has the capacity to corrode our thick relations, and thus contribute to ethical decomposition. To summarize, this would suggest that there can be a duty to 'forget', or rather to refuse to revisit or dwell upon, certain memories if the persistence of ethical relations permits and requires it. On this view, forgiveness can sometimes legitimately take the form of 'forgive and forget'. We saw that there are two hard limits, however: we should not forget a moral transgression, even though we might find the resources to forgive it; and for similar reasons we should not forget a betrayal, even though like a moral transgression it might present an opportunity to build thick relations anew in the light of hope and mutual goodwill.

The second problem raised by the argument I have made about nostalgia, grounded in the ideals of truth and relative comprehensiveness, is that it so far ignores the realities of oppressed persons struggling precisely to constitute memory, and hence community, in the ways that Margalit's framework theorizes. The ethical ideal of an unvarnished and comprehensive recall, even if this were possible, discounts the fact that certain people's links to the past are often *targeted* for erasure, or are *unequally exposed* to the risk of erasure. At the extreme limit of what Jonathan Lear calls 'cultural devastation', disorientation and loss of sense can be so extensive that we can speak of 'a breakdown of the field in which occurrences occur' (Lear 2006: 34). As such, the horizons of past and future crumble together into an oppressive, inert present. As Saidiya Hartman recounts,

> In every slave society, slave owners attempted to eradicate the slave's memory, that is, to erase all the evidence of an existence before slavery . . . . A slave without a past had no life to avenge. No time was wasted yearning for home, no recollections of a distant country slowed her down as she tilled the soil, no image of her mother came to mind when she looked into the face of her child. The pain of all she had lost did not rattle in her chest and make it feel tight. (2007: 155)

The problem, in sum, is that in worrying about nostalgia as an issue of comprehensiveness, we might ignore or downplay that some peoples or communities have been targeted for disarticulation *as such*. Put differently, some oppressed persons have been *robbed* of the robust weave of memories in which the selective recall we are discussing typically takes root. Therefore, the problem is not so much communitarian and hence ethical *decomposition*, as I have been using the term, as the difficulty of repairing or *recomposing* community, or perhaps of at the limit, *composing it* in the first place, through a new, intersubjective memorial comprehensiveness. The point here is not to position radically oppressed persons as passive victims, and as Hartman's analyses suggest, there is a continuity of tactics of resistance to consider. Rather, it is that the destruction of memory is used as a tactic for the destruction of the community, that this is a radical injury, and that the persons seeking to repair or to forge community anew must contend with it. This means that there is more to say in connection with comprehensiveness (and veracity for that matter) than the kind of memory work I have been taking for granted thus far.

The question facing us is what the ethics of memory could require of radically oppressed persons, to say nothing of others hoping to build back thick relations with them, in recognition of historical crimes. This last point bears emphasizing, since if it is a moral imperative to remember crimes against humanity, then we need to address the fact that those crimes *themselves* are often difficult to reconstruct, from any perspective let alone that of the victims. Sometimes records of the crimes were actively destroyed by the perpetrators, as in the Shoah, and sometimes the full humanity of those targeted is still persistently, systematically and structurally denied even after the crime is declared by the dominators to be over, as in anti-Black racism (Hartman 1997; Mbembe 2019; Wilderson 2020). Thus, the crime variously affects the very quality and public accessibility of the archive. Since 'ought' implies 'can', this is a serious barrier to consider.

To be clear, nostalgia as a memory-ethical issue is not absent from Hartman's discussion of the archive and afterlife of slavery; it appears both implicitly and explicitly. My point, rather, is to signal the fact that the descendants of slaves have been put in an unequal and therefore perhaps ethically different relation to the past. But even in the context of such a relation, they may nonetheless inhabit the 'pain of the return', and the overvaluation of aspects of the past that this implies. Hartman points, for instance, to 'the romance of origins' (2007: 98) and the fantasy of return as 'the last resort of the defeated' (2007: 99). She also cites Ayi Kwei Armah's description in *Two Thousand Seasons* of 'the folly of ex-slaves, who, blinded by filial loyalty, tried to return home' (2007: 105):

'The sickness of nostalgia', writes Armah, fixed the gaze of the wistful solely on the past. They were like children 'hankering after situations forever lost' and 'craving the love of blood relatives' who were better in memory 'than they could have ever been in their own flesh.' (2007: 105)

Hartman, who is concerned after all with the future (2007: 100), worries that she too is sick with nostalgia (2007: 106). This is striking because as a descendent of slaves, what she calls her 'nostalgia' would be one of lost origins, rather than a form of memory in the strict sense. Interestingly, she names *melancholy* as a characteristic of her possible sickness. This puts her into possible conversation with Nowak McNeice (2019), for whom, in a psychoanalytical register, one may 'lose' what one never had, and therefore speak in more encompassing terms than I generally have herein about one's relation to the past.

Allowing then that nostalgia registers, either as such or in a modified sense in persons whose communities of memory have been largely destroyed, Hartman's scholarship proves an invaluable resource in pursuit of the possible ethical difference involved when they reach into the past. She has contributed considerably to the memory of crimes against humanity in the context of American slavery and Reconstruction terror, fleshing out its archive and pushing its silences to speak in her classic *Scenes of Subjection* (1997). As she states therein, pursuing 'the history of the dominated' requires her to read her sources 'against the grain' (Hartman 1997: 10–1). This is because 'there is no access to the subaltern consciousness outside dominant representations or elite documents' (1997: 10). As such, she must 'excavate' the margins of monumental history, in view of sussing out the 'relentless proliferation of small acts of resistance' (1997: 14) and allowing Black agency in the face of terror and oblivion to belatedly emerge in the historical record. Hartman signals that she is engaged in the active reconstitution or reshaping of historical memory in some sense: she likens her method to 'a combination of foraging and disfiguration – raiding for fragments upon which other narratives can be spun and misshaping and deforming the testimony through selective quotation and the amplification of issues germane to [her] study' (1997: 12). Note that so far, it is possible to detect faint resonances with Didion on account of the methodological primacy of the particular. But here the analogy ends, since Hartman is engaged in a *struggle* that Didion simply is not.

Hartman subsequently develops and theorizes her methodology as 'critical fabulation', in connection with her attempt to tell the stories of two captive girls who died on the ironically named slave ship *Recovery* in the late eighteenth century (Hartman 2007, 2008). As she describes,

> The intention here isn't anything as miraculous as recovering the lives of the enslaved or redeeming the dead, but rather laboring to paint as full a picture of the lives of the captives as possible. This double gesture can be described as straining against the limits of the archive to write a cultural history of the captive, and, at the same time, enacting the impossibility of representing the lives of the captives precisely through the process of narration . . . . The method guiding this writing practice is best described as critical fabulation . . . . By playing with and rearranging the basic elements of the story, by re-presenting the sequence of events in divergent stories and from contested points of view, I have attempted to jeopardize the status of the event, to displace the received or authorized account, and *to imagine* what might have happened or might have been said or might have been done. (Hartman 2008: 11, emphasis added)

I have been speaking throughout the book as though imagination, which cognitively speaking is memory's close cousin, poses a kind of threat to veracity and hence to the ethics of memory. Both faculties you will recall trade in representations, but memory in the strict sense corresponds in a true (if only ever relatively comprehensive) way to its object; it is 'of the past' in a way that imagined events are not. The obvious objection to Hartman is that she contaminates memory with imagination, falsifying the past in some way. But this objection misses the point. An archive of silence, where slave voices are largely absent and others tend overwhelmingly to speak in their place, if at all, is already very far from being a 'relatively comprehensive' view of the past. In such a state, which it is crucial to remember was caused not through any 'natural' erosion of memory but through moral transgressions, through crimes against humanity, Hartman has no choice but to write 'with and against the archive' (Hartman 2008: 12).

My overall point in this chapter has been to warn via Didion of the way in which nostalgia can constitute a kind of second-order falsification of the past, through its affective investment and one-sided attention to certain memories at the expense of others. But Hartman draws attention to the fact that the comprehensiveness of existing communities of memory, and the archives out of which a nostalgic position could even be constructed in the first place, are in a state of drastic, imposed inequality. Using the imagination to breathe ghostly, speculative life into silent spaces could even be construed as an ethical act in and of itself, through its doomed attempt to reach backwards to the lost, in a kind of *post festum* solidarity; as Hartman describes it, she does not 'give voice' to the slave, but, rather, strives to write 'a history of an unrecoverable past' (Hartman 2008: 12). Reading her, one therefore gets an impression of exceptional courage and obstinacy in the face of memory's exorbitant ethical demands, much like the picture I drew from Didion, in Chapter 2. But whereas for Didion, it was a question of asserting memory in the face of *metaphysical* loneliness, Hartman must contend with an imposed *ethical* loneliness in Stauffer's sense. Hartman belongs among the teachers and exemplars we need, but for her the stakes are even higher because there is *moral* damage to contend with, and one must assert the very grievability of the lost in the act of critical fabulation.

Note that critical fabulation persists into Hartman's recent scholarship, but not simply to further enrich and challenge an archive of crime, suffering and resistance. In Hartman's *Wayward Lives, Beautiful Experiments* where the goal is to write a history of young, radical, modern Black women at the turn of the twentieth century, to provide 'an account of the wayward' and the largely forgotten beauty, freedom and courageous striving of their lives, she avows that here too she must 'employ a method of close narration, a style which places the voice of narrator and character in inseparable relation, so that the vision, language, and rhythms of the wayward shape and arrange the text' (2019: xiii–xiv). 'All the characters and events found in [the] book are real,' she assures us, but 'the authority of the archive and the limits it sets on what can be known, whose perspective matters, and who is endowed with the gravity and authority of historical actor' (2019: xiii) necessitate a work of creative, yet self-consciously critical intervention. On Hartman's view it is necessary to 'elaborate', 'augment', 'transpose', 'break open' archival documents; to 'press at the limits of the case file and the document', to 'speculate', 'imagine' and 'amplify' (2019: xiv–xv). All of this is done in the interest not of falsifying but of enriching the largely silent archive to reflect the current of fugitive and utopian strivings in historical black communities, their tireless attempt to consider 'how the world might be otherwise' (2019: xv) in the face of continuous if shifting oppression. We see here how where the archive falls silent, hope too clamours to make itself heard.

Hartman seems to suggest that it is not solely on the strength of memories of crimes against humanity that the community of memory can be built, but also through obstinate visioning and prefiguring of the very best of what a human life, lived with others, can offer.

At this point in the argument, I believe I have identified and affirmed Didion's pertinence to thinking through the problem of nostalgia. Moreover, thinking with her has been fruitful in prompting wider reflections, beyond what she explicitly offers on the norm of relative comprehensiveness in memory, on the topics of forgiveness and critical fabulation. In the book's final chapter, I will stay within the ambit of broadly 'public' problems but will focus the norms of veracity and comprehensiveness back onto the issue of *narrative* – specifically, the surface and deep narratives of American politics, as Didion reads them. Here it will be a question of how the ethics of memory exhorts us not to drop the threads of the power story undergirding our public representations. Though the theme is somewhat like that of nostalgia – guarding against dangerously and unfairly partial representations – Didion's newfound political energies in later works arguably see her more in the mode of constituting a history of the present, of keeping the story straight in a dizzying turnover of information and spin.

4

Political memory and memory as politics

Critical political realism and neoliberal life narrative

The previous chapter could be succinctly summarized in terms of ethical issues raised by remembering partially, including a particular focus through Didion on the ethical and political costs of letting an idealized, problematically partial version of the past stand in for the truth of how things really were. But if Didion was right to warn us of the pitfalls of nostalgia – despite her own nostalgic leanings, and the notable limitations of what she accomplishes in adopting a self-critical pose respecting them – her salience for the thinking of public memory is broader still.

I will focus here on two themes extending the discussion of more obviously 'public' aspects of the ethics of memory. These are, first, the apparent turn in the later Didion to a reinvigorated interest in narrative, under the sign of what I call a 'critical political realism', and second, the ideological employment of memoir as 'neoliberal life narrative' that has been contemporary with her later writings. The point of the chapter is to drive home *how memory ethics always intersects with politics*, and to insist that it would be a mistake to ignore its political dimension. Whether we like it or not, the normative stakes and standards of remembering, forgetting and related memory actions include the latter's *political* implications; this means that a reflection on memory's normativity must also include the dimension of the *strategically* normative. How we respond to these implications *as impactful for ethics*, I will explain, determines whether we cleave to a narrowly ethical or a more expansive moral position on public problems.

As this chapter will explore, there are ethical *and* political costs associated with remembering partially, certainly, but also with failing to remember accurately, or even failing to remember at all. To this extent an ethics of memory grounds and complements a critical political realism, which is to say, a realistic mapping and practice of power relations that does not unmoor itself completely from ethical or, above all, moral standards. Moreover, we will see that when we *do* remember, when we *do* let the lone voice add to the public archive of memory – no matter how accurately or inaccurately, no matter how comprehensively or partially – there is also the formal but equally ethical and political question of *which* life narratives to centre. In other words, we can ask which are best suited to the situation, the progressive demands of the current conjuncture and which we would do better to downplay, read 'against' or simply avoid.

As I will explain first in what follows, the later Didion in both her novels and her essays maps out a renewed vision of narrative to counter political forgetting. Distinct from the better known, more aloof, and sceptical pose she adopts in the 1960s and 1970s, Didion from the 1980s onwards banks upon the coherence of an underlying political narrative, a game of power beneath the surface froth of postwar democracy. This is what the chapter's subtitle designates as 'political memory'. Her framework for approaching this narrative can be understood in terms of a resistance to forgetting; not just the surreptitiousness but also the sheer complexity of power machinations strains against the construction of a commonsense, popular understanding of what is happening in the halls and backrooms of power.[1]

Second, it is remarkable that the later Didion's more personal 'memoir' writings arrived amid a landslide of published memoir writing, and the critical reactions that this engendered. Leigh Gilmore designates this phenomenon as the 'memoir boom/lash' of the late 1990s and early 2000s (2018: 86). Here we have a chance to consider memoir *itself* as a field of political contestation; this is what the chapter's subtitle indicates in terms of 'memory as politics'. I will argue that Didion starts out her career by replicating to a great extent the ideological drift of her time but ends up by refusing to furnish us with more of the 'neoliberal life narratives' overwhelmingly represented in the later, more reactionary sequence of the boom/lash. Instead, she offers a vision of memoir both more complex and grounded in philosophical obstinacy and shared vulnerability – hence, as more politically open, and promising. To this extent, certain of the 'lessons' about the ethics of memory we may draw from Didion concern the status of her writing as *both* reflective of mainstream ideology, *and* actively working against the grain of that ideology. This amounts to a complex political legacy, but one that is worth interrogating given the salience of the ethics of memory in our time.

Political memory: Critical political realism

To speak of a political turn in the later Didion perhaps risks overstating the case, since by all accounts she was already keen to politics early on. Having grown up around 'conservative California Republicans' in a postwar boom economy – before, she claims, the meaning of the word 'conservative' changed – she believed in low taxes, a balanced budget, a limited government and a presumption against governmental 'tinkering with the private and cultural life of its citizens' (Didion 2006: 735). She 'ardently' voted for Barry Goldwater in 1964, and was subsequently driven to register as a Democrat, the first in her family to do so, by what she describes as the personally offensive turn California Republicans made from Goldwater to Ronald Reagan (Didion 2006: 735–6). This decision was to prove formative for her developing political scepticism: 'That [changing parties] did not involve taking a markedly different view on any issue was a novel discovery, and one that led me to view "America's two-party system" with – and this was my real introduction to American politics – a somewhat doubtful eye' (Didion 2006: 736).

Apparently already jaded, the younger Didion's writings often engage, though by means of a characteristic peripherality or particularism, with defining political events and concerns of her time. This is, to be sure, an almost de-politicizing kind of engagement in politics in the earlier writings; I have described her as 'punching left' at new social movements in the 1960s and 1970s, even as she sometimes evinced what I believe was a genuine sympathy and longing for the ideals she coolly sought to demolish.

Since her 'wagon-train morality' offered no alternative to a robust moral vision such as the new social movements she targeted both represented and promised, critics have rightly pointed out Didion's tendency to 'enrage' many of her readers, espousing a version of conservatism even while she benefits personally from social progress (Chihara 2020). In the early Didion, conservatism was packaged in a deceptively 'postmodern' style, but there is no paradox here. As per Casey Shoop,

> Didion's stylistic operation portends a rather fatalistic world view. Her work reveals perhaps better than any other post-war writer how the formal strategies of postmodern metafiction are not synonymous with progressive politics. Narrative breakdown all too often becomes, in her hands, a form of existential quietism not only about the failure of the conventional national stories we tell, but also about any viable alternatives to them. (2016: 587)

Doubt and perspectivalism in her social and political reporting, in short, often dovetail with her moral scepticism to produce a stylish but fatalistic deference to the status quo.

What there is of a 'turn' in Didion's writings mainly concerns the shift of emphasis away from perceived social symptoms of narrative and ethical breakdown, and towards an almost obsessive investment in the underlying narrative of the political power moves beneath the surface of late capitalist society. As I interpret her, from at least the late 1970s, but certainly from *Salvador* onwards, Didion moves *away* from a relative quietism grounded in 'postmodern' scepticism. She moves, in fact, towards a vigorous political realism, without, however, abandoning the formal or apparently philosophical trappings of her sceptical period. In this respect, Didion parallels developments in continental political philosophy during the same era, particularly those of Ernesto Laclau and Chantal Mouffe (2014). These suggest that while there is apparently no putting the 'postmodern' genie back in the bottle, neither conservatism nor quietism must be the result. Rather, as per Laclau and Mouffe, the breakdown of received narratives and identities has had the salutary effect of reopening the question of political realism, or of politics under the guise of a mapping of and engagement with real as opposed to ideal or aspirational configurations of power.[2] But Didion is no cynical realist; if I recruit her to what I call a *critical* political realism, it is because she aims her interventions predominantly from *Salvador* onwards at the state and mainstream political discourse, evidently from a principled position, suggestive not just of communitarian ethics but of a more expansive norm of justice as fairness. If I am right, ultimately she jumps back into politics in a strategically and tactically realist way, but with a widely ethical or perhaps even a *moral* standpoint in the background.

It bears emphasizing that Didion may be generally categorized as an observer and commentator on *democracy*, particularly of American democracy and its peculiarities. As such, when she thinks in terms of what I have called the ethics of memory, she foregrounds the thick relations and norms constituting an increasingly atomized, arguably crumbling democratic society. This way of framing the issue allows the problem to emerge quite starkly: to ponder the ethics of memory in an advanced democracy, one characterized by rapid news cycles and technologically mediated, produced and disseminated disinformation, is to encounter a situation of rampant forgetting, and therefore a clear case of ethical decomposition. But this is not just an ethical issue; ethical decomposition redounds on democracy as a form of *political* society through the political implications of hyper-fragmentation. To this extent, the earlier Didion's anxiety about American society and politics, and her 'postmodern' style and moral scepticism, go hand in hand.

To be sure, Didion is no innovator here – though once again, as I have stressed throughout the book, she is someone from whom we might learn a great deal. Almost two hundred years ago, Alexis de Tocqueville had already sketched the general problem Didion encounters and had linked it to the specific history and characteristics of American society. Tocqueville draws a distinction between 'individualism' and 'egoism'. Egoism he defines as 'an ardent and excessive love of oneself which leads man to relate everything back to himself and to prefer himself above everything' (2003: 587). Egoism as such is antisocial. It is ancient and associated with no political regime in particular, whereas individualism is 'democratic in origin' and spreads as social and political equality increases (2003: 588). Individualism for its part stems initially from the circumstances of (male, white, 'average') Americans and is only incipiently antisocial. Distinct from egoism, it is 'a calm and considered feeling which persuades each citizen to cut himself off from his fellows and to withdraw into the circle of his family and friends in such a way that he thus creates a small group of his own and willingly abandons society at large to its own devices' (2003: 587). The problem is that individualism eventually *becomes* egoism; this it does by drying up 'the source of civic virtue' (2003: 588). Democracies in general, and American democracy in particular, thus lay the foundation for their own decomposition by fostering individualism. But individualism, we have seen, is only one step removed from the minimally ethical 'wagon train morality' or 'code of the West' that the younger Didion opposes to encompassing moral visions. In fact, such an ethic is perhaps already hypocritical, an idealization of more cynical, egoist motives, as Didion fears in *Where I Was From*.[3]

Why though does this slide into egoism happen? What does it mean exactly, to say that individualism dried up the source of civic virtue? Here it is worth noting how Tocqueville links American social and political equality, and therefore individualism, with classical liberal economics:

> As social equality spreads, a greater number of individuals are no longer rich or powerful enough to exercise great influence upon the fate of their fellows, but have acquired or have preserved sufficient understanding and wealth to be able to satisfy their own needs. Such people owe nothing to anyone and, as it were, expect nothing from anyone. They are used to considering themselves in isolation and quite willingly imagine their destiny as entirely in their own hands. (Tocqueville 2003: 589)

What Tocqueville describes here is strikingly like the exclusionist account of Californians and their story given by Didion. Moreover, the picture Tocqueville paints has direct implications for what I have called the ethics of memory. Construing oneself as an island loosens social bonds in the present, but also through time. As Tocqueville tells it,

> not only does democracy make men forget their ancestors but also hides their descendants and keeps them apart from their fellows. It constantly brings them back to themselves and threatens in the end to imprison them in the isolation of their own hearts. (2003: 589)

It would be fascinating to ponder here the ethics of memory and its intersection with politics in other types of political society. But Didion has her eyes trained on American democracy, and I will therefore cleave closely to it in what follows. In both her later novels and her later non-fiction, she tries, despite her well-documented scepticism, to keep focus on the power/money narrative, tries not to give up on public memory in a context that works against it. This obstinacy in charting a realist narrative of power is therefore a further echo of her exemplary embodiment of an ethics of memory. Additionally, it suggests that to remain genuinely *critical*, as I am using the term, a non-negotiable and expansively ethical if not properly *moral* horizon of justice as fairness is also required.[4]

Looking first at the later novels – *A Book of Common Prayer*, *Democracy* and *The Last Thing He Wanted* – we see precisely what I have described as

Didion's new or renewed preoccupation with the loss of public memory in a democracy. Memory is 'the "major cost" of public [i.e. political] life': 'you lose track. *As if* you'd had shock treatment' (Didion 1995: 51, emphasis in original). Such disorientation permeates both the style and the narratives of the novels themselves.

What Didion apparently worries about is the crumbling of not simply memory but also *history*.[5] As suggested by my reading of *A Book of Common Prayer* in Chapter 1, history is a kind of *human* orientation and scale for memory; it struggles not to sink into the temporal indifference or eternal, naturalistic changing-into-the-same of what I called 'the immemorial', or that Didion sometimes describes in terms of a 'geological' perspective. As the narrator, Grace, tells Charlotte of the fecund but rotting nation in which they live, 'Boca Grande has no history' (Didion 1977: 14). But supposing, even, that a historical perspective could be rescued from such naturalism, it is not for that reason safeguarded. This is because history, if it is possible, includes a longer and more obviously public and political perspective than the individual and her thick relations might tend to encapsulate.

As Didion states in *Democracy*, history or 'the long view' in general can be denied by the individual precisely because it represents 'the particular undertow of *having and not having*, the convulsions of a world largely unaffected by the individual efforts of anyone in it' (1995: 211, emphasis added).[6] Similarly, in *The Last Thing He Wanted*, the proliferation of largely derivative news sources figures as 'History's rough draft. We used to say. When we still believed that history merited a second look' (Didion 1996: 11). The narrator in that book will ultimately concede that she still does 'believe in history' (Didion 1996: 33). But she immediately amends that to mean that she believes it to be made 'exclusively and at random' by people like the character Dick McMahon – the protagonist's father, who has long had a hand in shady, subterranean deals (Didion 1996). History if it exists therefore figures as the province of power and money interests worked by amoral 'Western' archetypes, as a game of 'having and not having', emerging out of an 'immemorial' or 'geological' indifference rather gratuitously.

History in the novels therefore appears to be fatalistic or *random* from the individual's perspective, and these might amount to the same thing. Because of this, the preoccupation with forgetting as a public problem does not lead to any solid conviction on the possibility or for that matter the utility of political narrative reconstruction. Didion the narrator of *Democracy* implicitly expresses doubt about what 'novelists' 'usually' hold about human behaviour, that its apparent unpredictability indexes 'a higher predictability, a more complex pattern discernable only after the fact' (Didion 1995: 215). Faced with such doubt, and expressing it, but then *saying* in the novels anyway, Didion seems to suggest not so much a narrative confidence as something like a moral imperative, even an exorbitant or impossible one – much as one finds in the deceptively 'intimate' or 'private' sphere of memory ethics detailed in Chapter 2. Inserting herself, by name, into the narration of the novel *Democracy*, she describes how

> In 1955 [at Berkeley] I had first noticed the quickening of time. In 1975 [back on campus for a visiting fellowship] time was no longer just quickening but collapsing, falling in on itself, the way a disintegrating star contracts into a black hole, and at the scene of all I had left unlearned I could summon up only fragments of poems, misremembered. (Didion 1995: 72)[7]

Assuming this is an accurate impression of how Didion experienced time at the time, it is astounding to read it considering the further, exponential acceleration of events and information that has occurred since 1975. It is enough to lead a writer to 'resist narrative' altogether, to pretend to deliver only, with a minimum of interpretation, some of the 'documents that apply' (Didion 1995: 113). To cling to narrative *nonetheless* is to appreciate that 'the heart of narrative is a certain calculated ellipsis, a tacit contract between writer and reader to surprise and to be surprised, how not to tell you what you do not yet want to know' (Didion 1995: 162). Didion, as we know by now, appreciates 'the role played by specificity in this kind of narrative', the role played by 'the apparently insignificant detail' (Didion 1995: 162–3). But how can we ever *get to the point* when we are increasingly awash in such potential narrative detail, and in all areas of our lives? How possibly can the narrative hold us in suspense when the sheer overload of information risks submerging its thread completely? As Didion the narrator of *Democracy* warns us, 'I no longer have time for the playing out' (Didion 1995: 164). Yet this is in part because she inexorably works against herself, tending 'to elongate the time sequence, which was in fact quite short' (Didion 1996: 85).

Nonetheless, raising our ethics of memory to the level of public, political discourse demands exactly such patience, and therefore the *wager* that such patience can connect. The narrator of *The Last Thing He Wanted* does not confidently proceed to tell a story so much as wagers, gambles, plays:[8] 'I added it up . . . you could call this a reconstruction. A corrective, if you will . . .' A revisionist view of a time and a place and an incident about which, ultimately, most people preferred not to know. Real world' (Didion 1996: 13). She wagers that it is even possible to grasp a given period as one in which 'no information could be without interest', in which 'Every moment could be seen to connect to every other moment, every act to have logical if obscure consequences, an unbroken narrative of vivid complexity' (Didion 1996: 56). Here Didion aims, despite everything, to cut beneath ideology and mystification: such a 'real world' revision, as we saw, would be unpopular but salutary precisely because of how it differs from the 'magical' one we generally prefer (Didion 1996: 15). No matter if even at the time, 'nobody at all saw the whole' (Didion 1996: 203); the past still has consequences (Didion 1996: 211), and the 'imperfect memories' can still be mined for 'A hundred visions and revisions' (Didion 1996: 226).

Turning next to her later non-fiction, we can see how Didion the *journalistic* narrator wagers and arguably manages precisely the patience required for such 'real world' revision. She lays out how she construes her work *qua* political in an interview with Rebecca Meyer, and unsurprisingly perhaps, it fits with her literary approach: 'The whole way I deal with politics came out of the English department [at Berkeley, where Didion was an undergraduate]. They taught a form of literary criticism which was based on analyzing texts in a very close way. If you start analyzing the text of a newspaper or a political commentator on CNN using the same approach of close textual analysis, you come to understand it in a different way. It's not any different from reading Henry James' (Parker 2018: 73).

Such analysis of politics brings numerous inconsistencies and gaps in the official or 'surface' text to light, and these in theory can be presented to the public in a straightforward gesture reminiscent of Noam Chomsky or even Kant.[9] Though she adopts what is essentially a classical liberal understanding of the role of the public intellectual, Didion does it after her own fashion and with a dose of self-awareness. As Meyer points out, she portrays American democracy as 'fairly bankrupt' so there is both a recognizable effort on her part to stay engaged, and an awareness that she might be idealistic in doing so (Parker 2018: 73). As Didion puts it, 'I keep thinking that when everybody notices the inconsistencies [in American democracy], the way things don't add up, there will be a change. It's a romantic idea, I suppose, but I keep thinking it' (in Parker 2018: 73).

Such self-awareness, or such wariness of liberal ideology, lines Didion up with what Habermas calls the 'ambivalent' view of the public sphere in liberalism, for which he gives John Stuart Mill and – perhaps unsurprisingly, given what I have said earlier – Alexis de Tocqueville as exemplars (Habermas 1991: 129–40). As Habermas recounts in his reconstruction of the history of publicity, while it 'penetrated more *spheres* of society, it simultaneously lost its political *function*, namely: that of subjecting the affairs that it had made public to the control of a critical public' (Habermas 1991: 140, emphasis in original). We have passed increasingly from the putatively universal and broadly politically efficacious 'public sphere' or 'public of letters' of liberal ideology, to a multitude of 'intimate publics' of affective investment and affiliation. As such, Didion finds herself in the context of an increasingly generalized scepticism about human reason, and the resulting political conservatism and communities of feeling that she arguably contributed to constituting with her earlier works. This is why it makes sense to speak of a 'turn' in her later writings; it is as though the shock recounted in *Salvador* puts her on the 'Sisyphean' trail of writing about politics in a more classically liberal mode (Didion 2006: 736). She has to *wager*, like the characters of her later novels, that an old-fashioned liberal public will still be there, or can be called or willed into existence, to receive and engage with her political narrative reconstructions.

Ultimately, though the public sphere *as such* can be rightly made the object of an ambivalent attitude, it takes a certain vision of consistency, rationality and *justice* to actually *say* whatever one reconstructs of the truth in that sphere, when one could have turned one's efforts to different pursuits, or just stayed silent. Justice here is no narrowly communitarian 'frontier' justice, aimed solely at self-defence and ethical coherence; rather, it is a *moral* notion in the more abstract, universalistic sense I have been using. In this way, to repeat, Didion's 'political realist' turn is not a total concession to communitarian power interests; it is *critical*, in the sense of being rooted in a putatively extra-political normative horizon, one that is even wider than 'ethics' construed as the norms of thick relations.

Such a critical perspective of truth, consistency, and justice manifests in Didion's accumulation of evidence that American democracy fails in some way to add up to what its edifying narratives and fixed ideas express it to be.

To insist upon the inconsistencies of American democracy is not, to repeat, to give up on the idea of an underlying logic or sense. It is simply to insist that its real location is elsewhere than people tend to think, and that it does not measure up to the ideal version. More specifically, what underlying logic or sense there is in American democracy is not to be found in some ideal of consensus, or even in the give and take of democracy itself, even if these are precisely some of the norms forming the ground from which Didion launches her critique. Writing in the aftermath of the 9/11 terror attacks, she observes with prescience about issues like flag-burning and school prayer that

> When it comes to any one of these phenomena that we dismiss as 'politics', we tend to forgive, or at least overlook, the absence of logic or sense. We tell ourselves that this is the essential give and take of democracy, we tell ourselves that our elected representatives are doing the necessary work of creating consensus. We try to convince ourselves that somewhere, beneath the posturing, there is a hidden logic, there are minds at work, there is someone actually thinking out the future of the country beyond the 2004 election.
>
> These would be comforting notions were they easier to maintain. In fact we have created a political process in which 'consensus' is the last thing the professionals want or need, a process that works precisely by turning the angers and fears and energy of the few – that handful of voters who can be driven by the fixed aspect of their own opinions – against the rest of the country. (Didion 2003: 28–9)

What logic or sense there actually is, is to be sought beneath the surface of political democracy and it is, above all, *strategic* in nature. Knotting together several of the issues I have raised in the book so far, Didion can be read as suggesting that there is an ethical or even a moral presumption *not to mislay* the real logic or sense of democracy by clinging to obfuscating, comforting, perhaps sentimental or nostalgic notions about the political process. America may well have been a stable and comforting home to some of its citizens in the past, but it was always a machine built and operated in the interests of power and money.

Under Didion's critical eye, many long-standing political 'fictions', 'myths' and 'sentimental' attachments are shaken if not demolished. Some of these are relatively local, if suggestive of wider applicability. This is the case for example of her tracking of the race and class undercurrents of the 'sentimental narrative that is New York public life', in light of the 'central park jogger' case (Didion 2006: 686). *Miami*, for its part, remains a masterful exercise in following what there is of an underlying power-narrative – with obvious national connections and consequences, given the importance of Florida to America's political destiny since the book's 1987 publication.

Didion also sets her sights on national politics as such, and the state of American democracy in general. Despite what she detects as a creeping, cynical moralization of political discourse, where professed principles come to battle in increasingly sensational public displays, there is also an alarming narrowing of political difference and choice, foreshadowed in her early discovery that switching from Republican to Democrat failed to mean very much. The 'insider' nature of the American political process, the congealment of the two-party system into 'a permanent political class', belie the 'fable' that the political process in the US affords any real 'choice' to its citizens (Didion 2006: 736–7). Voting is reduced to a kind of 'consumer transaction' where the voter thinks she 'pays' with her vote for the ear of the politician, for access to the levers of power, but really gets only a 'sentimental' return on her investment that is not unrelated to the moralization of the parties' and candidates' discourse (Didion 2006: 738–9). Relatedly, the discussion is no longer about 'what the Democratic Party should advocate but about what it "must be seen advocating", not about what might work but about what might have "resonance," about what "resonates most clearly with . . . focus group participants"' (Didion 2006: 836). As Didion describes, 'This notion, that the citizen's choice among determinedly centrist candidates makes a "difference," is in fact the narrative's most central element, and its most fictive' (Didion 2006: 758).

The passages in question are stunningly prescient. It is not just that Didion shifts her erstwhile 'postmodern' scepticism back onto the question of who holds power, and who tells what fables to whom in the interest of keeping things that way. It is also the fact that in doing so, she maps the territory of what will become not just an American but a worldwide phenomenon of populist revolt against mandatory, manufactured neoliberal consensus. Read today, figures as hopeful as Bernie Sanders and Podemos, and as ghoulish as Donald Trump and Marine Le Pen, therefore haunt the pages of *Political Fictions*.[10]

Didion is also keen to emphasize how the imposed consensus at home redounds on other nations. For her, 'the real nature of the Reagan doctrine' pertains to how an administration with "little room to maneuver at home" may defuse democratic energies through 'sideshows abroad', through 'the creation of what pollsters call "a dramatic event", preferably one so remote that it remains an abstraction' (Didion 2006: 771). She goes on to link Washington and its ideologists to the El Mozote massacre, thus closing the loop with *Salvador*. But here again, note how Didion is not simply a sharp reader of the underlying power-narrative, but also chillingly prescient. Writing her foreword to *Political Fictions* not long before 9/11 and the 'War on Terror', she leverages the farce of the 2000 presidential election to underscore that 'the democracy we spoke of spreading throughout the world was now in our own country only an ideality' (Didion 2006: 742). This, quite troublingly, 'had come to be seen, against the higher priority of keeping it in the hands of those who already held it, as [a fact] without application' (Didion 2006: 742).

The last reference in particular, to 'exporting democracy', suggests how such critical realism as Didion espouses in *Political Fictions* belies what she calls the 'Sisyphean' aspect of writing about politics (Didion 2006: 736). The book was published on the eve of the terror attacks of 9/11, when 'sideshows abroad' ceased to be 'abstractions', redounding on American soil. Didion toured the country promoting the book in the weeks following, and this forced her to comment on the event, to link those comments to her book and in some respects to defend herself and other writers against the ideological closing of ranks that was occurring. The whole episode underscores how rapidly history moves in our times, despite whatever narrative coherence can be wrested from it.

The event of 9/11 and the way in which Didion handles it is, in fact, highly illustrative of the fault line between ethics and politics, and several of the themes I have already explored herein. Didion takes for granted 'the annihilating economy of the event', which is to say, 'the way in which it had concentrated the complicated arrangements and misarrangements of the last century into a single irreducible image' (Didion 2003: 8). On the one hand, she points out how 'what had happened was being processed, obscured, systematically *leached of history and so of meaning*, finally rendered less readable than it had seemed on the morning it happened. As if overnight, the irreconcilable event had been made manageable, reduced to the sentimental, to protective talismans . . . repeated pieties that would come to seem in some ways as destructive as the event itself' (Didion 2003: 8–9, emphasis added). Note that the invocation of 'meaning' here has the sense of 'true meaning', and that this requires faithful historical memory; throughout the text Didion excoriates the shallow, nostalgic, Manichean and 'pre-modern' meanings that were mobilized in the event's wake (Didion 2003: 14). Such talismans belie the obviously political stakes involved in interpreting the event: Didion explains how 'the entire event' of 9/11 'had been seized . . . to stake new ground in old domestic wars' (Didion 2003: 12).

Thus ethics, in Didion's handling of a calamitous event like 9/11, at least partly takes shape as an ethics of memory, and importantly as a principled one that does not forget the moral horizon. It points to a reconstruction of the event that concedes neither to nostalgia nor to outright illusion or error, and which works to construct a community of memory *qua* community of healing and mutual support, one that is potentially, aspirationally, even wider than New York or the United States. Didion's use of words like 'annihilating' and 'irreconcilable' in describing 9/11 therefore do not indicate that it was an unfathomable, absolute evil and therefore beyond comprehension let alone critical analysis. Rather, they highlight the *traumatic* nature of the event, in the sense explored in Chapter 2. The work of memory following the trauma proceeds in halting, necessarily inadequate steps, never fully capable of measuring up to the task – but nonetheless it hits upon the truth, if only in a local and cumulative sense, and is therefore normatively necessary.

In short, Didion's critical realism suggests how even a 'politics of memory' can honour an 'ethics of memory', if by 'politics' we mean a strategic normativity. It highlights how a *moral* horizon of memory is required to make a political realism genuinely *critical*. Arguably, Didion appeals not just to ethics but also precisely to such a horizon in her later political writings, as evidenced by her appeals to consistency and ultimately, often even implicitly, to justice.

Memory as politics: Life narratives, neoliberal or otherwise

I have already drawn out some of the political implications of nostalgia in Chapter 3, and so far in this chapter we have looked at Didion's more focused emphasis on political memory and forgetting, in the wake of her apparent 'turn' with respect to political narrative. But while many of her later works are, indeed, marked by their keen attunement to the underlying stories and intrigues of public life, Didion's most publicly resonant works from her later period are undeniably those which cleave closest to her intimate experience, as we saw in Chapter 2: specifically, the two versions of *The Year of Magical Thinking*, and *Blue Nights* (and to a lesser extent I would add, *Where I Was From*). The question arises then as to whether there is any real continuity here, between the putatively public and putatively private subject matters of Didion's writings from *Salvador* onwards, and how these bear or not upon the ethics of memory.

It is worth recalling that in general, the very distinction between a 'public' and a 'private' Didion is not absolute – as is the distinction between 'public' and 'private' in general. After all, the memoirs on grief are public-facing. And even if they were not, I have suggested how a person's 'private' reminiscences, though irreducibly private in a certain technical, phenomenological sense, are always already at home to varying degrees in public, normative cultures of value and feeling. In Chapter 2, I drew upon Lauren Berlant's (2008) notion of 'intimate publics' to capture this fraught nature of the putative private/public divide. But since the tone, style and subject matters of Didion's more obviously 'public' political writings and the more 'intimate' books on grief seem to differ considerably, the temptation might be to say that the latter texts form or appeal to an intimate public that is poles apart from her tracking of the narrowing of political choice and the impoverishment of political discourse. We must not, however, rest content with the idea that the memoirs form an 'intimate public', as opposed to the arguably liberal projection of a public sphere still operant in the political writings. The second term of the concept 'intimate public' reminds us that it is never an entirely isolated, insular, self-enclosed phenomenon. Its borders are negotiable and it is enmeshed in a wider set of public cultures, inhabiting therefore a broader political context. The question then remains: Is there an additional political or ethical story to tell of the putatively more 'intimate' Didion, a story we elided in the ethical focus of Chapter 2?

Here Leigh Gilmore's work is again helpful, permitting us to situate the memoirs on grief in an *ideological context*. She describes both the 'surge in life narratives published in the late twentieth century,' wherein 'women's life stories gained new prominence', as well as the backlash which quickly followed (2018: 85). She stresses how in the wake of Anita Hill's testimony and the rise of first-person literature by women of colour and queer writers, a subversive experimental period briefly blossomed wherein non-normative and potentially subversive representations of trauma and gender found a broader public (2018:

86). Gilmore then explores how such writings, their authors and the very genre of memoir itself met with swift reaction. First, 'They were tagged as both lies and inconvenient truths, and their authors were shamed, sidelined, and turned into examples of the excesses of identity politics, and increasingly of the pitfalls of memoir itself' (2018: 88). Second, and relatedly, representations of trauma including those connected to gender and non-normative identities 'migrated from memoir to self-help' (2018: 88). As Gilmore tells it, 'the potency, and threat, of nonnormative witnesses and narratives that catalyzed this period of vitality in life writing were absorbed and neutralized by a newly ascendant redemption narrative' (2018: 86–7). In short, following potent critical reaction to memoir, self-help as a genre effectively crowded out the brief efflorescence of non-normative testimonies by women in general and marginalized women in particular. All of this is extremely telling. What might seem to be a mere matter of changing interests and publishing trends suggests a deeper political, ideological story, where power interests have a hand in shaping *which intimate experiences have a chance at public reception and validation.*

Gilmore uses the term 'neoliberal life narrative' to denote the stereotyped redemption story that came to absorb and neutralize non-normative life writing.[11] She describes it in the following terms:

> the neoliberal life narrative features an 'I' who overcomes hardship and recasts historical and systemic harm as something an individual alone can, and should, manage through pluck, perseverance, and enterprise. The individual transforms disadvantage into value . . . . Neoliberal life narrative conditions readers to affirm and accept the redemption story as natural and desirable, and to embrace life stories that absolve readers of the requirement to do anything other than follow the writer's advice in their own lives because the writer has relieved readers of history's ethical claims on us. (2018: 89)

It is worth slowing down here to underscore what is at stake. It must be admitted that in a sexist and misogynist society, the first-person account of *any* woman, especially any marginalized woman, can be alive with critical potential.[12] This is true to the extent that it can lay bare to some extent how power functions in her society. But according to Gilmore, the woman's gesture of testimony is subject to a twofold neutralization. First, she is discredited through the coordinated efforts of critics speaking an ideologically orthodox 'critical' discourse. Second, what is subversive in her testimony (for example, how racism manifests as trauma) is recuperated through its absorption in discourses of overcoming and redemption.[13] In short, either it is insinuated or outright stated that the author is mistaken, or lying or dubiously motivated – or, if she is telling the truth, then she is construed as needlessly complaining, or manifesting or encouraging a 'victim mentality' if she refuses to spin that truth into a tale of optimism.

Significantly, Gilmore describes how neoliberal life narratives, in the form of self-help and redemption stories, 'do not impose an ethical demand on readers' (Gilmore 2018: 115). Though arguably the author of the neoliberal life narrative is increasingly framed as an accessible every-person, this is depoliticizing rather than democratizing; it is precisely her generic character that has an insidious, neutralizing effect, both politically and ethically. The reader to some extent encounters a cipher of herself, and she encounters this cipher in a redeeming narrative downplaying or even purified of the structural contributors and contexts of her trauma (for example, racism or sexism). The implication is that she, too – the reader – can and should overcome her trauma and her disadvantages through her own efforts. The effect is to take focus off the structural inequalities and injustices of her context, and to train it upon herself, via the challenge of self-improvement. While there is certainly nothing wrong with self-improvement as such, the problem is that neoliberal life narratives present it almost as though it happens in a vacuum. 'Ethics' obviously suffers here if it refers to an other-regarding stance or to one's thick relations, but so does politics – inasmuch as the individual is now engaged in a solitary, uncritical pursuit of redemption, or success or 'wellness'. What Gilmore describes under the rubric of neoliberal life narrative is, of course, only one aspect of how neoliberalism functions *qua* ideology. But it draws attention to a political context in which a genre of writing is recruited to leverage common sense into an uncritical, sacrificial submissiveness to economic reason.

As Gilmore further points out, however, neoliberal life narratives are not perfect tools for sapping ethical and political energies. They are haunted by what they suppress; they 'lack political analysis even as they teem with political potential' (Gilmore 2018: 106), and their autobiographical pretexts are 'pervasively traumatic, without being described as such' (Gilmore 2018: 114). The ideological operation of the backlash to non-normative memoirs is shot through with what it tries to suppress, leaving openings for further critical intervention. The recuperation of non-normative life writing was in any case by no means total, and testimony by women and marginalized persons remains an important political battleground.

This critical opening will be important to keep in mind when applying the concept of neoliberal life narrative to Didion, as I will explain a bit later. For now, note that the concept is apposite when discussing her, for at least three reasons. First, her 'wagon train morality' is one of bootstrapping, protecting one's own above all, and on the face of it, fits nicely with neoliberal ideology's individualism and its devolution of responsibility to the intimate family sphere (Brown 2015; Cooper 2019; Mounk 2019). Second, her attack on what she perceives as the infantilism and victim mentality suffusing 1960s and 1970s social movements like the women's movement shifts the discussion of social reconstruction onto the terrain of personal character, and therefore at best onto personal reconstruction and redemption. Finally, her explicit denial of 'privilege' in Quintana's case, on account of her personal struggles, obfuscates the structural forces contributing to relative advantages and the maldistribution of life chances (Wolff and De-Shalit 2013; Spade 2015; McLennan 2019).

Regarding 'wagon train morality', the potential for a relative depoliticization is obvious; if one adheres strictly to 'the code of the West' then the only political engagement worthy of ethical support can be a highly conservative one, protective of the close community. Any more substantive moral ideal or project of social improvement is to be rejected because it points towards disaster. Precisely this stance – bootstrapping, looking out for one's kin and relying upon them as one's only source of support and care – is quintessentially neoliberal as per Brown 2015 and Cooper 2019. But there is reason here not to conclude that Didion is an ideological prop to neoliberalism, full stop. I have suggested that 'wagon train morality' becomes nuanced through her career, being questioned in *Where I Was From*, for instance, in a hypothetical form: 'When you jettison others as not to be "caught by winter in the Sierra Nevada mountains," do you not deserve to be caught? When you survive at the cost of [others], do you survive at all?' (Didion 2006: 974). In fact, as Nowak McNeice (2019) points out, there is a palpable 'loss of ethics' in Didion's later novels, a *melancholic* investment in the Western code that ultimately fails to work for her female protagonists in her novels. Shoop also draws attention to the fact that it is the more cynical, rootless, *uncritically* politically realist male characters who tend to thrive in the world where wagon train morality has failed: such men, 'and they are always men', figure as 'cowboys of the geopolitical frontier whose competence at fixing problems always corresponds with their lack of political idealism' (2016: 587–8). In this sense, the later novels track the shift away from Didion's subsumption of politics to the dictates of a minimal, austere ethics, and towards the relocation of the real political narrative in the theatre of a critical, realist mode.

Regarding next the purported 'infantilism' and 'victim mentality' of those who do not 'accept the universe', here we find another evident support of neoliberal ideology. In taking aim at avatars of 1960s idealism and the women's movement, Didion aims a transparently depoliticizing operation at the left. In fact, she *moralizes* in an interesting way, not in the sense of upholding a moral horizon, but of chastising people's characters in light of her frontier ethics. Regarding Joan Baez, for example, the implication seems to be that it is her subject's sentimental *character* that in some sense disqualifies 1960s *ideals* (Didion 2006: 39–51). To be fair, this is again not to be taken as evidence that Didion serves as an ideological prop in any *simple* way. Her moralizing is equal-opportunity, politically speaking; she also levelled the same kind of mean-spirited irony at Nancy Reagan (Didion 2006: 565–78; Didion 2021: 30–7), though we have to be sensitive to the fact that whenever one critiques 'both sides' on an unequal playing field, one is by no means rising above or calling the field itself into question.

Finally, I have already commented at some length on Didion's mishandling of the concept of 'privilege' (McLennan 2019), and briefly revisited the discussion in Chapter 2. To summarize, in *Blue Nights* Didion takes umbrage at critics suggesting that her daughter Quintana was 'privileged'. Since Quintana struggled with her health and addiction, for example, she did not lead a privileged life in Didion's eyes. My claim was that to call Quintana 'privileged' is not to say that she was happy, or content, or that she led a good or even a decent life. Rather, it is to make the simple point that even in the face of her difficulties she had advantages that others in her society did not enjoy – a claim that is demonstrably true, given even a cursory knowledge of her life. But since privilege is a strategic concept in envisioning and building a more just society, Didion's denial amounts to an ideological concession to the status quo. We see here an example of how the moves she makes in her memoir writing can depoliticize suffering and therefore blunt social criticism.

As hinted at earlier, however, all of this is far from being the whole story. Though her 'wagon train morality', her attack on 'victim mentality', and the piece about privilege are all important, I argue that Didion's memoirs at any rate resist falling in any neat way under Gilmore's notion of neoliberal life narrative. Centrally important to this claim is that through their pessimism *they resist redemption*. About Marguerite Duras, Julia Kristeva remarks that her writing 'encounters, recognizes, but also spreads the pain that summons it' (Kristeva 1989: 229), and I think this could equally describe Didion. The risk is always that spreading such pain can dampen hope and political energies, thereby serving ideology in a different, contrary way. But as I warn my students, often to their initial surprise, 'positive thinking' is ultimately more dangerous than a certain measure of pessimism. We are not yet, as per Stauffer's concept, in a world of 'meaningful human rights', which would require not just institutions but also *all* individuals, including innocent 'bystanders' to crimes against humanity, to build a world in which all people can 'trust that they and the people they love will be safe' (2015: 66–7). While we must hope for such a future as we build it, we cannot hope for it in an altogether *trusting* manner and this is why pessimists like Didion will continue to have a place on my syllabus.

Though her younger self arguably does deliver neoliberal life narrative themes in earlier essays like 'On Self Respect' and 'The Women's Movement', the later memoirs are ultimately corrosive to the very idea of overcoming adversity through one's own efforts. Even if *The Year of Magical Thinking* especially can be bent into a kind of oddly harsh and dispiriting self-help narrative, or, rather, a stark *warning* about the pitfalls of grief, *Blue Nights* is all but ruinous to the idea of overcoming our losses. Rather than demonstrating personal growth through her trauma and grief, Didion shows how we will be totally undone by what can one day happen to us. We are in charge of picking up the pieces, though it is unclear if this finally matters. What I have characterized as Didion's obstinacy or courage shines through in the difference between a pessimistic and a nihilistic outlook, *despite* what she suffers, not finally on account of it. One can easily imagine failure to make even the minimally ethical gesture of *saying* that I explored in Chapter 2, but Didion makes it.

I have already drawn attention to Gilmore's claims that neoliberal life narratives 'do not impose an ethical demand on readers'. She goes on to say that 'They focus on one's relation to one's self rather than to others. They focus on what one person can do, and they distill politics and social change to an *n* of one' (Gilmore 2018: 115). Certainly there is a risk of depoliticization in view of Didion's pessimism, but is this really what her texts on grieving are doing? Are they rather not more radical and, I have argued, philosophical? Do they not as such *precisely* impose an exorbitantly heavy ethical demand on the reader? In my interpretation Didion does *not* construct a redemptive ideological narrative in which just one person's efforts can change the world. On the contrary, she exemplifies through her very saying the kind of obstinacy, courage and other-regarding stance one has to embody if one is to even continue to *live* in that world.

If, finally, there is anything 'neoliberal' or 'depoliticizing' about the Didion of *The Year of Magical Thinking* and *Blue Nights*, this comes in the form of their resolute, metaphysical individualism, and their apparently pessimistic subsumption of the political to ethical. But as I have suggested throughout this book, this fact points to a limitation of Didion's writing, and perhaps an over-investment in the metaphysical loneliness of modernity, and not of the ethics of memory per se. Contemporary thinkers of memory like Gilmore, Stauffer, Butler, Hartman and others all point to ways in which such an ethics, to truly aspire to a moral register, must point beyond itself to broader and often elided social issues. But this focus entails a messy engagement with politics, of the type that Didion herself had notably begun before the events of her intimate life eventually pushed her towards what has been, at the time of writing, a period of relative silence. I am comfortable at this point in the argument to have depicted Didion as a kind of popular, philosophical path-breaker, offering more by way of questioning and provocation than she does by way of answers, in short, a particularly salient if limited teacher in a wider communal effort.

Conclusion

Joan Didion and the future: Philosophical unsettlement and the right to be forgotten

The promise of this book regarding the theme of 'the ethics of memory' was, first, to have offered a way of interpreting Joan Didion's vast and diverse body of works and, second, to have suggested her power as a moral or ethical teacher or exemplar. In the Introduction I declared the second aim to be the more important of the two. This was because of the salience of the ethics of memory for our uncertain times, and because we appear to need teachers or exemplars respecting it. Throughout, I noted some important limitations to handling Didion in this way: centrally, the error and danger of extrapolating too far, of prematurely holding her lessons up as universal or sufficient or directly applicable when she has built her world using colonial tropes and has engaged in both testimony and self-criticism from within a privileged social location.

With these caveats in mind, I have also stressed that there is a hypothetical aspect to this study: Didion points in many ways towards the memory ethics we need if we are to remain *resolutely but critically modern* – that is, to build the future in a universalistic manner while remaining attentive to particularity, to difference, to the peripheral; to engage in memory ethics without forgetting memory morality, and vice versa; to ward off mythical entrapment in versions of the past that will harm us, or push us to harm or forget harm to others; and finally, to keep our eyes focused on the political power-narratives happening underneath the froth. But, to repeat, Didion herself exemplifies this critical modernism in her memory ethics only insofar as she has been socially permitted to practice it, and this suggests nothing less than a critical appropriation of her works welded to a programme for intellectual self-defence and social transformation.

How can we build a world in which we *all* have the same facility in getting down to the business of grieving? Of understanding and tracking the narratives that compose us as well as the distances we take from them? Of philosophizing over our losses, our regrets, even perhaps, gaining a non-deluded strength from our genuinely warm and sustaining memories? It may sound counterintuitive, but if we retain *veracity* as a driving ethical category and an important social value, then we will have to knock down barriers not just to knowledge in any positivistic sense, but also to *philosophical unsettlement*;[1] at issue here is the equitable opportunity for becoming unsettled and exploring our unsettlement, for considering the *elsewhere* that the truth might be found, for answering the call to philosophize that makes itself heard in most people, at least at some point in their lives. Quite apart from its being personally and socially useful, such unsettlement, I suggested in *Philosophy and Vulnerability*, can often express itself in terms of a deeply felt human need. The possibility I have kept in mind throughout is that Didion's works, in combination with those of others, could contribute to such a programme.

We have seen that striving for resolute but critical modernity requires fortitude and obstinacy, especially in the face of a pessimistic assessment of the universe. The same can be said of philosophy more generally, since as I argued in 2019, it trades not just in wonder but also in the pain of our human finitude. A key barrier here is material; there is a point of immiseration, evidently different for different people, where our philosophical inclinations can be snuffed out. I am *not* saying that the poor and the oppressed lack courage or fortitude; often they acquire it precisely on *account* of what they must deal with in their lives, though this is not to say either that their journeys amount to 'neoliberal life narratives' in Gilmore's sense. Indeed, in *Philosophy and Vulnerability* I cited my students in the Discovery University programme as testimony to this fact.[2] What I *am* saying is that a culture of opportunity for philosophical unsettlement should be one aim of a more encompassing vision of social justice, where material barriers to practising and developing it are overcome. And crucially, through the critical thinking it fosters, prefigurative moments of philosophical unsettlement, in the classroom and beyond, can themselves contribute to such a comprehensive programme. On the strength of her philosophical potency and the questions she raises, Didion may absolutely figure in such moments as part of a broader conversation.

Notably, however, such a presumption to equalize chances for philosophical unsettlement does not require total deference to the other basic ingredient of memory ethics, namely the ideal of *comprehensiveness*. Social justice does not have to mean, for example, that everyone becomes a searcher after truth, philosophical or otherwise. It just means that everyone has the genuine opportunity to,[3] and a host of other genuine opportunities, unhindered by material and structural barriers. And as we explored in Chapter 3, it also certainly does not mean that an unvarnished, totalizing look on the past is always a good thing.

Recently I thought about someone I once briefly knew, who made an impression on me and whom I have not seen in several years. I searched him online, and it turns out he lives in a jurisdiction where mugshots and arrest records are made public. More than half a dozen mugshots of him appear at the top of the search engine's list in connection with his name. I am instantly given a window onto his personal issues. He is haggard and obviously unwell. I see the pattern of his arrests, weigh it against the interactions I had with him, and I hazard a guess that there are significant mental health issues in the mix. All of this happens very quickly; no great effort on my part was required to get a sense of how his life has been going, simply to satisfy my curiosity in a bored moment.

By searching him and immediately finding him, I suppose I demonstrated the relative utility of our increasingly web-based and archived lives, with respect to memory – though as I have stated, really the only utility in this case lies in the satisfaction of my curiosity. What other purpose does this serve – his face on the internet, connected to his arrests, permanently on record for everyone to see? What is gained from putting this information out there, down to the very image of his seeming unwellness?

The point as I see it is obviously the shaming, humiliation and pre-emptive as well as permanent punishment of arrested individuals. Since the pictures are not tied, at least at the time they are posted, to any legal convictions, then, they raise an issue of justice: since shaming and humiliation are negatively impactful, then clearly a form of punishment already occurs here, outside of, before and even after the procedure of the courts. Barring further knowledge, for instance about his mental health and his chances of recidivism, it would also be a stretch to say that the community, let alone people on the internet worldwide, are kept safe by notifying them of his arrests in this way. I do not even live anywhere close to his community, but in searching him I am also instantly given access to knowledge about *anyone's* arrest where he lives. Along with his pictures, dozens of others appear of people I have never known. To repeat, this seems problematic from the perspective of both justice and of utility. It is quite clearly a question of pre-emptive and permanent punishment as retribution, in the form of shaming and humiliating.

It seems to me that a robust memory ethics of truth and relative comprehensiveness, as I have often drawn from Didion in these pages, therefore misses something important about my former acquaintance's case. While posting mugshots or other permanent records of alleged wrongdoing preserves something of the past, right down to the bloodshot eyes of the arrested person, this is not obviously a good thing. Shaming and humiliating some of its own members as policy, quite the contrary, is corrosive to ethics and renders a society 'indecent' as per Margalit (2007).[4] Humiliation in particular, as Margalit theorizes, communicates that the humiliated party is less than fully human, which he (problematically, to be sure) interprets in terms of being less than fully, which is to say morally, autonomous.[5] In posting a permanent record of an alleged transgression we treat someone implicitly as irredeemable. But to be irredeemable is on this view to be less than fully human; therefore, on the strength of this example alone, we have to consider the possibility that some forms of remembrance *dehumanize*.[6]

As we saw in connection with forgiveness, it can make sense to speak of a presumption to 'forget', or, more accurately, to stop revisiting the site of painful memories for one's own good, and for the good of the community. We cannot actually forget on purpose, but with the exceptions of moral transgressions and betrayals, a rule of 'forgive and forget', where we refuse to nourish resentment and feelings of vengeance by actively remembering, might be the appropriate way to go in many cases of transgression. The problem, of course, is that the internet makes it much harder to respect this rule. If I am on social media, I may, for example, engage in a form of 'digital self-harm' by scrolling through pictures of my ex-lover who wronged me and his/her/their new partner, constantly refreshing my resentment and my regrets. But more to the point, once on the internet, mugshots may keep alive a vision of the arrested person as flawed, bad, antisocial, a potential perpetrator and wrongdoer well beyond the point where his/her/their life may have actually been sorted out. In this connection, we might even defer to the person's moral autonomy as overriding whatever good could be had from keeping the permanent record publicly available. A 'right to be forgotten'[7] could be invoked, at least in certain cases.[8]

But if the internet poses a challenge to 'forgive and forget' by keeping past transgressions and alleged transgressions available for the whole world to see, then the increasing employment of automated and fine-grained rendering and predictive technologies, typical of 'surveillance capitalism' (Zuboff 2019), poses an additional problem. Wherever algorithms are employed to predict the future based upon past behavioural data, this can have life-altering consequences for individuals – for instance, those who are caught in the criminal justice system. As information scientists and other scholars have pointed out, 'garbage in' means 'garbage out'; in other words, if predictive algorithms are based upon already biased patterns, such as the intuitions and prejudices of programmers, then they will feed back and amplify such biases, ultimately widening inequalities and narrowing if not foreclosing individuals' life chances (O'Neill 2017; Noble 2018; Eubanks 2019; Trites 2019). Moreover, the ambition to completely render, predict and, ultimately, *control* human behaviour based upon people's past behaviours, whether for political or commercial purposes or both, raises the specter of an inhumane and nightmarish administrative post-politics (Zuboff 2019). Such a scenario would be a hypertrophic version of mandatory consensus Didion already sketched in *Political Fictions*, but to the point of foreclosing politics altogether.

A right to be forgotten then, both in the sense of having a fighting chance to have one's relatively minor transgressions forgiven by the community, and in the sense of not having one's future foreclosed by tools like predictive software, is tied to the right to an open future, indeed, the very *right to the future tense* as Zuboff describes it. As she states, 'Uncertainty is not chaos but rather the necessary habitat of the present tense' (2019: 337). Put differently, being fully and truly in the present, living a genuinely human life, means living with uncertainty, which itself entails the future *qua* horizon of possibility. This is not a technical or technological problem to be solved but is, rather, indicative of our very moral autonomy. If the future is beholden to the past, as I have implied it is throughout the book, then this cannot amount to the claim that the future be foreclosed, that we should henceforth inhabit a kind of 'technological immemorial' replacing the 'natural', 'tropical' one of Didion's imagining. It indicates not memory ethics as a potentially dystopian dream of total transparency, but, rather, memory ethics as a thoroughly *human* endeavour, respecting the opacities and uncertainties without which our lives will become unrecognizable.

What, finally, does all of this really have to do with Didion? Recall my claim that she is an exemplar, a kind of philosophical teacher with respect to memory ethics. While from one perspective this is not saying very much, it is also saying a great deal. Precisely on account of the urgency of issues like the preceding, we would do well to encounter obstinate philosophical thinkers for whom memory and its norms form an organizing theme. Finally, perhaps, and not unconnected to the issue of a putative right to be forgotten, Didion's works may be mined for a double lesson, perhaps somewhat against the grain of her pessimism. We are duty-bound to destroy, root and branch, the *myths* of our goodness. But we are also duty-bound to remember, for as far into the future as human memory extends, the *actual goodness* of which we are capable.

Notes

Introduction

1. Throughout the book, I will frequently refer to 'public memory' and 'communities'. This will be important because a major claim of the book is that Didion helps us to find our way or at least steel ourselves in a situation where public memory, and hence the communities that constitute themselves through it, are coming apart. I do not understand either, however, to be fixed or entirely coherent entities; public memory need not be and probably is never empirically universally valid among a given population, and there are no communities in any essentialist sense. Rather, I grant Ernesto Laclau's and Chantal Mouffe's concept of 'contaminated universality', in brief the view according to which hegemonic, empirical communities exist but 'no social identity is ever totally acquired' (Laclau and Mouffe 2014: xiii, 128), whenever I discuss public memory. I concur with Laclau and Mouffe that there is no society which is completely internally coherent – a greater or lesser element of antagonism always remains – but there is always a balance of power, and this determines both public memory and the community that understands itself on the basis of it. The claim that a given community may 'contest' its relation to the past means that it engages in an 'agonistic' confrontation between people who consider themselves members of the same community. At the limit, contesting the community's relation to the past may break into open antagonism, which in principle could result in the splitting of the community into two or more communities. I am interested mostly in the 'ethics' of memory, not the 'politics' of memory, but in the later chapters especially I will have occasion to explore the connections and hence the arguably uncertain division between the two.
2. In *Philosophy and Vulnerability* (McLennan 2019), I claim that philosophy is for most people, at some point in their life, a vital existential activity. I also make the case that this activity is bound up with vulnerability and inherently requires broad social support and nourishment. While I will not comment further on this here, it would be fair to say that for me the 'so what' and 'who cares' questions are always social and political in nature, touching as they do upon the support required to pursue a vital activity.

3 Murdoch's point of view, in which I may better my mental standing towards someone through fair and devoted attention, belongs in the Platonic tradition according to which evil is a kind of failure, specifically a failure of focus or 'attention' upon the good. But it is possible that not all ethically dubious or unethical acts, mental or otherwise, are failures in this sense. What if I claim to repudiate the good as such (something Plato denied being possible) and accordingly adopt an actively negative attitude or behaviours? This resonates with Terry Eagleton's description of evil as 'metaphysical, in the sense that it takes up an attitude toward being as such, not just toward this or that bit of it. Fundamentally, it wants to annihilate the lot of it' (Eagleton 2010: 16). Tying this observation in to the ethics of memory sheds light upon phenomena like the Nazi destruction of documentation of the Final Solution, where it was a matter of erasing not just the actual Jews, Roma, homosexuals, disabled, Slavs and communists themselves, but also the very memory of their erasure.

4 Though I do take researching and writing very seriously, it is not hard to come up with higher-stakes examples along these lines. My children were born four years apart, and when my youngest son was born, I was presented with the choice of re-installing and reusing various baby safety gear either 'from memory', or after rereading the instructions (in addition to checking, not without a certain suspicion of planned obsolescence, if items were now recalled, obsolete or considered substandard). I chose the latter option, on the understanding that *even if I was confident in my ability to remember* – which I was – it would be in some sense unethical not to check. The specific sense in which this use of memory would be unethical would involve the risks it would implicitly judge as acceptable when it came to my youngest son.

5 Elsewhere, I have commented on Margalit's limitations with respect to who belongs in the ethical as well as the wider moral community. Being a broadly Kantian thinker, he accords non-human animals only indirect or honorary ethical and moral status; as such, a theme that I develop and challenge him on is that of our norms of public remembrance to non-human animals (McLennan 2018b).

6 Margalit rightly points out that 'Memory is veridical: if you remember p, then p is true' (2017: 73). This is the aforementioned 'cognitive' aspect of memory examined by Ricœur (2006). But Margalit also warns that 'what is shared in shared memory is hardly veridical, especially when the shared memory involves many individuals' (Margalit 2017: 73). As he describes it, 'Shared collective memory is in many cases a shared memory of an alleged memory . . . . But even when it is veridical, shared collective memory is shrouded in a fusion of facts and

fiction' (2017: 74). Annie Ernaux nicely describes this in terms of the 'collective novel' written by her community members through oral gossip (1997: 66). At the limit, 'Shared collective memory of the past is more a memory of past memory than a memory of a veridical event' (Margalit 2017: 74). All this has interesting implications for the discussion of nationalism, and Margalit underscores some of these. The important point is that the further out we stray from the very thickest of one's relations, the more stress is put on the cognitive aspect of memory, and therefore, arguably, the more pressing the ethical question of memory becomes.

Here again, Ricœur supplements the discussion in an illuminating way, providing a category that would help us distinguish between different levels of thick relations. Between 'the living memory of individual persons and the public memory of the communities to which we belong,' he posits 'the level of our close relations, to whom we have a right to attribute a memory of a distinct kind' (2006: 132–3). My *close relations* differ from the wider community because in a lived sense, they grow old with me. They are those for whom both my birth and my death are of particular importance – whereas for society at large, these may only be of demographic interest. What happens in between these events is also important to my close relations in a way that, for the broader community, it is likely not. As Ricœur put it, 'my close relations are those who approve of my existence and whose existence I approve of in the reciprocity and equality of esteem . . . what I expect from [them] is that they approve of what I attest: that I am able to speak, act, recount, impute to myself the responsibility for my actions' (2006: 132). Close relations may therefore be critical of me, but in a constrained sense: 'I include among my close relations those who disapprove of my actions, but not of my existence' (2006). In sum, close relations seem linked to me, and have a particular stake in the veridical nature of our shared memories, in a way that the wider community is not.

7 Perhaps a limit-case of what I have in mind here is in Huebner (2006). Huebner illustrates the communal nature of memory by connecting the thick relations of the Mennonite church with his grandmother's Alzheimer's disease:

> In the church we are called to be materially present to one another. But what I want us to consider is that this is at the very same time to be memorially present to each other as well. The church is not merely a context in which we share our bodies with one another. It is a context in which we provide each other with memories as well . . .
>
> If memory is detached from the concrete practices and embodied habits that define the church as a particular kind of community, a body, then

> we abandon victims of Alzheimer's disease to a long and painful process of solitary destruction. But if memory can be understood as a skill that is shared and schooled in the context of the entire community, then Alzheimer's need not represent a kind of permanent excommunication from the church . . .
>
>> much of what is problematic is the very idea of remembering as something that is done by individuals, whether they are Alzheimer's patients or not. It is not autonomous individuals who remember. Rather, memory is a function of the entire community, the body of Christ. (2006: 173–5)
>
> I owe a debt of gratitude to Jason Peters for gifting me this remarkable text many years ago. I also owe gratitude to my mom for tracking down, photographing and texting the pages I vaguely remembered but needed to reread, stored away in my old room in the home I once shared with her. I am no expert on the Mennonite church, but I believe that taken as a general claim, Huebner overstates the community's preeminence. His point is in any case nicely illustrated through the help I received from others in order to write 'my' book.

8   Note finally that it is also possible, as in the case of the scientific or broader international scholarly community, to stand in a moral but not necessarily ethical relation to one's peers, relating purely through rational discussion and abstract respect. See Kant 1983 and Margalit, 2002: 145–6.

9   Margalit's distinction between ethics and morality belongs to a broadly Kantian tradition in moral philosophy. It finds contemporary echoes, for example in Habermas (1990a).

10 Members of morally unconstrained communities usually feel that, overall, they are moral people. This is because taking care of 'one's own' often requires sacrifices and can provide a sense of purpose, even nobility. As Margalit puts it, 'The unselfishness of ethical individuals, in an ethical and immoral society, gives them the illusion that they belong to a moral order, since they identify morality with individual unselfishness' (2010: 123). This short-circuiting of morality is, of course, a barrier to building morally better communities. It might also explain to some extent the extreme reactions, incomprehension and overall 'fragility' of individuals who are called to be morally better in the current climate – for example, white people being challenged to acknowledge their own racism and the part they play in structural racism (DiAngelo 2018).

11 Margalit bases his definition of the moral community upon moral autonomy, cashed out in terms of the presumption that each human being has the capacity to radically change his or her life, that is, to start over and do better, morally

speaking (2007: 72–6). I have commented (McLennan 2018b) on how this broadly Kantian definition of the moral community by Margalit creates problems in terms of how to include sentient human beings with apparently diminished moral autonomy. I agree with Margalit that such humans should be included fully in the moral community. But if he lends them an honorary status *despite* his autonomy criterion, then this raises the question of why non-human animals, many of whom are sentient but also lack moral autonomy, should be excluded on his view.

12 I am using the word 'transgressions' loosely here, but for Margalit, 'betrayal' has a specific sense that ties into memory. For Margalit, 'Only when the harm and the offense serve as good reasons for questioning the meaning of the thick relation can we talk of betrayal' (2017: 83). I will discuss this idea at some length in Chapter 3.

13 An indispensable resource on moral repair following crimes against humanity is Jill Stauffer's *Ethical Loneliness* (2015). Drawing extensively from the phenomenological tradition, Stauffer describes 'ethical loneliness' as 'the experience of being abandoned by humanity compounded by the experience of not being heard' (2015: 9). She goes on to describe 'meaningful human rights' in terms of receiving reassurance that we are, indeed, after all 'living in a world with others, one where [we] will be protected when [we] are under threat' (2015: 67). This reassurance obviously entails that our stories of abuse be heard, that they are recognized and included and thus that we are recognized and brought back into the wider community. Stauffer's vision is thus revealing for an account of 'the ethics of memory', inasmuch as it foregrounds narrative practice and listening.

14 There is a sequence in the television adaptation of Margaret Atwood's *The Handmaid's Tale* that illustrates this point perfectly. The series takes place in a dystopian near future. In the episode 'Unwomen', protagonist June is on the run from her fascist captors, who exemplify the idea of 'ethics without moral constraint'. She hides out in the abandoned headquarters of the *Boston Globe*, and finds evidence that the former employees of the newspaper were executed there. All alone, she sets up a memorial to them using their personal effects and prays for them. This gesture could be construed as something of a message in a bottle, wherein June transmits evidence to future witnesses that the moral perspective has survived here, holding all persecuted human strangers in its embrace even in the darkest of times. But even assuming for the sake of argument that her gesture will never be received by anyone, she has, nonetheless, through it reconstituted her commitment to her own humanity. Iris Murdoch's previously discussed point about purely 'internal' actions resonates here: even if June's gesture had had no

outward form, it could still be judged as ethically salutary on account of what it affirms or centres.

15 I take for granted here Wendy Brown's analyses of neoliberalism as a distinct antidemocratic mode of governance that refashions subjectivity (Brown 2015), as well as its tendency in recent years to buckle under the strain of the political, cultural and moral reactions it has unleashed (Brown 2019).

16 Brown (2015) is a key source on 'responsibilization' of individuals through the imposition of neoliberal governance. The basic idea here is that individuals are increasingly and unreasonably burdened with responsibility for their life outcomes. Melissa Cooper (2019) nuances this idea by showing how in the United States, public responsibility has devolved more and more to immediate families and to private religious institutions and programmes. A good further resource on what Brown calls responsibilization is Yascha Mounk (2019).

17 This retreat has been noted, using different terms, in the embattled field of human rights. See Brysk (2018).

18 See Habermas (1990a) for an exploration of the link between discourse ethics, social pragmatics and the personal development of the moral point of view. Like Margalit, Habermas cleaves to a basically Kantian account opposing morality to ethics, and he construes the moral point of view as a relatively abstract one predicated upon the child's embeddedness in an ethical community. Habermas builds his account from a developmental tradition in morality stemming from Piaget and Kohlberg.

19 In taking a normative stance on uncritical indulgence in nostalgia, I assume here that the person or community in question *has the option* of remembering in a fairly comprehensive way. Historically oppressed persons often do not have this option, because, for example, their cultures and communities were targeted for assimilation or broken apart through terror. As such, their engagement with the past, searching for better times – even when this borders on 'fabulation' – may be judged in a more nuanced way. I will address this issue in Chapter 3, where Saidiya Hartman and her concept of 'critical fabulation' will be in play.

20 A comprehensive account of Canada's colonial and imperial history, and the myths that have obscured it, is given in Shipley (2020).

21 See Hartman (2007: 91–8). Hartman's case study, highly pertinent to what I am saying here, is the short-lived slave rebellion on St. John in 1733.

22 As Devin Zane Shaw points out in a different context (Shaw 2016), the very fact of addressing someone and exhorting him/her to understand you or to do something implies a recognition of that person's equal basic intelligence. This is true even of authoritarian communications of the type 'You must do as I

say' or 'You are not worth as much as I am'. Such tacit recognition of equality, if we put store in the worth of intelligence, further implies the equal *value* of that person. At the limit, as we will see later discussing Margalit's (2007) notion of humiliation, even a (non-pathological) dehumanization of another person recognizes the humanity, hence the equal value, of the humiliated. In Didion, as in any 'conservative' or 'libertarian' writer, there is precisely such an implicit expansion of normative scope beyond the narrowly personal sphere of close relations. For her part, she explicitly recognizes the 'intrinsic worth' of her readers.

23 Though largely skirting academia, Didion was schooled in New Criticism as an undergraduate at Berkeley, and had occasion to reflect upon this legacy when she returned as a visiting scholar.

24 Notice what happens if we take the earlier Didion strictly at her word, that is, that meaning is elusive and fragmentary. Does she mean this, or not? Do we understand what she is saying, or not? This is equivalent to refusing to find coherent meaning in her texts and thus, in a sense, we are led to refuse to take her at her word that meaning is elusive and fragmentary. This wraps us in circles. It would thus be better, I think, to simply recognize that there are good reasons, both within and without her text, to approach her in a creative and appropriative fashion. What I am describing here might sound like a particularly freewheeling approach to an author, but it amounts to little more than working with Didion as philosophers in general tend to do with their sources, at least on my interpretation of philosophical activity. There is meaning in her texts, but probably more than one meaning, and perhaps even more or other meanings than she may have intended. This opens up possibilities and accounts for why philosophizing with texts can be at once *difficult* and highly compelling, even *exhilarating*.

Chapter 1

1 Roughly, drawing my working definition of modernity from Habermas (1990b), I am interested in the fact that Didion's works express and to some extent nuance or challenge a disenchanted philosophical outlook, expressed in terms of a largely future-oriented and instrumental time-consciousness. The question of how to classify Didion in literary terms is interesting but is not my concern here.

2 As Inez Victor states in Didion's novel *Democracy*, even being tough 'never stopped any plane from crashing' (Didion 1995: 205). The risk of framing us as

equally vulnerable to the universe in this way is that it masks social inequalities. We see this in the COVID-19 pandemic, where claims that the virus is 'an equal opportunity killer' or that we are 'all in the same boat' mask disproportionate infection and death rates, for instance, along the lines of race and class. As for Didion, I discuss her missteps on privilege in McLennan (2019), and I offer further commentary on this issue in Chapter 2.

3 There is evidence in Didion to the effect that the weather *in general* shapes a person's outlook and self-understanding, which leaves room for a self-conscious scepticism about the universalizability of her own view. In the bargain, this gives a further reason to be careful about ascribing any 'metaphysics' to Didion herself. Driving through Oxford, Mississippi, she describes how 'the wind came up, sudden and violent, and the sky darkened and there was thunder but no rain. I was afraid of a tornado. The suddenness and unpredictability of this shocked me. The weather around here must shape ideas of who and what one is, *as it does everywhere*' (Didion 2017: 85–6, emphasis added). And elsewhere: 'Well, I grew up in a dangerous landscape. I think people are more affected than they know by landscapes and weather . . . . Those extremes affect the way you deal with the world. It so happens that if you're a writer the extremes show up. They don't if you sell insurance' (Parker 2018: 49).

4 Joseph Conrad is a frequent point of reference in Didion, and, in fact, the novel *Heart of Darkness* is briefly referred to in the same essay where she speaks of 'the heart of darkness . . . in man's blood' (Didion 2006: 329).

5 Didion confirms what struck me as the oddity of studying 'shopping-center theory': 'One thing you will note about shopping-center theory is that you could have thought of it yourself, and a course in it will go a long way toward dispelling the notion that business proceeds from mysteries too recondite for you and me' (Didion 2006: 314).

6 I am highly sceptical of the idea that anyone would bother *arguing* for nihilism, as though it is important, in its *passive* sense; there is no good reason to spread the bad news, unless one's intention is simply to pass the time, or to actively destroy.

7 Granting that there is a difference between psychiatric evaluation and 'analysis', Didion's inclusion of part of her psychiatric evaluation is of interest considering the comments she makes elsewhere:

> at one point I would have described myself as a neurotic . . . . I don't know now. I really don't think in terms of neurosis. I think in terms of only extreme psychosis and normal. I mean or you're getting along all right . . . . I actually wouldn't want to go into analysis because if I found out too much

about myself I might stop working, which is more important to me than being good at a dinner party (Parker 2018: 8).

8 Lumping Laski's revolutionary communism in with other 'opiates' hearkens back to Marx. Marx claims in the Introduction to *A Contribution to the Critique of Hegel's Philosophy of Right* that 'Religious suffering is, at one and the same time, the expression of real suffering and a protest against real suffering. Religion is the sigh of the oppressed creature, the heart of a heartless world, and the soul of soulless conditions. It is the opium of the people' (1843). No Marxist herself, it is likely Didion is being ironical here. But there is a substantive point to make: Marxism *qua* philosophy and *qua* method is a rigorous but *open* system, not a closed 'religious' or 'paranoid' system of the type apparently exemplified by Laski's communism.

9 It is suggestive that when she sketches the dispositional roots of her writerly focus on particularity, Didion recounts failing to concentrate on 'the Hegelian dialectic' (Didion 2021).

10 The suppression of truth as surprise or exception also accounts for the unremittingly *boring* quality of dialogue with dogmatists, conspiracy theorists and proselytizers.

11 Note that 'redemptive wilderness' is an idea that should sound foreign to Didion, if my interpretation along the lines of 'earthquake weather' has been convincing. I think, however, it is possible to square this idea with 'earthquake weather' by noting, first, that it belongs 'to the western imagination', not necessarily Didion's own imagination – an interesting possibility, in which she signals her critical irony with respect to her formative community – and second, that Didion evidently modulates her anxiety through fixation on the possibility of *redeeming nature*, for instance, through infrastructure projects or cultivating flowers. Her position with respect to the natural world, though fraught, is by no means uniformly negative.

12 Didion presciently notes that most American southerners 'are political realists: they understand and accept the realities of working politics in a way we never did in California' (2017: 71).

13 We will see in Chapter 2 that a certain modernity, to which Didion ascribes at a critical distance, expresses itself through a focus on the future and an erasure of the past – up to and including a denial of death, and a muting of funerary memorialization. The South is in this sense something of an exception. Driving through Mississippi, Didion describes 'the graveyards everywhere . . . . Death is still natural and ever present in the South, as it is no more in those urbanized parts of the country where graveyards are burial parks and relegated to unused or unusable land far from sight' (2017: 80–1).

14 See Lyotard (2001) for a philosophical and aesthetic study of Malraux emphasizing the theme of the infernal, immemorial cycle. It is revealing how in Malraux (1970), Mao Tse-Tung's modernizing revolution is almost incredulously received, his personal aura almost mythically described, because of his having supposedly wrenched a monolithic 'immemorial' society into the industrial age.

15 An arresting image of Grenada, Mississippi, comes in the form of 'a five-year-old in baseball pajamas playing catch with a black maid in a white uniform, the ball going back and forth, back and forth, suspended in amber' (Didion 2017: 83). The ball is moving, so in what sense is it 'suspended in amber?' Possibly in the sense of suggesting the Southern air's sultriness and thickness, but more interestingly perhaps through the activity's very futility, its motionlessness via cyclical character. Note further that in this sense, *the whole scene* is likewise 'suspended in amber', an artefact of unequal, gendered race relations in the US whose dismal presence, perhaps, goads the writer into recording it.

16 Sara Davidson paints a revealing picture of Didion's process working on the book:

> Her office is a chamber in which to dream waking dreams. There are props and cue cards. While she worked on *A Book of Common Prayer* a map of Central America hung on the wall. Set out on a table were postcards from Columbia, a newspaper photo of a janitor mopping up blood in a Caribbean hotel, books on tropical foliage and tropical medicine and a Viasa Airlines schedule with 'Maracaibo-Paris' circled in blue. 'Maracaibo-Paris – I thought those were probably the perimeters of the book,' Joan Didion said. (Parker 2018: 21)

17 Recall again that in 'Why I Write', Didion depicts herself as incapable of concentrating on Hegel. I think she understands rather more of him than she lets on, the use of the term 'contradictions' here alluding to his dialectical account of history (or to Marxist variants thereof, which penetrated Latin American liberation movements). Hegel himself describes nature as the most external, remote, almost intractable element of his system; see Hegel (2004).

Chapter 2

1 See Wittgenstein 2001 for the classic argument against the notion of a 'private language'. One, indeed, lives in the world phenomenologically, from a first-person perspective, but this perspective is enmeshed, 'at home' so to speak, in

language. Ricœur describes how 'In its declarative phase, memory enters into the region of language; memories spoken of, pronounced are already a kind of discourse that the subject engages in with herself. What is pronounced in this discourse occurs in the common language, most often in the mother tongue, which, it must be said, is the language of others' (2006: 129).

Further in this vein, Annie Ernaux describes the languages or idioms of her youth as those that 'constituted' her (1997: 40). They prescribed 'uses of the world' that she and her parents held in common, which is to say, 'what one should do with one's body and with things' (1997: 58, my translation). Interestingly, the existence of these languages also poses a *challenge* to memory; elsewhere, Ernaux despairs of reconstructing all the languages composing the 'inner discourse' of her girlhood (Ernaux 2016: 33).

2 Keep in mind Ricœur's (2006) distinction between memory in the active and in the passive sense. I may have experiences tied to memory and forgetting, for example, the return of a traumatic memory, in a seemingly *passive* mode. Whether or not these are guided, provoked or determined as salient in any way by public norms – as opposed to, say, my neurological and psycho-sexual history – is an interesting but separate question that I will bracket for reasons of scope.

3 Annie Ernaux describes how, as per Proust, our memory is anchored 'outside of us', for example, in the regularities of nature that produce feelings of security and identity over time. But she despairs in her own case, and perhaps that of her entire generation:

> For me – and perhaps for everyone from my era – for whom memories are attached to a hit summer song, a belt that was in fashion, to things that are destined to disappear, memory furnishes no proof of my permanence nor of my identity. It makes me feel and confirms for me my fragmentation and my historicity. (Ernaux 1997: 102, my translation)

Elsewhere, she makes the revealing comment that her memories prior to 1968 are in black and white, and then after that, in colour: 'Hasn't memory followed the passage of film and television from black and white to colour?' (Ernaux 2000: 105).

4 We could even hearken back here to Margalit's specific sense of 'ethics of memory', and propose that phenomenological aspects aside, talk of 'private' memory is just a way of referring to memories at the level of our very thickest relations. Indeed, this is reflected in the contestable notion that the family is in some sense a truly 'private' sphere. As Maurice Halbwachs points out (1980: 33, 41), childhood memories – usually considered to be the most intimate, because formative – are usually not simple impressions, but, in fact, are awash in a social

5. There is a vast literature supporting the notion that autonomy is in some sense real, but that it supervenes upon community and the supportive environment. As a father to two young children, I am partial to D. W. Winnicott's and John Bowlby's writings in this vein; see Winnicott 1991, 2006; Bowlby 2005a, 2005b.

6. Regarding the substantial question – *am* I really the same person I remember being? – I quite like the answer Ernaux gives in *Mémoire de fille*:

> That girl there in 1958, who fifty years on is still capable of rising up and provoking an interior debacle, has therefore a hidden presence, irreducible in me. If the real is, according to the dictionary definition, what acts and produces effects, then this girl is not me, but is real in me. A kind of *real presence*. (2016: 23, my translation, emphasis in original)

7. Elsewhere, Ernaux describes her relation to her past selves using the metaphor of Russian nesting dolls: even if she 'prefers herself now', the remembered self, towards which she is indifferent, remains present, nested in with 'millions' of others (2001: 99–100).

8. Interested readers may pursue this discussion in McLennan 2020, where I explore the breakdown of personal identity through dementia and age-related 'decline' as a conceptual and ethical issue for Simone de Beauvoir.

9. I hope I will be forgiven for citing the 2005 and 2007 versions of *The Year of Magical Thinking* interchangeably, since I am above all interested in reconstructing Didion's doubly ethical gesture involved in recounting her grief, as I will describe. This is something that remains consistent between the two versions.

    I am aware that there are important differences between the book and the play; notably, the play debuted after and recounts Quintana's death, which did not figure in the book. In this respect, it would be interesting to look at the play on its own, as a bridge between *Magical Thinking* 2005, and *Blue Nights*, in which Didion recounts events surrounding the play.

10. Interestingly, because of her guilt, Didion also veers hard the other way in a similarly magical mode. She is faced with the fact of the time lag between 10.05 pm when the ambulance left her building, and 10.18 pm when John is officially pronounced dead: 'I had to believe he was dead all along. If I did not believe he was dead all along I would have thought I should have been able to save him. Until I saw the autopsy report I continued to think this anyway, an example of delusionary thinking, the omnipotent variety' (Didion 2005: 22).

11 In a beautiful passage, arguably the climax of the memoir, Didion opens the door a crack to self-pity:

> It is the blight *man* was born for.
>
> We are not idealized wild things.
>
> We are imperfect mortal beings, aware of that mortality even as we push it away, failed by our very complication, so wired that when we mourn our losses we also mourn, for better or for worse, for ourselves. As we were. As we are no longer. As we will one day not be at all. (Didion 2005: 198, emphasis in original)

12 It is possible, as per Nelson's suggestion (2017: 172), that *Blue Nights* will be the last 'new' work by Didion, who is 86 years old at the time of writing. Since its publication, *South and West* has appeared (Didion 2017), but it revisits a travel notebook and essay from the 1970s. Similarly, the collection *Let Me Tell You What I Mean*, appearing in early 2021, gathers previously uncollected essays. Since *Blue Nights*, Didion has not been altogether silent, however. She has appeared in interviews and in her nephew Griffin Dunne's documentary *Joan Didion: The Center Will Not Hold* (2017).

13 Nelson notes how in *Blue Nights*, Didion abandons style – fearing, in fact, that this new absence of style is imposed, 'systemic', tied to her newfound frailty (Nelson 2017: 172; Didion 2011: 110–1). She intimates that this loss of style, and the letting-in of self-pity, is the end of Didion as the public has come to know her:

> her momentum is arrested. Didion is not going anywhere. And in fact, the memoir predicts that she never will. Entwined with Quintana's narrative is that of Didion herself – remorseful mother, grieving mother, an aging and frail woman, in the dyadic form of autobiography. It predicts that without her style and emotional hardness, Didion will dwell on it for the rest of her life. (Nelson 2017: 172)

Nelson makes much of Didion's style as a function of her moral outlook, and vice versa. She goes so far as to claim that Didion's 'sense of morality and her sense of style . . . cannot be separated' (2017: 151). While my own comments on the issue of style will be minimal in this book, I concur that it should be grasped in conjunction with ethics, in the broad sense, including how ethics wrestles with emotion. To highlight this function of style in Didion, in *Philosophy and Vulnerability* I made a quick comparison with Marguerite Duras. There the claim was that

> At the risk of oversimplifying, Didion would thus be something of an American counterpart to Marguerite Duras, whose 'Stylistic awkwardness would be the discourse of dulled pain' (Kristeva 1989: 226). Like Duras's, Didion's writing 'encounters, recognizes, but also spreads the pain that summons it' (Kristeva 1989: 229). This it does, as I have suggested, for eminently ethical reasons: Didion spares no one's feelings, not even her own, in her duty-bound quest for the unvarnished delivery of the truth. (McLennan 2019: 80)

14 Recall Didion's claim in 'Why I Write' (2021) that the writer is a 'secret bully'. If all writers are bullies, an important distinction is that Didion thinks she does it for our own good. But interestingly, another difference is that in doing so, she lays her cards on the table, revealing the 'secret' both explicitly and through her style. As Nelson claims, 'The truthfulness of style lies not only in the accurate reporting of particularity but in a syntactical candor about its own aggression' (2017: 155). Perhaps my favourite example of such transparent aggression in Didion, admittedly not in her 'reporting' but in the novel *Democracy*, is when she begins a chapter: 'See it this way' (1995: 75).

15 Brown (2015) is a good resource for understanding how neoliberalism, often construed as a quintessentially modern logic of governance on account of its economism and financialization of everyday life, actually functions with the help of religious and moral-political 'supplements', such as the imperative to 'sacrifice' (215–6). Brown (2019) pursues this line of thinking to the point of demonstrating how neoliberalism's supplements or excesses serve to undermine it in the current conjuncture.

We will see that Urbain's analysis of modern, Western death and dying practices links up nicely with critiques of neoliberalism as a mode of governance. Under neoliberalism, I am in general *responsibilized*, in the sense of disciplined to believe that I am radically responsible for how my life goes (Brown 2015). As for life, so for death: if I die, then I should have taken better care of myself, made better choices. The logical extension of this kind of thinking is the often-cultish pursuit of 'wellness' by neoliberal subjects, devoting their very lives to prolonging their lives.

16 Urbain and other critics of modernity have gotten good traction out of the notion of 'individualism', but I think any picture of our crumbling neoliberal conjuncture should also stress the somewhat perverse return of the *family*. As Melinda Cooper argues, the family has for decades increasingly taken on the strain caused by privatization (2019). The COVID-19 pandemic, at the time of writing, drives home the function of the family as a social safety net or pressure valve in very stark terms.

Interestingly, Didion – who is often styled by commentators as an iconoclast, as an individualist, a cool and detached 'style icon' (Gilmore 2016b: 611) – grapples with the ethics of memory *precisely at the familial level* in her memoirs of grief. And she takes exception to implications that her family ties were in some sense unhealthily tight:

> Many people have pointed out that John and Quintana and I were 'unusually dependent' on one another.
>
> Is 'unusual dependency' another way of saying 'marriage'? Husband and wife? Parent and child? (Didion: 2007: 24)

Similarly, in 2005: 'Unusual dependency (is that a way of saying "marriage"? "husband and wife"? "mother and child"? "nuclear family"?) is [according to the literature] not the only situation in which complicated or pathological grief can occur' (Didion 2005: 54).

17 Urbain's fascinating and wide-ranging study, most of which lies outside of my scope, connects the modern idea of death as accident and failure to a plethora of contemporary phenomena surrounding death and dying. To take only one example, he describes 'the purging of all traces of the past from the epitaph' (Urbain 2005: 223, my translation). He notes the disappearance over time of the verb in the deceased's biography – 'He was a good father and husband' becomes 'Good father, good husband' – thus rendering his qualities atemporal and thereby purging *time*, precisely *this person as a real historical being* from the very writing bearing witness to him (Urbain 2005: 223–4). In effect, through its inability to properly reckon with death, with the past, with what is lost, modern culture increasingly stages the cemetery as a site of disappearance and forgetting, not remembrance. Modernity on this interpretation has implications for the very zoning of where we lay our dead to rest.

Again, Didion's memoir lines up with Urbain's analysis: 'One way in which grief gets hidden is that death now largely occurs offstage' (Urbain 2005: 60). But recall that Didion in 2017 makes an exception for the South, where memory exerts more of a persistent hold. Driving through Grenada, Mississippi, she describes 'the graveyards everywhere . . . . Death is still natural and ever present in the South, as it is no more in those urbanized parts of the country where graveyards are burial parks and relegated to unused or unusable land far from sight' (80–1).

18 This is a version of the classic argument of Max Horkheimer and Theodor Adorno in *Dialectic of Enlightenment*: myth, or the pre-modern, returns in a virulent modern form as a *myth of enlightenment* (2002). While I do not wish

to pursue this connection too far, note what it might mean with respect to modern death and dying: 'secular' subjects like Didion will engage in magical thinking and rituals faced with loss *precisely because* there is seemingly no other recourse.

19 There is a hard limit to the geological viewpoint: solar heat death, in which the Earth will be consumed, to say nothing of cosmic heat death in general. For a philosophical meditation on solar heat death and the possibility of the survival of something like a human perspective, see Lyotard (1991: 8–23).

20 Note, parenthetically, that Urbain's bleak modernity is not the whole story. There exist resources in modern philosophy to at least *conceive* of a kind of substantial, metaphysical preservation or 'resolution', through memory, of what is lost – even if this does not literally amount to personal survival after death. Marxism, as we briefly discussed in Chapter 1, offers a vision of History in which the individual can find meaning and purpose. And Ricœur, to take another example, explores modern philosophical grounding for the Biblical idea that no hair goes uncounted by God, that the first will be the last – in essence, that the individual's life will be preserved forever, in the consciousness of God (Ricœur 2014: 81–4). His direct source for construing this idea in modern terms is the process philosophy of Alfred North Whitehead (Ricœur 2014: 77–8), but this line of thinking can be traced even further back to Baruch Spinoza. For Spinoza, a kind of immortality or 'eternity' inheres in the fact of temporality being one of God's (or Nature's, as he uses the terms interchangeably) infinite attributes. From this perspective, it is no matter if one dies, and no matter if no one remembers. From a metaphysical perspective, one will always have been, and nothing is ever truly lost (Spinoza 1992: 213–4). Arguably, all of this is cold comfort – but the point here is that there are modern ways of framing the universe and its relation to memory that Didion does not pursue.

21 'Memory does not only bear on time: it also requires time – a time of mourning' (Ricœur 2006: 74).

22 In note 13, I related Nelson's comment that Didion will dwell on the narrative of her life, entwined with Quintana's, for the rest of her life (Nelson 2017: 172). See also Freud (1964).

23 In McLennan (2019), I explored at some length the image of swimming with others as a metaphor for our interdependency. Water and swimming imagery is pervasive in Didion, but in that context it was a question of unpacking the metaphor as it appears in Audre Lorde.

24 There is a passage in *Blue Nights* that appears to complicate if not undermine my interpretation. Describing the discovery of an aneurysm at the base of her brain

in 2009, Didion 'realized that I was no longer, if I had ever been, afraid to die: I was now afraid not to die, afraid that I might damage my brain (or my heart or my kidneys or my nervous system) and survive, continue living' (2011: 24–5). Here it seems not to matter to Didion that she dies, and, in fact, it might be preferable to living with diminished capacities.

    I have two responses to this difficulty. First, Didion describes discovering her loss of the fear of death during the period when, if my interpretation is correct, she is still working through her trauma and thus has no conscious knowledge of her preciousness with respect to her memories of Quintana. It is perfectly conceivable that she would express a contrary opinion here – especially if we put any stock in the psychoanalytical metaphor, in which the truth is in some sense blocked or unconsciously disavowed. Second, note that two of the possibilities Didion lists – damaging her brain and her nervous system – could amount to the same thing as death, in terms of wiping out her memories of Quintana, and having to live on without them.

25 The distinction between 'saying' and 'said' – *le dit* and *le dire* – animates ethical thinking in psychoanalysis, phenomenology and post-structuralism. There is an echo of Freud and *Nachträglichkeit* here: there is *what* is said, as distinct from the bare fact *that* it is said. And again, an echo of Ricœur: there is memory in its *cognitive* aspect, and memory in its *pragmatic* aspect.

26 I will refer to 'saying,' and to 'a saying' where it is a specific case of saying. This is because I am straightforwardly talking about Didion and other persons who 'say' things. I should note that although I cite Lyotard (1988) in this connection, he favours the term 'phrase' in that text, which unfolds at a much deeper, ontological level than mine. He attempts to do away with any vestiges of anthropomorphism when it comes to language; the problem on this view is that 'saying' implies a sayer (whereas a 'phrase' is simply an occurrence, viewed pragmatically, and it is always possible that the 'addressor' be unmarked).

27 This remains true even though readers and reviewers have questioned Didion's choices with respect to what she divulges. Daugherty's unauthorized 2015 biography is a good resource. For takes bordering on the sensationalist, see Matesa 2011 and Sauers 2011.

28 Wiesel relates the following story:

> When the great Rabbi Israel Baal Shem-Tov saw misfortune threatening the Jews it was his custom to go into a certain part of the forest to meditate. There he would light a fire, say a special prayer, and the miracle would be accomplished and the misfortune averted.

> Later, when his disciple, the celebrated Magid of Mezritch, had occasion, for the same reason, to intercede with heaven, he would go to the same place in the forest and say: 'Master of the Universe, listen! I do not know how to light the fire, but I am still able to say the prayer.' And again the miracle would be accomplished.
>
> Still later, Rabbi Moshe-Leib of Sasov, in order to save his people once more, would go into the forest and say: 'I do not know how to light the fire, I do not know the prayer, but I know the place and this must be sufficient.' It was sufficient and the miracle was accomplished.
>
> Then it fell to Rabbi Israel of Rizhyn to overcome misfortune. Sitting in his armchair, his head in his hands, he spoke to God: 'I am unable to light the fire and I do not know the prayer; I cannot even find the place in the forest. All I can do is to tell the story, and this must be sufficient.' And it was sufficient. (Wiesel 1972: 168)

Wiesel comments further, however, that it is 'no longer sufficient' in a world where 'the threat' to the Jewish people 'has not been averted. Perhaps we are no longer able to tell the story' (Wiesel 1972). The ethics of memory appears here again as a kind of limit case of ethics: it is the very minimum of any hope, and of community. See also Lyotard (1988: 47).

29 At the time of writing, *Blue Nights* represents the last new book by Didion published in about a decade; *South and West* (2017) was based on writings in an old notebook and *Let Me Tell You What I Mean* (2021) collects previously uncollected essays. It is therefore tempting to speculate as to what this 'silence' from Didion means. I have mentioned in other notes that Nelson, for her part, pictures a remorseful, grieving and frail Didion dwelling 'for the rest of her life' on her and Quintana's entwined narratives (2017: 172). Having gone to the very limit, it is possible that for Didion there is no more to say.

30 See Ricœur (2006: 234–80) for a broader discussion of representation and the historian's craft.

31 Lyotard's comments on silence are given in connection with the oft-noted silence of Shoah survivors. We saw that silence is a 'phrase', or a case of saying, and that this saying can bear on either addressee, referent, sense, addressor or some combination of these. Their silence on the Shoah therefore does not necessarily testify 'in favor of the non-existence of gas chambers, as [the negationist] believes or pretends to believe' (1988: 14). The problem is that this silence nonetheless undermines the case for the referent. Lyotard tells us that 'If one wishes to establish the existence of gas chambers, the four silent negations must be

withdrawn: There were no gas chambers, were there? Yes, there were. – But even if there were, that cannot be formulated, can it? Yes, it can. – But even if it can be formulated, there is no one, at least, who has the authority to formulate it, and no one with the authority to hear it (it is not communicable), is there? Yes, there is' (1988).

32 Similarly, Agamben holds that 'to bear witness is to place oneself in one's own language in the position of those who have lost it, to establish oneself in a living language as if it were dead, or in a dead language as if it were living' (1988: 161). As such, there is simultaneously something noble and something quixotic about witnessing.

33 As Ricœur puts it, Freud's clinical lesson is ultimately that 'Memory does not only bear on time: it also requires time – a time of mourning' (2006: 74). For a similar problematic in a theological register, see Agamben 2005.

34 The same goes for the present self and the future self. My point here is that in othering oneself through the medium of time, it is possible to take a properly 'other-regarding' stance to that other, and to that extent, ethical questions are on the table. It is common, for instance, for people not to like the person they used to be, in some measure. The choice is therefore between leaving this past, disliked otherness alone, as a brute fact, or 'dialoguing' with it in such a way that it is neither forgotten, nor assimilated to the present (see Beauvoir 1976: 27 for a similar but ultimately contrary take regarding our past actions). Similarly, it is possible to not like oneself *now* and to commit oneself to a project of self-improvement whereby one will be judged by one's future self.

35 I referred in Note 14 of the Introduction to a sequence in the television adaptation of *The Handmaid's Tale* that speaks to this idea.

36 For Lyotard, the non-human animal is the paradigm of the victim: it cannot testify, because its cries are not even registered as speech (1988: 28).

37 Note how Stauffer's analysis resonates with Margalit's distinction, explored in the Introduction, between ethics and morality: 'ethical loneliness' would be a case where a person is denied their full humanity, so there is a moral injury and a moral duty of memory and repair. A way of describing a person's 'ethical loneliness' thus might be: because her humanity is not recognized (immoral), she is not included in the community (unethical). As such, Stauffer's analysis also resonates with Margalit's notions of the 'decent society', where there is no institutionalized humiliation, and the 'civilized society', where individuals do not humiliate each other (Margalit 2007: 13). Note further that Stauffer does engage with Margalit (Stauffer 2015: 131–3), on the topic of forgiveness.

38 The substance of Butler's intervention is that 'all lives matter', but this is not her slogan – precisely because the slogan is usually used in bad faith, to *counter* the claim that 'Black lives matter'.

39 Daugherty 2015 gives a compelling narrative of Quintana's personal struggles, often alluding to the home and family circumstances that may have exacerbated them.

40 Gilmore centres women and girls, but does it through an intersectional approach, in Gilmore 2018 and Gilmore and Marshall 2019.

41 Gilmore examines several high-profile cases in her book, but its publication also proved very timely for developing events in the US. The handling of the testimony of Christine Blasey Ford during Brett Kavanagh's Supreme Court Confirmation hearing, postdating the publication of *Tainted Witness,* is treated in Gilmore 2019. Therein she explicitly evokes 'frames' in Butler's sense.

42 Like Didion in *The Year of Magical Thinking*, Mamie Till-Mobley told her public that 'We cannot afford the luxury of self-pity' (Mobley-Till and Benson 2003: x). Although Didion's losses were terrible and her suffering great, how much more striking is it that Mobley-Till – whose son was lynched – can make a stand against self-pity?

43 For POC-centred analyses and commentary on #BlackLivesMatter, see for example, Taylor 2016; Puar 2017; Khan-Cullors and bandele 2020.

Chapter 3

1 The story about Swiss mercenaries is only one possible origin story for the word 'nostalgia'. It is given in the *Historical Dictionary of the French Language*. It attributes the word 'nostalgia' to a doctor, Jean-Jacques Harder, who classified it as an illness. This makes it reminiscent of 'myalgia' or 'neuralgia'. Cassin cites two other possible origins, both of which also stress nostalgia as a perceived medical issue (2016: 5–6).

2 Perhaps Didion's celebrated essay 'Goodbye to All That', which eulogizes her time living and working in New York, is the piece of hers which best captures what Kant is suggesting here. Didion secured a job at *Vogue* magazine and moved across the country for it, at age twenty, working there for seven years. In the essay, she stresses how open her horizons were in the city: 'Nothing was irrevocable; everything was in reach. Just around every corner lay something curious and interesting, something I had never before seen or done or known about . . . . I could make promises to myself and to other people and there would

be all the time in the world to keep them. I could stay up all night and make mistakes, and none of it would count' (Didion 2006: 171). As she summarizes, 'was anyone ever so young? I am here to tell you that someone was' (Didion 2006: 169). Interestingly, Didion loses her connection to New York before she even moves away, disenchanting the city before even having the chance to leave it and return to it; 'it is distinctly possible to stay too long at the fair' (Didion 2006: 175). This corresponds to her feeling the weight of the past catching up to her, to her horizons closing, which is precisely one aspect of how one becomes older, from a phenomenological perspective (McLennan 2020). Didion recounts how 'That was the year, my twenty-eighth, when I was discovering that not all the promises would be kept, that some things are in fact irrevocable and that it had counted after all, every evasion and every procrastination, every mistake, every word, all of it' (Didion 2006: 173).

3 'Attachment theory', in the tradition of John Bowlby, could give insight here into manners of evaluating one's past in light of one's attachment history. See Bowlby (2005a, 2005b). We could, of course, update Kant's comments to reflect how people who are poor *but still swept up in the mobility of capital* might suffer deficits of attachment.

4 The work of Ann Cvetkovich is now classic in theorizing 'public feelings'; see Cvetkovich (2003, 2012).

5 The reader may notice virtue ethics being invoked here; I hope I will be forgiven for implicitly assimilating it to a form of consequentialism. My point is simply to raise the possibility that character is one of the goods that can be damaged by nostalgia.

6 Regarding aesthetics, Margalit's brief treatment of nostalgia (2002: 61–2) incorporates a discussion of the closely related tendency towards '*kitsch* representations of the past'.

7 Nowak McNeice devotes an entire chapter to 'the loss of ethics' that is highly pertinent to my argument. Didion's 'wagon train morality', which I argued forms a rough and early template to which she gradually adds nuance, is in Nowak McNeice's view 'lost' and melancholically invested. For the heroines of her novels, who are either Westerners or transposed or transported Westerners, 'This ethical system . . . proves to be inadequate, as the world does not adhere to the same set of beliefs, which leaves the characters frustrated and dejected' (Nowak McNeice 2019: 134). My way of expressing much the same in Chapter 2 was to draw attention to the fact that the protection of one's kin, even when it is only done through the minimal gesture of memory, persists as the ethical core of the late Didion – but that, steeped in the anxious modernity of the 'earthquake

weather' universe, she recognizes its inadequacy. Necessity and inadequacy thus merge in an unhappy, normatively burdened consciousness.

Didion in *Where I Was From*, in fact, signals her own symbolic failure to live up to her pioneer ethics, explicitly linking this failure to her family's failure in respecting one aspect of the ethics of memory:

> I asked how exactly it had come to pass that the family did not own the Kilgore cemetery.
>
> 'I presume somebody sold it,' my mother said.
>
> I thought about this.
>
> I also thought about having seen the rattlesnake slide from the broken stone into the grass.
>
> I had seen the rattlesnake but I failed to get out of the car and kill it, thereby violating, in full awareness that I was so doing, what my grandfather had told me was 'the code of the West'.
>
> If 'not killing the rattlesnake' violated 'the code of the West', what about 'selling the cemetery'? Would that qualify? (Didion 2006: 1080–1)

To make a final point, however, Didion's pose here of self-criticism and implicit criticism of her family perhaps elides too much. As Michelle Chihara points out, the real story of Didion's and her family's land ownership, and their own role in changing California, is quite other than her obliquity and use of the passive voice would often suggest (Chihara 2020). For Chihara, 'The entire memoir [*Where I Was From*] sits as a book-length effort to look at and then mystify the Didion family's structural intervention in the California real estate markets' (Chihara 2020). As such, the book has serious limitations both as a self-criticism, and as a work of memory ethics.

8 There is an irony to Didion's 1967 essay 'On Going Home', wherein she sketches in an early form some of the musings on nostalgia that will carry forward to *Where I Was From*. She describes being 'home' for Quintana's first birthday, defining her home not as the house where she lives with her husband and daughter in Los Angeles, but 'the place where my family is, in the Central Valley of California' (Didion 2006: 125). This is revealing; marriage and moving away, exogamy, is described 'the classic betrayal' (Didion 2006). At least it was such to Didion's generation, the last to have posed 'the question of whether or not you could go home again' before the 'children born of the fragmentation after World War II' rendered it irrelevant (Didion 2006: 126).

Didion describes the baby's birthday party, and how

> after she has gone to sleep, I kneel beside the crib and touch her face, where it is pressed against the slats, with mine. She is an open and trusting child, unprepared for and unaccustomed to the ambushes of family life, and perhaps it is just as well that I can offer her little of that life. I would like to give her more. I would like to promise her that she will grow up with a sense of her cousins and of rivers and of her great-grandmother's teacups, would like to pledge to her a picnic on a river with fried chicken and her hair uncombed, would like to give her *home* for her birthday, but we live differently now and I can promise her nothing like that. I give her a xylophone and a sundress from Madeira, and promise to tell her a funny story. (Didion 2006: 127, emphasis in original)

As I read it, the irony of this piece is that Didion worries about providing Quintana with 'home' when here, at least, she is already giving it to her in very clear terms. The reference points will be different, and perhaps much forgotten, but even while setting Quintana up as a 'child born of fragmentation', Didion reveals a core commitment to 'family life', to the ethical community, that perdures. To nuance this view, see Daugherty 2015. Cassin closes her study of nostalgia with a similar but evidently more hopeful recognition of the fundamental mobility of 'home', its link to a community that is not necessarily rooted in place: 'When are we ever at home? When we are welcomed, we ourselves along with those who are close to us, together with our language, our languages' (2016: 63).

9   One could perhaps forget some types of crime against the community 'for the sake of the community', but we do our communities no favours by forgetting crimes against humanity. And in what sense could one forget a crime against humanity 'for the sake of humanity'?

10 Stauffer insists upon the legitimacy of survivors' *refusal* to forgive, while allowing that forgiveness could still be possible. A precondition would be the construction and defence of 'meaningful human rights', which would require not just institutions but also *all* individuals, including innocent 'bystanders' to crimes against humanity, to build a world in which all people can 'trust that they and the people they love will be safe' (2015: 66–7). As a Canadian who comes from historically poor settler families, I find one of the main virtues of Stauffer's book to be its reminder that *no one* is morally speaking off the hook whenever crimes against humanity are perpetrated.

11 Recall again that I challenge Margalit's moral humanism in McLennan 2018b.

12 This speaks to the Kantian theme of indirect duties to humanity. In destroying or disrespecting something that stands for a symbol of human reason, I indirectly disrespect humanity itself. See Kant 1984: 239–42.
13 DiAngelo (2018) is a good resource for understanding and refuting the defensive moves of 'nice', 'colour-blind' white people living in systemically racist societies.
14 Once more see McLennan (2018b) for a discussion of some philosophical implications and difficulties raised by Margalit's definition of the moral sphere in terms of moral autonomy.

Chapter 4

1 Annie Ernaux captures the spirit of ideological atomization I am referring to here in an arresting passage of *Ce qu'ils disent ou rien*: for people in the teenage protagonist's milieu it is always a question of criticizing and gossiping about 'people one by one, never a word on the factory, the school, the institutions the civics prof taught us about, did they even know all that existed, yes surely, but they didn't think we could discuss it' (1977: 67, my translation). See also Sartre 2004 on the concept of 'seriality'.
2 In McLennan (2018a) I make a similar argument about Lyotard vis-à-vis Laclau and Mouffe; his extreme scepticism ends in a kind of exorbitant and paradoxical moralism, whereas Laclau and Mouffe pick up on it to reinvigorate a new political realism. What I find remarkable about Didion is how she appears to make this move herself, from a roughly postmodern quietism to a politically realist position. But whereas Laclau and Mouffe elide the more robustly normative question of politics in favour of voluntarism, Didion seems to hang on to a vision of American democracy *as it should be*. This seems to entail a picture of justice as fairness, and for this reason I designate hers a *critical* political realism, guided as it is by a morally as opposed to strategically normative horizon.
3 In Didion (2006: 968–74) the myth of the 'redemptive power of the crossing' overland to California is tested by reading crossing accounts and diaries, and the 'darkness' they reveal. Abandoning an orphaned girl and her younger brother discovered on the trail so as 'not to be caught by winter in the Sierra Nevada mountains' 'might have seemed difficult to reconcile with the conviction that one had successfully met the tests or challenges required to enter a new life' (2006: 974).
4 Just as in *A Book of Common Prayer* the narrator announces both her intention and finally her failure to witness, in *Democracy* she declares that the latter 'is

not the novel I set out to write, nor am I exactly the person who set out to write it' (Didion 1995: 232). But precisely because of her failure, 'the options remain open'; here too we see the tension between a finished, fixed narrative, where the calculated ellipse and omission of the full wealth of the particular establishes sense, and the interminable ethical *labour* of testifying and storytelling, where what is at stake is a true and relatively comprehensive witnessing (Didion 1995: 233).

5   Though it falls outside of the scope of my discussion, Ricœur (2006) meticulously draws the connections between cognitive and pragmatic aspects of *memory* as opposed to cognitive and pragmatic aspects of *history*.

6   The narrator goes on to say: 'that Inez's experience had tended to deny. She had spent her childhood immersed in the local conviction that the comfortable entrepreneurial life of an American colony *in a tropic without rot* [Hawaii] represented a record of individual triumphs over a hostile environment' (Didion 1995: 211, emphasis added). Hawaii figures here as a 'Western' rather than a 'Southern' locale, in this way fully American (though designated as a colony) and much like the mythical California. The impression of individual triumphs over nature, precisely those that could not be won in what are for Didion perhaps the true, entropic tropics of *A Book of Common Prayer*, leads one to deny 'history'. This makes history something not unlike what I have called 'the immemorial' and 'the geological point of view'. For all that, history does not cease to be an eminently public object of contemplation.

7   This comment about Didion's experience of the acceleration of time and events is interestingly not free of self-criticism. I have noted the pervasive moral colouration she gives to some cognitive failures, especially when they suggest a defect of character. In *The Last Thing He Wanted*, she describes the character Treat Morrison's incapacity to 'see the thing straight' as a kind of radical 'dishonesty' (1996: 136).

8   Gambling is an interesting trope in Didion; see Didion 1970 and the chapter 'The Loss of Ethics' in Nowak McNeice (2019).

9   This brackets, of course, the newer and highly important issue of content micro-targeting, especially political micro-targeting; see O'Neil (2017) and Zuboff (2019). As demonstrated, for instance, in *Political Fictions* and *Fixed Ideas*, Didion, however, was not at all naïve in the 1980s, 1990s, and 2000s about the media's power to frame issues differently for the purpose of manipulating different audiences.

10 Reagan himself is something of a cipher in Didion's account of American politics, a symbol or figurehead, and not where one should look to find the real story. See

'Many Mansions' (Didion 2006: 227–31) and 'In the Realm of the Fisher King' (Didion 2006: 565–78).

11 A good example of such a redemption narrative given by Gilmore is Jeanette Walls's *The Glass Castle* (Gilmore 2018: 89).

12 Note that my emphasis is on critical *potential*. Because of sexism and misogyny, I am sure that even Ivanka Trump and Marine Le Pen could contribute testimony shedding light on and critical of the gendered patterns of how power functions. But because of their embeddedness in power interests that are *supportive* of that sexism and misogyny, in addition to the impoverished vantage point they present *qua* intersectional life writing, I doubt that their memoirs will ever become classics of critical thinking.

13 In Butler's terms, the cost of being a 'grievable' subject of memoir would be coding oneself as a kind of post-racial, post-feminist neoliberal individual.

Conclusion

1 One should not miss the chance to link 'unsettlement' – the state of feeling unsettled, or uneasy – with un-settlement, un-settling, in the sense of challenging settler colonialism. Didion's self-criticism, as explored in Chapter 3, is from this perspective limited but at least points the way to a kind of unsettlement or decolonization of memory. To repeat, she is far from perfect here – she has glaring limitations that cannot be papered over, and that must be read in dialogue with other thinkers. But she can form part of a critical literary programme, of which Katarzyna Nowak McNeice's study (2019) is perhaps the best recent example.

2 In winter 2020 I had a second chance to teach for Discovery University, this time on the theme of 'Science and Social Values'. Like the first time it was a wonderful experience – but cut a few weeks short, unfortunately, by the pandemic.

3 See Wolff and De-Shalit (2013) on the notion of 'genuine opportunity'.

4 A society is 'decent' as per Margalit if its institutions do no not humiliate people. It is 'civilized' if its citizens do not humiliate each other (2007: 13).

5 Margalit 2007 (89–111) surveys different respects in which people can be humiliated, which is to say dehumanized. Interestingly, the specific cruelty of humiliation is the fact that it continues to recognize the humanity of the individuals it dehumanizes. This it has to do, because humiliation is among other things a *message* the humiliated party is intended to receive. If I humiliate a woman through objectifying her, I treat her *as if* she is an object; only the pathological case, the sociopath, treats her *as* an object, truly not getting on some

level that she is a human being. The upshot of this is that when we humiliate individuals in the strict sense, we should know better, and, in fact, we do know better. This means we are more blameworthy than the sociopath, who is after all a pathological case.

6 Posting mugshots is not the only form of potentially 'dehumanizing' memory I have in mind here. The presence online of leaked nude photos, for example, is humiliating and allows at any time for the re-humiliation of the injured party; hence, the possibility of revisiting the humiliation is part of the humiliation.

7 This is not my coinage; a 'right to be forgotten', as put into effect in the European Union and Argentina, limits third-party access to certain personal information and can entail the scrubbing of public records. See Trites (2019).

8 While I am no criminologist and have nothing to say about exactly which types of cases would qualify, in a rough and ready way it is possible to imagine, for example, misdemeanors classed differently from violent offences (where 'violence' means violence to persons, not damage to property).

Bibliography

Agamben, G. (2002), *Remnants of Auschwitz: The Witness and the Archive*, translated by D. Heller-Roazen, New York: Zone Books.
Agamben, G. (2005), *The Time That Remains: A Commentary on the Letter to the Romans*, translated by P. Dailey, Stanford: Stanford University Press.
Antonini, F. (2019), 'Pessimism of the Intellect, Optimism of the Will: Gramsci's Political Thought in the Last Miscellaneous Notebooks', *Rethinking Marxism: A Journal of Economics, Culture & Society*, 31 (1): 42–57.
Aristotle (2018), *On the Soul: And Other Psychological Works*, translated by F. D. Miller Jr., Oxford: Oxford University Press.
Bascaramurty, D. (2017), 'A Horrible History: Four Indigenous Views on Canada 150', *Globe and Mail*, 30 June. Available online: https://www.theglobeandmail.com/news/national/canada-150/canada-day-indigenous-perspectives-on-canada-150/article35498737/ (accessed July 21, 2020).
Battiste, M. (2013), *Decolonizing Education: Nourishing the Learning Spirit*, Vancouver: Purich Publishing.
Beauvoir, S. de (1976), *The Ethics of Ambiguity*, translated by B. Frechtman, New York: Citadel Press.
Benatar, D. (2017), *The Human Predicament*, New York: Oxford University Press.
Berlant, L. (2008), *The Female Complaint: The Unfinished Business of Sentimentality in American Culture*, Durham: Duke University Press.
Bowlby, J. (2005a), *A Secure Base*, London: Routledge.
Bowlby, J. (2005b), *The Making and Breaking of Affectional Bonds*, London: Routledge.
Brown, W. (2015), *Undoing the Demos: Neoliberalism's Stealth Revolution*, New York: Zone Books.
Brown, W. (2019), *In the Ruins of Neoliberalism: The Rise of Antidemocratic Politics in the West*, New York: Columbia University Press.
Brugère, F. and Le Blanc, G. (2017), *La fin de l'hospitalité : L'Europe, terre d'asile?*, Paris: Flammarion.
Brysk, A. (2018), *The Future of Human Rights*, Cambridge: Polity Press.
Butler, J. (2016), *Frames of War: When is Life Grievable?*, London: Verso.
Butler, J. (2020), *The Force of Nonviolence: An Ethico-Political Bind*, London: Verso.
Cassin, B. (2016), *Nostalgia: When Are We Ever at Home?*, translated by P.-A. Brault, New York: Fordham University Press.

Chihara, M. (2020), 'In Renouncing the Myths of Old California, Did Joan Didion Deflect Responsibility? Michelle Chihara Digs Through the Didion Family's Land Records', *LitHub*, 14 February. Available online: https://lithub.com/in-renouncing-the-myths-of-old-california-did-joan-didion-deflect-responsibility/ (accessed 25 August 2020).

Cooper, M. (2019), *Family Values: Between Neoliberalism and the New Social Conservatism*. New York: Zone Books.

Critchley, S. (2013), *Infinitely Demanding: Ethics of Commitment, Politics of Resistance*, London: Verso.

Cvetkovich, A. (2003), *An Archive of Feelings: Trauma, Sexuality, and Lesbian Public Cultures*, Durham: Duke University Press.

Cvetkovich, A. (2012), *Depression: A Public Feeling*, Durham: Duke University Press.

Daugherty, T. (2015), *The Last Love Song: A Biography of Joan Didion*, New York: St. Martin's Press.

DiAngelo, R. (2018), *White Fragility: Why It's So Hard for White People to Talk About Racism*, Boston: Beacon Press.

Didion, J. (1970), *Play it as it Lays*, New York: Farrar, Straus and Giroux.

Didion, J. (1977), *A Book of Common Prayer*, New York: Vintage Books.

Didion, J. (1994), *Run River*, New York: Vintage Books.

Didion, J. (1995), *Democracy*, New York: Vintage Books.

Didion, J. (1996), *The Last Thing He Wanted*, New York: Vintage Books.

Didion, J. (2003), *Fixed Ideas: America since 9.11*, New York: New York Review Books.

Didion, J. (2005), *The Year of Magical Thinking*, New York: Vintage International.

Didion, J. (2006), *We Tell Ourselves Stories in Order to Live: Collected Nonfiction*, New York: Alfred A. Knopf.

Didion, J. (2007), *The Year of Magical Thinking: The Play*, New York: Vintage International.

Didion, J. (2011), *Blue Nights*, New York: Vintage International.

Didion, J. (2017), *South and West: From a Notebook*, New York: Alfred A. Knopf.

Didion, J. (2021), *Let Me Tell You What I Mean*, New York: Alfred A. Knopf.

Doughty, C. (2015), *Smoke Gets in Your Eyes & Other Lessons from the Crematory*, New York: W. W. Norton.

Eagleton, T. (2010), *On Evil*, New Haven: Yale University Press.

Ernaux, A. (1977), *Ce qu'ils Disent ou rien*, Paris: Éditions Gallimard.

Ernaux, A. (1997), *La honte*, Paris: Éditions Gallimard.

Ernaux, A. (2000), *La vie extérieure*, Paris: Éditions Gallimard.

Ernaux, A. (2001), *Se perdre*, Paris: Éditions Gallimard.

Ernaux, A. (2016), *Mémoire de fille*, Paris: Éditions Gallimard.

Eubanks, V. (2019), *Automating Inequality: How High-Tech Tools Profile, Police, and Punish the Poor*, New York: Picador/St. Martin's Press.

Foucault, M. (1977), 'What is an Author?', *Language, Counter-Memory, Practice: Selected Essays and Interviews*, translated by D. F. Bouchard and S. Simon, Ithaca: Cornell University Press.

Freud, S. (1964), 'Analysis Terminable and Interminable', in *The Standard Edition of the Complete Psychological Works of Sigmund Freud Volume XXIII (1937–1939): Moses and Monotheism, An Outline of Psycho-Analysis and Other Works*, 211–53, translated by J. Strachey, London: The Hogarth Press and the Institute of Psycho-Analysis.

Freud, S. (2011), *Deuil et mélancolie*, translated by A. Weill, Paris: Éditions Payot & Rivages.

Gilmore, L. (2001), *The Limits of Autobiography: Trauma and Testimony*, Ithaca: Cornell University Press.

Gilmore, L. (2016a), 'Conclusion: Joan Didion's Style', *a/b: Auto/Biography Studies*, 31 (3): 614–7.

Gilmore, L. (2016b), 'Public Grief: Reading Joan Didion in the Context of #BlackLivesMatter', *a/b: Auto/Biography Studies*, 31 (3): 610–4.

Gilmore, L. (2018), *Tainted Witness: Why We Doubt What Women Say About Their Lives*, New York: Columbia University Press.

Gilmore, L. (2019), 'Frames of Witness: The Kavanaugh Hearings, Survivor Testimony, and #Me Too', *Biography*, 42 (3): 610–23.

Gilmore, L. and E. Marshall (2019), *Witnessing Girlhood: Toward an Intersectional Tradition of Life Writing*, New York: Fordham University Press.

Habermas, J. (1990a), *Moral Consciousness and Communicative Action*, translated by C. Lenhardt and S. Weber Nicholsen, Cambridge, MA: The MIT Press.

Habermas, J. (1990b), *The Philosophical Discourse of Modernity: Twelve Lectures*, translated by F. G. Lawrence, Cambridge, MA: The MIT Press.

Habermas, J. (1991), *The Structural Transformation of the Public Sphere: An Inquiry into a Category of Bourgeois Society*, translated by T. Burger with the assistance of F. Lawrence, Cambridge, MA: The MIT Press.

Hadot, P. (2004), *What Is Ancient Philosophy?*, translated by M. Chase, Cambridge, MA: The Belknap Press of Harvard University Press.

Halbwachs, M. (1980), *The Collective Memory*, translated by F. J. Ditter and V. Y. Ditter, New York: Harper Colophon.

Haraway, D. (2016), *Staying with the Trouble: Making Kin in the Chthulucene*, Durham: Duke University Press.

Hartman, S. V. (1997), *Scenes of Subjection: Terror, Slavery, and Self-making in Nineteenth-century America*, New York: Oxford University Press.

Hartman, S. V. (2007), *Lose Your Mother: A Journey Along the Atlantic Slave Route*, New York: Farrar, Straus and Giroux.

Hartman, S. V. (2008), 'Venus in Two Acts', *Small Axe*, 12 (2): 1–14.

Hartman, S. V. (2019), *Wayward Lives, Beautiful Experiments: Intimate Histories of Riotous Black Girls, Troublesome Women, and Queer Radicals*, New York: W. W. Norton & Company.

Hegel, G. W. F. (2004), *Hegel's Philosophy of Nature*, translated by A. V. Miller, New York: Oxford University Press.

Horkheimer, M. and T. W. Adorno (2002), *Dialectic of Enlightenment: Philosophical Fragments*, translated by E. Jephcott, Stanford: Stanford University Press.

Huebner, C. K. (2006), *A Precarious Peace: Yoderian Explorations on Theology, Knowledge, and Identity*, Waterloo: Herald Press.

Joan Didion: The Center Will Not Hold (2017), [Film] Dir. G. Dunne, USA: Netflix.

Kant, I. (1983), 'An Answer to the Question: What is Enlightenment?', *Perpetual Peace and Other Essays on Politics, History, and Morals*, translated by Humpfree, Indianapolis: Hackett Publishing Company, 41–8.

Kant, I. (1984), *Lectures on Ethics*, translated by L. Infield. Indianapolis: Hackett Publishing Company.

Kant, I. (2006), *Anthropology from a Pragmatic Point of View*, translated by R. B. Louden, New York: Cambridge University Press.

Khan-Cullors, P. and a. bandele (2020), *When They Call You a Terrorist: A Black Lives Matter Memoir*, New York: St. Martin's Griffin.

Kristeva, J. (1989), *Black Sun: Depression and Melancholia*, translated by L. S. Roudiez, New York: Columbia University Press.

Laclau, E. and C. Mouffe (2014), *Hegemony and Socialist Strategy: Towards a Radical Democratic Politics*, London: Verso.

Lahary, J. -P. and E. Vannier (1980), *Mourir à New York (crimes Extraordinaires et Autres Histoires)*, Paris : Fayard.

Lear, J. (2006), *Radical Hope: Ethics in the Face of Cultural Devastation*, Cambridge, MA: Harvard University Press.

Locke, J. (2008), *An Essay Concerning Human Understanding*, Oxford: Oxford University Press.

Lyotard, J.-F. (1993), *Libidinal Economy*, translated by I. Hamilton Grant, Bloomington: Indiana University Press.

Lyotard, J.-F. (1988), *The Differend: Phrases in Dispute*, translated by G. Van Den Abbeele, Minneapolis: University of Minnesota Press.

Lyotard, J.-F. (1990), *Heidegger and "the jews"*, translated by A. Michel and M. Roberts, Minneapolis: University of Minnesota Press.

Lyotard, J.-F. (1991), *The Inhuman: Reflections on Time*, translated by G. Bennington and R. Bowlby, Stanford: Stanford University Press.

Lyotard, J.-F. (1993), 'The Survivor', in R. Harvey and M. S. Roberts (eds), *Lyotard: Toward the Postmodern*, 144–63, translated by R. Harvey and M. S. Roberts, Atlantic Highlands: Humanities Press.

Lyotard, J.-F. (2001), *Soundproof Room: Malraux's Anti-Aesthetics*, translated by R. Harvey, Stanford: Stanford University Press.

Malabou, C. (2012), *The New Wounded: From Neurosis to Brain Damage*, translated by S. Miller, New York: Fordham University Press.

Malraux, A. (1970), *Antimemoirs*, translated by T. Kilmartin, New York: Bantam Books.

Margalit, A. (2002), *The Ethics of Memory*, Cambridge, MA: Harvard University Press.

Margalit, A. (2010), *On Compromise and Rotten Compromises*, Princeton: Princeton University Press.

Margalit, A. (2007), *La société décente*, translated by F. Billard, Paris: Flammarion.

Margalit, A. (2017), *On Betrayal*, Cambridge, MA: Harvard University Press.

Marx, K. (1843), 'A Contribution to the Critique of Hegel's Philosophy of Right: Introduction', *Marxists Internet Archives*. Available online: https://www.marxists.org/archive/marx/works/1843/critique-hpr/intro.htm (accessed 17 July 2020).

Matesa, J. (2011), 'Is Joan Didion in Denial About Her Daughter's Alcoholism?', *The Fix*, 8 December. Available online: https://www.thefix.com/content/Joan-didion-quintana-roo-blue%20nights-pancreatitis7033 (accessed 17 July 2020).

May, T. (2017), *A Fragile Life: Accepting our Vulnerability*, Chicago: The University of Chicago Press.

Mbembe, A. (2019), *Necropolitics*, Durham: Duke University Press.

McLennan, M. R. (2018a), 'Differend and "Post-Truth"', *French Journal For Media Research*, 9/2018. Available online: https://frenchjournalformediaresearch.com:443/lodel-1.0/main/index.php?id=1437 (accessed 17 July 2020).

McLennan, M. R. (2018b), 'Norms for the Public Remembrance of Nonhuman Animals', *Ethics, Politics & Society*, 1 (1): 63–81.

McLennan, M. R. (2019), *Philosophy and Vulnerability: Catherine Breillat, Joan Didion, and Audre Lorde*, London: Bloomsbury Academic.

McLennan, M. R. (2020), 'Beauvoir's Concept of "Decline"', *Feminist Philosophy Quarterly*, 6 (2): : 1–17.

Mouffe, C. (2018), *For a Left Populism*, London: Verso.

Mounk, Y. (2019), *The Age of Responsibility: Luck, Choice, and the Welfare State*, Cambridge, MA: Harvard University Press.

Murdoch, I. (2007), *The Sovereignty of Good*, London: Routledge.

Nelson, D. (2017), *Tough Enough: Arbus, Arendt, Didion, McCarthy, Sontag, Weil*, Chicago: The University of Chicago Press.

Noble, S. U. (2018), *Algorithms of Oppression: How Search Engines Reinforce Racism*, New York: New York University Press.

Nowak McNeice, K. (2019), *California and the Melancholic American Identity in Joan Didion's Novels: Exiled from Eden*, New York: Routledge.

Nudelman, F. (2016), 'Reporting Nuclear Dread: The Stranger at Didion's Door', *a/b: Auto/Biography Studies*, 31 (3): 591–6.

O'Neil, C. (2017), *Weapons of Math Destruction: How Big Data Increases Inequality and Threatens Democracy*, New York: Broadway Books.

Parker, F., (ed.) (2018), *Conversations with Joan Didion*, Jackson: University Press of Mississippi.

Plessner, H. (2019), *Levels of Organic Life and the Human: An Introduction to Philosophical Anthropology*, translated by M. Hyatt, New York: Fordham University Press.

Puar, J. (2017), *The Right to Maim: Debility, Capacity, Disability*, Durham: Duke University Press.

Ricœur, P. (1990), *Soi-même comme un autre*, Paris: Éditions du Seuil.

Ricœur, P. (2006), *Memory, History, Forgetting*, translated by K. Blamey and D. Pellauer. Chicago: The University of Chicago Press.

Ricœur, P. (2014), *Vivant jusqu'à la mort. Suivi de Fragments*, Paris: Éditions du Seuil.

Sartre, J.-P. (2004), *Critique of Dialectical Reason Volume One*, translated by A. Sheridan-Smith, London: Verso.

Sauers, J. (2011), 'Did Alcoholism Kill Joan Didion's Daughter?', *Jezebel*, 13 December. Available online: https://jezebel.com/did-alcoholism-kill-joan-didions-daughter-5867725 (accessed 17 July 2020).

Schine, C. (2011), 'Elegy to the Void', *The New York Review of Books*, 24 November. Available online: http://www.nybooks.com/articles/2011/11/24/elegy-void/ (accessed 27 March 2017).

Shaw, D. Z. (2016), *Egalitarian Moments: From Descartes to Rancière*, London: Bloomsbury Academic.

Shipley, T. A. (2020), *Canada in the World: Settler Capitalism and the Colonial Imagination*, Black Point: Fernwood Publishing.

Shoop, C. (2016), 'Joan Didion's Style: A Revisionist Western', *a/b: Auto/Biography Studies*, 31 (3): 586–91.

Spade, D. (2015), *Normal Life: Administrative Violence, Critical Trans Politics, and the Limits of Law*, Durham: Duke University Press.

Spinoza, B. (1992), *The Ethics; Treatise on the Emendation of the Intellect; Selected Letters*, translated by S. Shirley, edited by S. Feldman, Indianapolis and Cambridge: Hackett Publishing Company.

Stauffer, J. (2015), *Ethical Loneliness: The Injustice of Not Being Heard*, New York: Columbia University Press.

Taylor, K.-Y. (2016), *From #BlackLivesMatter to Black Liberation*, Chicago: Haymarket Books.

Till-Mobley, M., and C. Benson (2003), *Death of Innocence: The Story of the Hate Crime That Changed America*, New York: The Random House Publishing Group.

Tocqueville, A. de (2003), *Democracy in America and Two Essays on America*, translated by G. E. Bevan, London: Penguin Books.

Trites, A. (2019), 'Black Box Ethics: How Algorithmic Decision-Making is Changing How We View Society and People: Advocating for the Right for Explanation and the Right to be Forgotten in Canada', *Global Media Journal – Canadian Edition*, 11 (2): 18–30.

Truth and Reconciliation Commission of Canada (2015), *Final Report of the Truth and Reconciliation Commission of Canada, Volume One: Summary: Honouring the Truth, Reconciling for the Future*, Toronto: James Lorimer & Company Ltd., Publishers.

Urbain, J.-D. (2005), *L'archipel des Morts: Cimetières et mémoire en Occident*, Paris: Éditions Payot & Rivages.

Virilio, P. (2005), *L'accident originel*, Paris: Galilée.

Wiesel, E. (1972), *Souls on Fire: Portraits and Legends of Hasidic Masters*, translated by Marion Wiesel, New York: Random House.

Wilderson, F. III. (2020), *Afropessimism*, New York: Liverlight Publishing Corporation.

Winnicott, D. W. (1991), *The Child, the Family, and the Outside World*, London: Penguin Books.

Winnicott, D. W. (2006), *The Family and Individual Development*, London: Routledge, 2006.

Wittgenstein, L. (2001), *Philosophical Investigations*, translated by G. E. M. Anscombe, Oxford: Blackwell Publishers.

Wolff, J. and A. De-Shalit (2013), *Disadvantage*, Oxford: Oxford University Press.

Zuboff, S. (2019), *The Age of Surveillance Capitalism: The Fight for a Human Future at the New Frontier of Power*, New York: PublicAffairs.

Index

9/11 terror attacks   111, 141, 143–4

accident, death as   73–81, 94, 173 n.17
Adorno, Theodor   173 n.18
Agamben, Giorgio   89, 177 nn.32–3
anamnēsis   8, 83, 88, 118
archive   5, 18–19, 64, 106, 126–9, 132, 155
Aristotle   6
autonomy   65, 170 n.5
    moral autonomy   122–3, 156–7, 162–3 n.11, 182 n.14

Baez, Joan   149
Beauvoir, Simone de   170 n.8, 177 n.34
Benatar, David   49
Berlant, Lauren   67–8, 92, 145
betrayal   16, 30, 39, 44, 66, 89, 106, 119, 121, 123–5, 156, 163 n.12, 180 n.8
#BlackLivesMatter   69, 99–101, 178 n.43
Bowlby, John   170 n.5, 179 n.3
Breillat, Catherine   31
Brown, Wendy   148, 164 nn.15–16, 172 n.15
Brysk, Alison   164 n.17
Bush, George W.   20
Butler, Judith   33, 64–5, 69, 95, 97–9, 101, 105

Cassin, Barbara   107, 178 n.1, 181 n.8
Chihara, Michelle   180 n.7
Chomsky, Noam   139
close relations   26–8, 119, 161 n.6, 165 n.22
colonial irony   56–7, 61
communism   53, 167 n.8
comprehensiveness   9–11, 20, 25, 29–30, 33–4, 39, 53, 105–6, 110, 115, 118, 120, 124–30, 132, 155–6, 164 n.19, 183 n.4
Conrad, Joseph   57, 60, 166 n.4

Cooper, Melinda   148, 164 n.16, 172 n.16
cosmic horror   46–9
crimes against humanity   16, 23, 120, 123, 126–8, 130, 150, 163 n.13, 181 n.9, 181 n.10
Critchley, Simon   47
critical fabulation   34, 106, 124–30, 164 n.19
critical political realism   55, 59, 61, 131–44, 182 n.2
Cvetkovich, Ann   179 n.4

Daugherty, Tracy   90–1, 175 n.27, 178 n.39, 181 n.8
death camps   91, 123
DiAngelo, Robin   162 n.10
Discovery University   154, 184 n.2
Donner-Reed Party   25, 28
Doughty, Caitlin   73
Dunne, Griffin   171 n.12
Dunne, John   70, 76–80, 92, 97, 170 n.10, 173 n.16
Dunne, Quintana Roo   70, 73, 78, 80–2, 85–93, 96–8, 102, 116–17, 148–9, 170 n.9, 171 n.13, 173 n.16, 174 n.22, 175 n.24, 176 n.29, 178 n.39, 180–1 n.8
Duras, Marguerite   150, 171–2 n.13

Eagleton, Terry   160 n.3
earthquake weather   41–3, 48, 51, 53–4, 59–61, 63, 68, 73–4, 85, 102, 167 n.11
El Mozote massacre   59, 143
El Salvador   57–60
Ernaux, Annie   65–6, 161 n.6, 169 n.1, 169 n.3, 170 nn.6–7, 182 n.1
ethical loneliness   69, 96–7, 101–3, 122, 129, 163 n.13, 177 n.37
ethics (as distinct from morality)   14–17
ethics of memory (general sense)   5–12
ethics of memory (specific sense)   12–17

ethos   18, 28, 33, 53–4, 60, 71, 79, 92, 102

failure, death as   73–9, 94, 173 n.17
False Memory Syndrome   6, 9
Floyd, George   69, 101
forgiveness   30, 34, 106, 118–19, 121–4, 130, 156–7, 177 n.37, 181 n.10
frailty   81–6, 93, 97, 171 n.13, 176 n.29
frames of testimony   69, 95, 99, 101, 103, 178 n.41
Freud, Sigmund   6, 7, 68, 82, 174 n.22, 175 n.25, 177 n.33
   Nachträglichkeit   82–4, 175 n.25

gambling   183 n.8
Garza, Alicia   101
gender   55, 98, 101, 145–6, 168 n.15, 184 n.12
geology   41–2, 45, 48, 78–80, 137, 174 n.19, 183 n.6
Gilmore, Leigh   18, 32–4, 67, 69, 95, 99–101, 103, 105, 132, 145–7, 150–1, 154, 173 n.16, 178 nn.40–1, 184 n.11
Gramsci, Antonio   3
grievability   69, 95–102, 129, 184 n.13

Habermas, Jürgen   74, 122, 140, 162 n.9, 164 n.18, 165 n.1
Halbwachs, Maurice   169 n.4
Haraway, Donna   31–2
Hartman, Saidiya   34, 106, 125–30, 151, 164 n.19, 164 n.21
Hegel, G. W. F.   167 n.8, 168 n.17
   Hegelian dialectic   24, 167 n.9
history   2, 8, 20–1, 29, 52, 55–9, 67, 93, 112–13, 117, 120–1, 127–30, 137, 143, 146, 164 n.20, 168 n.17, 174 n.20, 183 nn.5–6
Horkheimer, Max   173 n.18
Huebner, Chris   64, 161–2 n.7

imagination (as distinct from memory)   6, 8–9, 21, 33, 86, 106, 108, 110–11, 118, 124, 128–9
immemorial   56–8, 78, 115, 137, 157, 168 n.14, 183 n.6
intersectionality   101, 178 n.40, 184 n.12

intimate public   67–8, 79, 89, 92, 94, 97, 102, 140, 145

Kant, Immanuel   108–9, 115–17, 120, 139, 160 n.5, 162 nn.8–9, 163 n.11, 164 n.18, 178 n.2, 179 n.3, 182 n.12
Khan-Cullors, Patrisse   101
Kristeva, Julia   69, 150, 172 n.13

Laclau, Ernesto   134, 159 n.1, 182 n.2
Laski, Michael   52–3, 167 n.8
Lear, Jonathan   125
Le Pen, Marine   142, 184 n.12
liberalism   136, 139–40, 145
Locke, John   65
Lorde, Audre   31, 174 n.23
Lyotard, Jean-François   41, 68, 82–3, 87–9, 168 n.14, 174 n.19, 175 n.26, 176 n.28, 176–7 n.31, 177 n.36, 182 n.2

magical thinking   70–80, 92–4, 100, 174 n.18
Malabou, Catherine   65
Malraux, André   56–7, 168 n.14
Mao Tse-Tung   168 n.14
Margalit, Avishai   10–19, 23, 26, 28, 30, 32, 38–9, 69, 91, 93, 103, 106, 109–10, 118–25, 156, 160 n.5, 160–1 n.6, 162 nn.8–10, 162–3 n.11, 163 n.12, 164 n.18, 165 n.22, 169 n.4, 177 n.37, 179 n.6, 181 n.11, 182 n.14, 184 n.4, 184–5 n.5
Marx, Karl   167 n.8
   Marxism   167 n.8, 168 n.17, 174 n.20
melancholy   54, 112–14, 118, 127, 148, 179
memory, *see anamnēsis; mnēmē*
metaphysical loneliness   67–9, 80, 86, 89–90, 95–103, 107, 129, 151
Mill, John Stuart   140
misogyny   184 n.12
mnēmē   8, 83, 88, 118
modernity/modernism   1–3, 38, 47, 56, 59, 61, 68–70, 73–81, 88–9, 92–5, 100, 102–3, 114–15, 151, 153–4, 165 n.1, 167 n.13, 168 n.14, 172 nn.15–16,

173 n.17, 173–4 n.18,
   174 n.20, 179 n.7
morality (as distinct from ethics)   14–17
   moral transgression   119–
      25, 128, 156
   wagon train morality   25, 44, 115,
      133, 135, 148–50, 179 n.7
Mouffe, Chantal   17, 134,
   159 n.1, 182 n.2
mourning   6–7, 23, 70, 78, 93, 97–100,
   112, 174 n.21, 177 n.33
Murdoch, Iris   7–9, 11–2, 124,
   160 n.3, 163 n.14

names, forgetting and
   remembering   6, 11–2, 64
nature   36, 43–6, 54, 56–9,
   167 n.11, 168 n.17, 169 n.3,
   174 n.20, 183 n.6
   human nature   60
Nazism   15
   concentration camps   123
   Final solution (*see* Shoah)
Nelson, Deborah   23–5, 28, 36, 47, 71–3,
   79, 171 nn.12–13, 172 n.14,
   174 n.22, 176 n.29
neoliberalism   2, 5, 17–18, 39, 75, 142,
   147–9, 151, 164 nn.15–16,
   172 nn.15–16, 184 n.13
   neoliberal life narrative   34, 131–2,
      146–51, 154
nihilism   46–7, 49, 94, 102, 105
nonhuman animals   15, 17, 91, 160 n.5,
   163 n.11, 177 n.36
nostalgia   9, 20–2, 30, 33–4, 103, 105–18,
   121, 124–31, 144, 164 n.19,
   178 n.1, 179 nn.5–6, 180–1 n.8
Nowak McNeice, Katarzyna   54,
   112–14, 127, 148, 179 n.7,
   183 n.8, 184 n.1
Nudelman, Franny   43

ontology   35–6

pessimism   3, 43, 49–51, 57, 78, 94–5,
   150–1, 154, 158
philosophy   4, 14, 30–1, 35–6, 38, 57,
   95, 134, 154, 159 n.2, 162 n.9,
   167 n.8, 174 n.20
   philosophical unsettlement   154–5

Plato   160 n.3
Podemos   142
postmodernity/postmodernism   32, 39,
   50, 134–5, 142, 182 n.2
post-truth   18, 34
practico-inert   43
privacy   100–1
privilege   2, 56, 98–100, 102–3, 148–50,
   153, 166 n.2
psychoanalysis   9, 83, 175 n.25
public intellectuals   139
public sphere   97, 99, 102, 140, 145

racism   1–2, 15, 19–21, 60, 93,
   97, 100, 120–1, 126, 147,
   162 n.10, 182 n.13
   in Canada   19–21, 120–1
   racist monuments   1–2, 93
Reagan, Nancy   149
Reagan, Ronald   183, 142, 183 n.10
   'Reagan Doctrine'   142
residential school system   2
Ricoeur, Paul   6–8, 19–20, 26, 29, 52,
   65, 68, 72, 83, 87, 91, 108–10,
   118, 160–1 n.6, 169 nn.1–2,
   174 nn.20–1, 175 n.25, 176 n.30,
   177 n.33, 183 n.5
right to be forgotten   21, 124, 157–
   8, 185 n.7
Rolland, Romain   3

Sanders, Bernie   142
Sartre, Jean-Paul   14, 43, 182 n.1
saying (as opposed to said)   87–95, 138,
   150–1, 175 nn.25–6, 176 n.31
Schine, Cathleen   84
self-delusion   27–8, 39, 44, 49, 71, 73,
   92, 94, 111
self-pity   28, 71–2, 79, 171 n.11,
   171 n.13, 178 n.42
sexism   147, 184 n.12
Shaw, Devin Zane   164 n.22
Shipley, Tyler   120–1, 164 n.20
Shoah   126, 176 n.31
Shoop, Casey   134, 148
social movements   43, 49, 52, 133, 148
Spinoza, Baruch   174 n.20
Stauffer, Jill   33, 69, 90–1, 96–7, 101, 103,
   105, 119, 122–3, 129, 150–1,
   163 n.13, 177 n.37, 181 n.10

stoicism 49
surveillance capitalism 21, 157

Taylor, Breonna 101
tensor sign 41, 54, 60
thick relations 13–17, 19–20, 23, 26, 30, 106, 111, 116–17, 120–6, 135, 137, 140, 147, 161 nn.6–7, 170 n.4
thin relations 14–17, 19, 23, 91–2, 120
Till, Emmet 100
Till-Mobley, Mamie 100, 178 n.42
Tocqueville, Alexis de 135–6, 140
Tometi, Opal 101
trauma 6, 33, 42, 61, 66, 68, 70, 72, 76, 81, 83, 112, 144–7, 150, 169 n.2, 175 n.24
Trump, Donald 18, 20, 142
Trump, Ivanka 184 n.12
truth, *see* comprehensiveness; veracity

universalism/universality 14–15, 17, 25, 28–9, 32, 36–7, 39, 96, 102, 122, 140, 153, 159 n.1, 166 n.3
aristocratic 25, 29, 32, 36, 39, 102
contaminated 159 n.1
Urbain, Jean-Didier 68–9, 75–6, 81, 172 nn.15–16, 173 n.17, 174 n.20

veracity 8–11, 20, 29, 39, 72, 86, 88, 105, 107, 126, 128, 130, 154

Walls, Jeanette 184 n.11
Whitehead, Alfred North 174 n.20
Wiesel, Eli 88, 175–6 n.28
Winnicott, D. W. 170 n.5
Wittgenstein 5, 168 n.1
women's movement 28, 148–9

Zuboff, Shoshana 21, 124, 157, 183 n.9

www.ingramcontent.com/pod-product-compliance
Lightning Source LLC
Chambersburg PA
CBHW061831300426
44115CB00013B/2332